State and Society in Nigeria

Second Edition

Other Books Edited by Gavin Williams

Sociology and Development (with Emmanuel de Kadt)*,* Tavistock, 1974,
   reprinted 2003, 2013, 2018.
 Nigeria: Economy and Society. Rex Collings, 1975
Rural Development in Tropical Africa (with Judith Heyer and Pepe
   Roberts) Macmillan, 1981
Sociology of Developing Societies: sub-Saharan Africa. with C.H. Allen.
   Macmillan, 1982
*Classes, States and Democratic Politics in Ghana and Nigeria: A Critical
   Appreciation of the Work of Björn Beckman.* Centre for Research
   and Documentation, Kano, 2004

Publications Editor

Ruth First, *Black Gold: the Mozambican Miner: Proletarian and Peasant.*
   with Rosalynde de Lanerolle. Harvester, Hassocks, and St Martin's
   Press, New York, 1983

Editorial Contribution

Renfrew Christie, *Electricity, Industry and Class in South Africa*, St
   Antony's Macmillan Series, 1984

State and Society in Nigeria

Second Edition

Gavin Williams

m a l t h o u s e $\mathcal{XP}$

Malthouse Press Limited

Lagos, Benin, Ibadan, Jos,Port-Harcourt, Zaria

© Gavin Williams 2019
First Published 1980
Second Edition 2019
978-978-56575-8-6

Published and manufactured in Nigeria by
Malthouse Press Limited
43 Onitana Street, Off Stadium Hotel Road,
Off Western Avenue, Lagos Mainland
malthouselagos@gmail.com
Tel: +234 (01) 0802 600 3203

Distributors:

African Books Collective Ltd, Oxford, UK
Email: abc@africanbookscollective.com
Website: http://www.africanbookscollective.com

Dedication

To

Rosa Abayomi and Keir Ayodele
and
Raufu Mustapha

Acknowledgements and Preface

The First Edition of *State And Society In Nigeri*a was published in 1980 by Afrografika Press with permission from the late Rex Collings to reprint 'Nigeria: a political economy'; to the Nigerian Institute for Social and Economic Research, to reprint 'Ideologies and Strategies of Rural Development, a Critique'; to Cambridge University Press to reprint 'Politics in Nigeria'; and to Tavistock Press to reprint 'Political Consciousness among the Ibadan Poor'. The second edition of *State and Society in Nigeria* book brings together five essays on the sociology and political economy of Nigeria, written between 1972 and 1977, with a Preface to the volume. It is in memory of the late A. R. (Raufu) Mustapha who was for me, as he was for others, my closest friend and colleague in Oxford.

The original essays remain mainly as they were originally published, except for changes in tenses and grammatical corrections and of references to some more recent publications, especially in the sections on religious and ethnic topics. Most alterations and additions to the text and to the notes are in the Introduction. Part I. and in Part IV, which takes over material originally discussed in Parts II and III. This second edition adds to the original edition Part VII, 'Politics and Society' which revised the text of a lecture that I gave at the University of Ibadan to the original edition. Charles Akinde, the publisher of Afrografika Press, published the first edition of these essays, which aimed to make them available in the first instance to a Nigerian audience. He subsequently encouraged me to produce this extended edition. Adigun Agbaje gave generously of his time and academic solidarity to bring the publication of this extended volume to fruition. I thank Dafe Otobo and Malthouse for their support for this new edition.

My interest in Nigeria was awakened in 1965 when, as a naïve graduate student recently arrived in Oxford from South Africa, I had the remarkable good fortune to be taught by the great socialist scholar Thomas Hodgkin. His encouragement and friendship continued to provide an example of breadth of learning and political principle.

My wife Gillian and I were able to live in Nigeria in 1970 and 1971. We enjoyed meeting and friendships with Nigerians and people from other parts of the world. Segun Oke was a warm friend from our first meeting on the *M.V. Apapa* en route to Lagos in 1970, and enabled Gill and me to be accommodated in Ibadan. Olu Otunla was a good friend; he made it possible for me to continue with some of my research. I was able to make subsequent visits in 1975 and 1978 and again in 2010. Madam Ajayi made me at home when I returned to Nigeria in 1975. After 1990, I was free to return to South Africa, where I could take my Nigerian experience with me and make a contribution to research and teaching.

Research and writing are collective activities. I remain indebted for their guidance to my teachers and colleagues in Stellenbosch, Oxford, Durham, and Ibadan. These essays draw on the knowledge and comments of numerous friends and colleagues, many of whom, sadly, are no longer with us. I shared my research in Nigeria with Adrian Peace in 1970 and 1971. Peter Lloyd initiated and directed the project, which made it possible for us to undertake the research on which these essays have drawn.

Gillian Williams carried out archival research on the *Agbekoya*. Femi (now Professor) Durosaro and Raufu (now Chief) Yesufu assisted and guided my field research in Ibadan. I learned about rural Ibadan from, among other farmers, Lasupo Obisesan. They all contributed to making it possible to produce Part V, which may make the most innovative contribution in this volume.

Ken Post, the most perceptive analyst of the politics of Nigeria guided and criticized my studies of Nigeria and of Marxism. In Durham, Philip Corrigan showed me how better to understand relations between states and societies historically. I benefitted from Ruth First's great experience, political commitments, intellectual impatience, and shared companionship. J.D.Y. (John) Peel gave personal kindness and intellectual generosity throughout his career. His thorough empirical research and social theory exemplified the historical sociology to which I can only aspire. At Oxford, Abdul Raufu shared teaching with me the politics of Africa and the historical sociologies of rural societies and we worked together with innovative and meticulous research students.

Christopher Beer generously collaborated in writing on the politics of the Ibadan peasantry. Terisa Turner and I wrote the joint article that appears in this volume. I was able to work with Paul Clough and to benefit from his meticulous research and understanding of Hausa rural society. Shehu Othman and I collaborated in writing about how Nigerian politics works. In 1975, Mike Cowen and Bob Shenton published their study, which clarified the *Doctrines of Development.* Bob has always done me the favour of not agreeing with me.

Since 1980, I have been able to learn about Nigerian history, politics, and society from my graduate students: Tajudeen Abdulraheem, Adekeye Abebajo, Paul Bagobiri, Paul Clough, Obed Mailafia, Ruth Marshall, Kate Meagher, Raufu Mustapha, Kathryn Nwajiaku-Dahou, Ike Okonta, Shehu Othman, Ruth Watson, and Dan Zelikow.

To these names, I can only list some of the numerous others on whose knowledge and insights I have been able to draw: Philip Abrams, Chris Allen, Bolanle Awe, Gerald Aylmer, Jairus Banaji, Sara Berry, Henry Bernstein, Teddy Brett, Julian Clarke, Robin Cohen, Carolyne Dennis, Jan-Georg Deutsch, Billy J. Dudley, David Ehrhardt, Ruth First, Tom Forrest, Bill Freund, Chris Gerry, David Goldey, Sarah Graham, Peter Gutkind, Jane Guyer, John Harriss, Barbara

Harriss-White, John Hargreaves, Teresa Hayter, Judith Heyer, Adam Higazi, Jamil Hilal, Robert Home, Tony Hopkins, Jibrin Ibrahim, Jeremy Jackson, Cecile Jackson, Attahiru Jega, Asma'u Joda, R.W. Johnson, Richard Joseph, Tony Kirk-Greene, Murray Last, Colin Leys, Paul Lubeck, Ian Maddison, Archie Mafeje, Otonti Nduka, Adebayo Olukoshi, Segun Osoba, Dafe Otobo, Oliver Owen, Richard Palmer-Jones, Charmaine Pereira, Dorothy Remy, John Rex, Pepe Roberts, Derek Sayer, Ami Shah, Ricardo Soares de Oliveira. Michael Stephen, Stanley Trapido, Justin Tseayo, Emmanuel Tumusiime-Mutebile, Tina Wallace, Peter Waterman, Michael Watts, John Weeks, Anne Whitehead, Christine Whitehead, Laurence Whitehead, Lindsay Whitfield, and Philip Williams.

It was my good fortune to be appointed to Lectureships at Durham University and then at The University of Oxford to a Fellowship at St Peter's College. In Durham, the Political Economy group provided an unusual academic and political forum. In Oxford, the university seminar on The History and Politics of Africa was started in 1970 and hosts an annual Thomas Hodgkin Lecture. Gerald Aylmer, Philip Corrigan, and Derek Sayer initiated an annual workshop of 'The English State from 1000 to 1834"; I learned a lot. St Peter's has welcomed students from and doing their research on Nigeria and other African countries. It has also provided a venue for significant international workshops on Nigeria's political economy and more recently on Lusophone Africa.

Our initial research project was based at the University of Sussex from 1970 to 1972 and funded by the Social Science Research Council of the United Kingdom. The Centre of Islamic and Middle Eastern Studies at the University of Durham paid for my second period of research, which coincided with the overthrow of the Gowon government, which enabled me to bring my knowledge of political events in Nigeria up to date and to prepare the paper on ideologies and strategies of rural development which appears here. My 1978 visit was funded by the International Labour Office to prepare a study on rural inequalities in Nigeria. It did not find favour at the ILO and was published instead as a Working Paper by the Centre for Development Studies at the University of East Anglia.

These three visits were all facilitated by the Nigerian Institute of Social and Economic Research at Ibadan and in 1975 by the Department History at the University of Ibadan. In 1975, Dr Ekundayo Akeredolu-Ale, made me welcome and encouraged my research at the Nigerian Institute of Economic Research (NISER) in Ibadan, on which Part VI is based. I enjoyed the company and learned from the knowledge of my fellow South African, Sam Nolutshungu. Sadly, his early death prevented him taking up the Vice-Chancellorship of the University of the Witwatersrand and deprived South Africa of a fine scholar. I must extend my thanks to Professor T. N. Tamuno, then Head of the Department of History and subsequently Vice-Chancellor of the University of Ibadan, and to Professor R. O. Adegboye for their help.

My research would not have been possible without the assistance of librarians and archivists: in Nigeria at the Kenneth Dike Library at the University of Ibadan; NISER; the Nigerian Archives at Ibadan, the Institute of Agricultural Research at Samaru, and the National Archives in Ibadan; in Britain, at the libraries of the Centre of West African Studies at the University of Birmingham, the Institute of Commonwealth Studies in London, the University of Durham, Rhodes House, Social Studies, and Queen Elizabeth House (all three now all within the Bodleian Libraries), St Peter's College, the British Library and the British Newspaper Library, and above all from Bob Townsend, Librarian at Queen Elizabeth House at the University of Oxford.

Ulandi du Plessis and Rosa Williams prepared and edited, and re-edited the text and corrected my errors and infelicities. Without Keir Williams' assistance I would have been unable to complete this study. Alison Wiblin provided extensive assistance far beyond the call of duty. My greatest debts are to the people of Ibadan City, and particularly of Oje, and of Ibadan Division, especially in Akanran and neighbouring villages and hamlets, for giving so patiently of their time and knowledge.

The final chapter, Part VII, extends the text of a lecture at the University of Ibadan, given at the suggestion of Professor Adigun Agbaje. It was subsequently given at the Aminu Kano Centre in Kano, at the invitation of the Vice-Chancellor, Professor Attahiru Jega, and in Abuja at the Centre for Development and Democracy thanks to Dr Jibrin Ibrahim, and at the University of Abuja. My visit to Nigeria was made possible by an invitation from Professor Femi Durosaro to give the keynote address entitled 'The academic vocation in an era of commoditization' at a Conference on Globalization and Higher Education at the University of Ilorin on 7 March 2010, I am most grateful to Professor Durosaro, to the University of Ilorin, and to my friends and colleagues in universities and research institutions in Kano and Abuja for their warm welcome and their generosity in hosting me during my visit.

Gillian Williams made it possible for me to enjoy love, humour, and friendships, and our time in Nigeria. She has given me the support and tolerance, which has enabled me to complete these essays and to share our lives with Rosa and Keir, for whom this book is written, and with our grandchildren.

Contents

Part I

Ideas on Development

Nigeria is a class society. The class and state relations in Nigerian society, and their places within international capitalism were central to my studies of Nigeria from the time I wrote my B.Phil thesis in 1967. These studies are represented here in research on four issues: the ways in which capitalism 'underdevelops' Nigeria; the class bases of political conflict; the resistance of workers and peasants to their subordination and exploitation by the state and capital; and the ideologies and practices of rural development policies. The social relations of class, status, and state domination; and political economy, politics and policies have not, indeed cannot, lose their relevance. I have continued to bypass gender and generation, which are integral to all of these themes. I can only beg the reader's tolerance.

My understandings of the subjects and my analytical vocabulary have changed since I submitted my thesis in 1967. [1] My uncritical adjectival use of 'bourgeois' has altered since 1967. I would avoid referring to 'neo-colonialism', which is where I had started from, or any other of the 'neo'- prefixes. As I said of 'neo-patrimonialism' in Part VII, these are lazy

---

[1] G. Williams, The Political Sociology of Western Nigeria, B. Phil. thesis, University of Oxford, 1967. *Revised January 1980*

concepts, that attach labels at the expense of explaining the interactions within and among institutions. The concept and practice of 'development' should not be taken at face value. As Cowen and Shenton have shown, *Doctrines of Development*[2] have continued the legacies of progress and improvement embedded in Comte's positivism and Fabian colonialism.

The title 'Development' is today more than ever embedded in the names of development institutes, policies, and projects. International and national agencies and (I)NGOs 'do development' for good or often ill in the discourse of 'devspeak'. Research in 'developing countries' is explicitly intended and publicly funded to provide governments and international agencies with the information they need to carry out their goals of 'development'. These goals are rarely subjected to critical scrutiny, nor the capacities of government agencies to achieve them or are the interests which development agencies serve critically questioned. It may be more important than practising development 'to study development and explain policy.'[3]

In Scotland in the eighteenth century Adam Smith observed, in the title of one of his chapters in *The Wealth of Nations,* that 'The Division of Labour is Limited by the Extent of the Market.' He compared trade from the remote Highlands in Scotland to the 'very considerable commerce' between London and Calcutta, which 'by mutually affording a market, give a good deal of encouragement to each other's industries.'[4] In

---

[2] M.P. Cowen and R. W. Shenton, *Doctrines of Development* (London, 1995), p. 27.

[3] G. Williams, 'Studying Development and Explaining Policy' *Oxford Development Studies*, 31 (1) 2003.

[4] Adam Smith, *An Inquiry into the Nature and Causes of the Wealth of Nations* (1759) (Chicago, 1982), Book 1, ch. 1. and Book IV, ch. I, II. It is commonly presented selectively. It should be read with *The Theory of Moral Sentiments* {1759} A.L. Macfie and D.D. Raphael (eds),

nineteenth century Britain, T. F. Buxton[5] and other evangelicals expected 'legitimate trade' (in palm produce) and the operations of the British navy to bring an end to the Atlantic slave trade, which Britain had abolished in 1808. Slavery itself was only abolished in British colonies in 1838; the end of the trade awaited the abolition of slavery in Brazil in 1888.

At the end of the century, imperialists like Chamberlain[6] argued that the expansion of the Empire would develop the 'undeveloped estates' of the tropics to the mutual benefit of the peoples of Britain and its colonies. In 1937, Bernard Bourdillon, the Governor of Nigeria, pronounced to the Royal Empire Society that 'The exploitation theory is dead... and the development theory has taken its place.'[7] 'Development' was incorporated into the Colonial Welfare and Development Acts in 1940 and in 1945, and with an excess of imagination, the 'Ten-Year Plan of Development'. Its most evident project in Nigeria was the failed Mokwa Agricultural Project, Nigeria's match to the Tanzanian Groundnut Scheme.[8]

In 1944, the World Bank was founded as the International Bank for Reconstruction and Development. Its 'two ambitious goals' are to 'End Extreme Poverty within a Generation and

---

(Indianapolis, 1984), esp, Introduction, pp. 13-14 and pp. 183-5, 233-4, and D. D. Raphael, *Adam Smith* (Oxford, 1985).

[5] Thomas Fowell Buxton, *The African Slave Trade and Its Remedy* (London, 1839). See R. Law (ed.), *From Slave Trade to 'Legitimate' Commerce: The commercial transition in nineteenth-century West Africa* (Cambridge, 1995).

[6] Speech in the House of Commons, 22nd August, 1895, cited F. Lugard, 'The Extension of British Influence (and Trade) in Africa' *Proceedings, Royal Colonial Institute*, 27 (1896), p. 7.

[7] B. Bourdillon, 'Address to the British Empire Society' *West Africa*, 30 Jan. 1937, cited Cowen and Shenton, *Doctrines of Development*, pp. 7, 366. On the political significance of the 1930 Act, see K.W. J. Post, *Arise Ye Starvelings: the Jamaican Labour Rebellion of 1938 and its aftermath* (The Hague, 1978).

[8] K.D.S. Baldwin, *The Niger Agricultural Project: an experiment in African development* (Oxford, 1957); G. Williams, 'Taking the Part of Peasants: rural development in Nigeria and Tanzania' in P.C.W. Gutkind and I. Wallerstein (eds), *The Political Economy of Contemporary Africa* (Los Angeles, 1976/ 1985).

Boost Shared Prosperity'.[9] Its position as an international lender enables it to confer the status of 'development' upon its policies, projects and intentions.[10] As Philip Abrams said of the 'state-idea', the idea of 'Development' is a 'social fact'.[11] It is not imaginary, it is real in its consequences.[12] As there is a 'state-system', so there is a 'development-system', in Abrams's words 'a nexus of practice and institutions', which is masked by the Idea of Development.[13]

Contentions among academics and practitioners did not begin by asking the prior question: do we know what we mean by 'development'? Cowen and Shenton find the doctrine of 'trusteeship' embedded into the 'construction of development' during the first half of the nineteenth century. At its inception in 1889, the Republic of Brazil took August Comte's 'Ordem e Progresso' for its national flag from August Comte's *Positive Philosophy*: 'Progress is the development of Order under the influence of Love.' [14] The doctrines and practices of 'development' are visibly present, and at the same time, they are obscured by their assimilation into the language of 'devspeak'.[15]

From 1967, Marxist writers changed the ways in which they defined the problems of 'underdevelopment' and 'class

---

[9] Worldbank.org.

[10] T. Hayter, *Aid as Imperialism* (Harmondsworth, 1971); E.S. Mason, and R.E. Asher, *The World Bank Since Bretton Woods* (Washington, 1973); G. Williams, 'The World Bank and the Peasant Problem,' in J. Heyer, P. Roberts and G. Williams (eds), *Rural Development in Tropical Africa* (Basingstoke, 1982).

[11]   E. Durkheim, *Rules of Sociological Method* {1895} (New York, 1982), p. 35.

[12] W.I. Thomas and Dorothy Swaine Thomas, *The Child in America: Behavior Problems and Programs* (New York, 1928), pp. 571-2.

[13] P. Abrams, 'Notes on the Difficulty of Studying the State' {1977} *Journal of Historical Sociology*, 1, 1 1988).

[14] August Comte, cited Cowen and Shenton, *Doctrines*, p. 27.

[15] G. Williams, 'Les contradictions de la Banque Mondiale et le crise l'État en Afrique' en *L'État contemporaine en Afrique*, sous la direction de Emmanuel Terry' (Paris, 1987), p. 363.

relations'. These were the apparent failures of 'underdeveloped countries' to emulate the achievements of capitalism in Europe, North America, and Japan. Consequently, the question was: can capitalism create the development of capitalism?[16] The debates on the development of capitalism were squarely within the classic traditions of Marxism. In Russia, Marxists ('Social Democrats') originally distinguished themselves from populists (*narodniki,* 'Socialist-Revolutionaries') by their insistence that capitalism would have to develop its 'productive powers'[17] sufficiently for a socialist revolution to be possible.[18]

Could this task be left to capitalists, national or imperial? Marxist political economists could be found in both side of the debate. Andre Gunder Frank argued that international capitalism 'underdeveloped' Latin American countries. He held on to the notion of 'development', but turned it inside out.[19] If capitalism underdeveloped Latin America and Africa, the state would have to take on the responsibility: a resurrection of 'socialism in one country'.

Bill Warren rejected theories of underdevelopment and argued that imperialism promoted the development of capitalism.[20] He challenged the new orthodoxy by going back

---

[16] See A. Philips, 'The Concept of Development' *Review of African Political Economy* (*ROAPE*) 8 (1977) for a critique of the question; M.P. Cowen and R.W. Shenton, 'The Invention of Development' in *Doctrines*, pp. 3-59, and in W. Cooke (ed.), *Power and Development* (London, 1995), pp. 27-63.

[17] I have replaced the common translation into English of *produktivkräfte* as 'forces of production' with 'productive powers', and at times changed my own use of 'forces' (of production) into the simple 'capacities'.

[18] A. Walicki, *The Controversy over Capitalism* (Oxford, 1969).

[19] A.G. Frank, *Capitalism and Underdevelopment in Latin America* (Harmondsworth, 1967). There is no reference in Frank's book to Brazil's motto: *ordem e progresso*. On underdevelopment theory, see H. Bernstein (ed.), *Underdevelopment and Development: the Third World Today* (Harmondsworth, 1973).

[20] B. Warren, 'Imperialism and Capitalist Industrialisation,' *New Left Review*, 81 (1973).

to Marx on Germany and Lenin on Russia. They suffered not from only from the development of capitalist production but also from the backwardness of the incompleteness.[21] In the opening chapter of his *History of the Russian Revolution*, Trotsky identified the 'advantage of backwardness'.[22] The solution to the 'backwardness of capitalism', and ultimately the condition for a transition to socialism, is the development of capitalism.

If capitalists were unable to achieve the development of capitalism, they would have to ally themselves with the state. Alexander Gerschenkron demonstrated in his studies of Tsarist Russia and Imperial Germany how the direction of the economy by an alliance of the state and financial institutions and capitalist companies opened the way for an alternative response to the dilemma of economic backwardness.[23] Japan was the Asian example of the delayed development of capitalism. Chalmers Johnson bridged the gap from 'late industrialization' to the 'developmental state'. In his book on the Ministry of Trade and Industry in post-war Japan, Johnson concluded that 'In states that were late to industrialize, the state itself led the industrialization drive, that is it took on developmental functions.[24] In Korea and Taiwan, Japan's successors to the title of 'developmental state', export-led growth was a necessity as well as an opportunity.

[21] K. Marx, The Future Results of British Rule in India' {22 July 1853}) 'Preface' to the first German edition of *Capital*, vol. 1 ({1867} Harmondsworth, 1976) p. 91, in K. Marx and F. Engels, *Collected Writings*, (CW, vols. 12, 32a) and in D. McLellan, *Karl Marx: Selected Writings*, 2nd ed. (Oxford, 2000) (KM) ch. 26, 32A); V.I. Lenin, *The Development of Capitalism in Russia, Collected Works*, vol. 3 ({1899}1960) p. 600).
[22] L. Trotsky, *History of the Russian Revolution* ({1930} London, 1934), pp. 23-28.
[23] A. Gerschenkron, *Economic Backwardness in Historical Perspective* (Cambridge MA, 1962); Alec Nove, *An Economic History of the USSR* ({1969} Harmondsworth, 1993).
[24] C. Johnson, *MITI and the Japanese Miracle, 1925-1975* (Palo Alto, CA, 1982), p. 19; and *Who Governs? The Rise of the Developmental State* (London, 1996).

Authoritarian structures of government gave scope to professional officials to direct policies in a reciprocal relation with business conglomerates.[25] Systemic corruption can be price of these forms of rule.

The standpoint of the essays in this volume is a radical rejection of 'development' through the exploitation and subjection of producers, whether in the name of 'socialism' or 'liberalism'. and a commitment to the 'emancipation of labour', the creation of conditions which enable people to produce freely in co-operation with one another rather than under the direction of capital and the state.

---

[25] M. Woo-Cummings, The Developmental State (Ithaca NY, 1999); R. Wade, *Governing the Market: Economic theory and the role of government in East Asian industrialization* (Princeton NJ, 1990); Alice H. Amsden, *Asia's Next Giant. South Korea and late industrialization* (Oxford, 1992). For the original, Japanese 'example', see Johnson, *MITI,* pp. 242-4. On Africa, see Thandika Mkandawire, 'Thinking about Developmental States in Africa' *Cambridge Journal of Economics* (2012); on South Africa, see W. Freund, South Africa as a Developmental State? Changes in the social structure since the end of apartheid and the emergence of the BEE elite,' *Review of African Political Economy* 114 (2012); *'Twentieth-Century South Africa – A Development History* (Cambridge University Press, 2019).

Part II

Nigeria: a Political Economy[1]

The Origins of the Colonial Political Economy

Prior to the development of the trans-Atlantic trade, production in Africa was predominantly agricultural. Africans did produce manufactures and traded in a variety of commodities. However, long-distance trade was limited largely to certain vital necessities, such as salt, and luxuries consumed by a wealthy and powerful few. Scarce population and high transport costs limited the demand for the production of goods for other than local trade. The domestic economy was able to reproduce itself[2] but not to transform itself.[3]

From the sixteenth century, European traders came to the Guinea coast in search of a variety of commodities, among which slaves increasingly though never exclusively predominated. Africa's intercontinental trade links, previously limited to the costly Saharan routes, were extended and Africa integrated into the expanding Euro-American economy as a supplier of precious metals, agricultural commodities, and labour.

---

[1] From Gavin Williams, ed. *Nigeria: Economy and Society*, Rex Collings, London, 1976.
[2] C. Meillasoux, 'Introduction' to *The Development of Indigenous Trade and Markets in West Africa* (Oxford, 1971).
[3] This paragraph and much of my analysis of the pre-colonial political economy follows A.G. Hopkins, *An Economic History of West Africa* (London, 1973).

As Akinjogbin has pointed out, slaves tended to become the 'sole export crop'.[4] The 'production' and exchange of slaves was 'the business of kings, rich men and prime merchants'.[5] They appropriated the profits of the trade and spent them on importing relatively expensive items for consumption and exchange, notably cloths, and on guns, which were needed to procure further exports. The institutional foundations of pre-colonial coastal trading were established to serve the slave trade. Various trading currencies came into operation, and a credit system, 'trust', financed the distribution of imports by African traders throughout the interior in order to procure commodities for export. The incorporation of Africa into international exchange through the expansion of the trans-Atlantic slave trade failed to increase the capacities to produce exports, other than of slaves. Domestic agricultural production for subsistence and for the market was discouraged. Africa contributed to the development of European capitalism and to European commercial domination of the world, and thus to its own subordination to the dictates and vagaries of capitalism. The adaptation of African states and societies to the requirements of the slave trade produced conflicts within African societies, between warriors and merchants and between rulers and their subjects, as well as between African states.[6] But the ending of the trade in slaves and the creation of opportunities for producing a very different sort of commodity was not the outcome of these conflicts but of changes in the requirements of European and particularly of British capitalism.

---

[4] I.A. Akinjogbin, 'The Oyo Empire in the Eighteenth Century' *Journal of the Historical Society of Nigeria*, (JHSN), 3 (1966), pp. 458-9.
[5] Barbot, late seventeenth century, cited Hopkins, *Economic History*, p.105.
[6] Meillasoux, 'Introduction' pp. 51-6; Akinjogbin, 'Oyo Empire'.

At the beginning of the nineteenth century, the European demand for vegetable oils increased, while the price of European manufactures, notably cloth, fell. The production of vegetable oils could be undertaken by small producers, and the bulking and bulkbreaking of exports and imports created new opportunities for petty trading. Exports of palm products increased dramatically in the forest zone.[7] The development of smallholder production threatened the political position of the military aristocracies of West Africa, which had rested on their control of the slave trade. They responded to this challenge in various ways: they continued slave raiding, they conquered and plundered neighbouring peoples, they sought new political alignments, they put slaves to work on plantations, and they sold commodities for export. None of these strategies could resolve 'the crisis of the aristocracy in nineteenth-century West Africa, a social and political crisis stemming from a contradiction between past and present relations of production' which continued in various societies, and particularly in Yorubaland, right up to the imposition of colonial rule at the end of the century.[8]

The system of coastal trade inherited from the slave trade continued to serve 'legitimate commerce' throughout the nineteenth-century. European and African merchants exchanged imports at coastal 'factories', where each side protected its profit margins by limiting competition among themselves. The firms involved in the trade did change. The shift towards small producers and traders made it easier for upstarts to make a start in trading from which they could

---

[7] Hopkins, *Economic History*, pp. 125-30; A. McPhee, *The Economic Revolution in British West Africa* (London, 1926).

[8] Hopkins, *Economic History*, p. 143. This argument is decisively criticized by S. Berry, *Cocoa, Custom and Socio-Economic Change in Rural Western Nigeria*, (Oxford, 1975), p. 28.

challenge the established traders. Among both European and African traders, the typical form of oligopolistic competition repeated itself: a newcomer, perhaps a defector from an established trading house, undercut prices. If they failed to eliminate him, the established houses had to offer him a place in their ring or find themselves excluded by the upstart. In the Niger Delta, legitimate commerce built up the political power of 'merchant princes'.[9]

The development of legitimate commerce united the material interests of Victorian capitalism with the moral issues on which the evangelical movement chose to focus its concerns. Missionaries established elementary and secondary schools, and encouraged the development of cash-crop production to recruit and finance their flock, root out slavery and polygamy, and serve the greater glory of God. African Christians, often ex-slaves returning from Brazil or Sierra Leone, were to be the agents of this civilizing mission, though its financial support and much of its leadership and direction remained in white hands.[10] Legitimate commerce also brought colonial political authority to the Nigerian coast. The elimination of exports of slaves and the regulation of commerce between Europeans and Africans led to the establishment of a colonial government in Lagos and of consular authority over the Niger Delta.[11]

Between 1860 and 1890, the export trade in vegetable oils was faced by an acute crisis, which was determined by its dependence on European capitalism. The demand for West

---

[9] Hopkins, *Economic History*; C. Gertzel, 'John Holt' (D.Phil, Oxford, 1959); O. Ikime, *Merchant Prince of the Niger Delta* (London, 1968); G.I. Jones. *The Trading States of the Oil Rivers* (Oxford, 1963).

[10] J.F.A. Ajayi, *Christian Missionaries in Nigeria, 1841-91* (London, 1965); E.A. Ayandele, *The Missionary Impact on Modern Nigeria, 1842-1914* (London, 1966); and *Holy Johnson* (London, 1970).

[11] K.O. Dike, *Trade and Politics in the Niger Delta, 1830-85* (Oxford, 1956).

African vegetable oils slumped. Developments in transport and finance increased opportunities for competition in West Africa. The invention of the Gatling and Maxim guns made coercion cheaper and easier. European powers eventually resolved the crisis by bringing all African territories under formal colonial rule. African rulers defended their sovereignty in vain.

The several European powers sought to protect their own commercial and strategic interests in Africa by defining their own spheres of influence, ensuring access to one another's territories, and eliminating indigenous constraints on their commercial activities. Treaties of protection paved the way for formal colonial administration. Particular industries, notably textiles on the one hand and steel and engineering on the other, planned to secure new markets and sources of raw materials by encouraging the expansion of cotton production in Africa and the building of railways, which would evacuate cotton and carry textiles to the interior. The depression in demand from Europe and the rise in mineral and vegetable substitutes cut the profits of the palm oil trade. The development of scheduled steam-ships, the increasing use of freely convertible francs and shillings, and the development of banking services independent of the established coastal firms increased competition and threatened the bilateral oligopolies of the coastal traders. Merchants on both sides sought to pass on the costs of the slump to one another, producing conflicts over quality and price of goods, currency exchange, and repayment of debts, over the return of escaped slaves, over spheres of influence, and over the political autonomy of African states. Imperialist ideology now defined the task of 'civilizing' Africa as the white man's burden. Africans were excluded from ecclesiastical and administrative office as well as commercial opportunities and institutions, in favour of European officials and firms. Diplomacy and ideological mission combined to give effect to the requirements of economic expediency.[12]

The system of 'legitimate commerce', established in the wake of the slave trade, encouraged the development of peasant production of export commodities. However, the expansion of production was limited by the fluctuating requirements of the European market and by the high cost of transport to the coast and margins of profit in the coastal trade. It could only be developed further by the extension of cheap bulk transport, which at that time meant railways into the interior and the introduction of more competitive trading arrangements. This required the extension of formal colonial rule in the absence of an indigenous state able and willing to guarantee foreign loans and protect foreign commercial interests. The fetters on the development of productive powers were removed by the expansion of colonial rule, a product of contradictions specific to the relations of production and exchange in Africa and of contradictions within the wider international capitalist system.

The Development of the Colonial Political Economy

The establishment of the colonial state made possible the development of commodity production by African producers and traders. The colonial state financed the development of railways and harbours. It rationalized the currency, and encouraged the use of money. It abolished the trading monopolies of coastal principalities, internal tolls, and the arbitrary interference, from the point of view of the European

---

[12] Hopkins, *Economic History*, pp. 132-66; J. Hargreaves, *Prelude to the Partition of West Africa* (London, 1963), 'The Loaded Pause', *JHSN*, 7 (1974), and *The Loaded Pause* (London, 1975); Ajayi, *Christian Missions*; Ayandele, *Holy Johnson*.

trading firms, of African rulers with the free conduct of commerce. It organized the forcible and voluntary recruitment of labour both for state purposes, railway and road building and portering, and for private purposes. Military occupation and the signing of treaties, as necessary to imperial control, were swiftly followed by the extension of the jurisdiction of colonial courts to cover the activities of mercantile companies and their agents, which facilitated the extension of their commercial activities into the interior. The increase in the demand for export crops in the early years of the century encouraged firms to advance credit for the purchase of cash crops, which financed the sale of imported goods. In turn, the expansion of export production and the increase in the money supply in the form of produce advances increased opportunities in trading, in craft production, and in the production of food for the market.[13] The mutual benefits of increased production helped to reconcile Nigerians to colonial rule, though without ever eliminating resistance to the imposition of colonial authority throughout the country, and gave a certain substance to the 'Dual Mandate',[14] which served alongside cruder notions of racial superiority and the white man's burden to justify colonial rule and the profits of colonial commerce.

In order to develop new crops, African traders and farmers adapted existing social institutions to organize the regulation of access to land, the mobilization of savings and credit facilities, and the recruitment of slave, 'pawn', and free labour

---

[13] Hopkins, *Economic History*, pp. 198-209.
[14] Cf. Lugard, *The Dual Mandate in British Tropical Africa* (London, 1922), and 'The Extension of British Influence'.

to clear, weed, and manure land and to plant trees.[15] The successful establishment of export production by African traders, planters, and peasants contrasted favourably with the failures of government and company plantations, and suited European trading companies, if not always suiting cotton and soap manufacturers who wanted to control the price and quantity of their own supplies.[16] Thus in Nigeria, colonialism enabled Africans to develop peasant production, and stimulated the development of petty commodity production generally. Mercantile firms were able to make commercial profits but plantations were not given the opportunity to develop at the expense of peasant production and capitalist production was limited to the Jos tin mines, while the state developed the Enugu coalfields.

In each of the areas in which colonial policy contributed to the development of peasant and petty commodity production, colonial administration and commerce restricted its further development. Despite Chamberlain's vision of the development of the 'undeveloped estates' of the tropics, the colonial government in Nigeria left this task largely in the 'invisible' hands of the market. Its major direct contribution was the building of the railway and the development of harbours. Administrative measures were used to encourage and regulate the production of cotton for export, but their success was limited by the Government's inability to enforce cotton

---

[15] P. Hill, *Studies in Rural Capitalism* (Cambridge, 1970), and *Rural Hausa* (Cambridge, 1972); S. S. Berr, *Cocoa, Custom and Socio-Economic Change* 'Christianity and the Rise of Cocoa Growing Ibadan and Ondo' *JHSN*, 4 (1968), Berry, 'Cocoa and Economic Development in Western Nigeria' and J. Hogendorn, 'The origins of the goundnut trade in Northern Nigeria' C.K. Eicher and C. Liedholm, (eds) *Growth and Development of the Nigerian Economy*, East Lansing, 1970,

[16] W.K. Hancock, *A Survey of British Commonwealth Affairs*, vol. 2, part 2 (Oxford, 1942), pp. 173-200; Hopkins, *Economic History*, pp. 209-16.

cultivation in the face of better returns from other crops, notably groundnuts.[17] Railway investment and encouragement of cotton production were both stimulated by the requirements of specific metropolitan industries and the railway debt was charged to colonial revenue. State investments had to be financed out of current revenue, which was dependent on the fluctuating value of exports, even where they would have brought a profitable return to British trading firms and augmented government revenue as in the case of motor roads in the hinterland of the cocoa belt. Its investment in railways led the Government to discourage the building of roads and the development of private motor transport services where these competed with the railway. Road and rail routes were determined by the military and administrative criteria of linking administrative centres, rather than encouraging trade and production.[18]

The initial expansion of colonial rule encouraged competition in the distributive trades. Trading firms advanced credit, primarily to secure themselves a share of the crop rather than to encourage its initial cultivations as was done by Hausa merchants in the case of groundnuts. When both barter and income terms of trade turned against the producers after World War I, the large firms protected their markets and profits by restrictive tactics, such as pool agreements, and by amalgamations and the exclusion of smaller competitors,

---

[17] Hogendorn, 'Nigerian Groundnut Exports; cf. M. Johnson, 'Cotton Imperialism in West Africa', *African Affairs*, 291 (1974). E.A. Brett, *Capitalism and Underdevelopment in East Africa: the Politics of Economic Change, 1919-1939* (Heinemann, 1973); A.S. Barnett, 'The Gezira Scheme: Production of Cotton and the Reproduction of Underdevelopment', in I. Oxaal. T. Barnett and D. Booth (eds), *Beyond the Sociology of Development* (London 1975); T. Forrest, 'Agricultural Policies in Nigeria, 1900-1978' in Heyer, Roberts and Williams, *Rural Development*

[18] Cf. Brett, *Capitalism and Underdevelopment*; G. Kay, 'Introduction' to *The Political Economy of Colonialism in Ghana* (Cambridge, 1972).

which enabled them to pass low prices on to African middlemen and producers. While protecting the firms' freedom to trade, the authorities did not restrict their 'freedom to combine'.[19] When war required action, they institutionalized rather than restricted the monopolistic trading position of the companies.[20] At the turn of the century, the development of banking facilities and rationalization of currency had encouraged competition and the expansion of the market. But the ultra-conservative currency and credit policies of the Government and the banks made the money supply dependent on the fluctuations of export incomes and accentuated their effects. The banks simply served the mercantile firms, and denied most African traders direct access to bank credits, thus ensuring that African traders remained dependent on the firms. Secure in the profits accruing from staple lines, the firms did not attempt to introduce new lines or encourage new productive activities. It was left to smaller, usually African traders 'to import and operate commercial vehicles, to market sewing machines, to build cinemas, and to establish a bread-making industry' for the first time.[21] 'Surplus' money was repatriated to mercantile firms, and was much of the high salaries of the firms' and Government's agents. Although the colonial state initially encouraged the development of production for export, the restrictive policies of the Government and the firms limited their further development.

---

[19] Gertzel, 'John Holt' p. 8.
[20] *Report of the Commission of Enquiry into the Marketing of West African Cocoa* (Chairman, W. Nowell) Cmnd. 5485 (London, 1938); Hancock, *Survey*, 2, 2, p. 209-36; J. Mars, 'Extra-territorial Enterprises' in M. Perham (ed.), *Mining, Commerce and Finance in Nigeria* (London, 1948); Bauer, *West African Trade*; R. W. Shenton and W. Freund, 'The Incorporation of Northern Nigeria into the World Capitalist Economy' *ROAPE*, 13 (1979).
[21] Hopkins, *Economic History*, p. 204, more generally pp. 188-209, 258-67.

Class Relations in the Colonial Political Economy

Colonialism transformed the class relations and political institutions of Nigerian society. Pre-colonial institutions governing kinship, land tenure, nobility, and kingship survived and even flourished. But they were adapted to meet new requirements within a different structure of relations to market and state, and between indigenous and foreign cultures. Peasants, farmers, and traders became dependent for their livelihood on the metropolitan market for export crops. Racist rules and attitudes, and monopolistic practices by the colonial administration, churches, and firms excluded Africans from access to 'the recognised functions, and rewards, of a middle class'.[22]

The Government imposed on Nigeria a 'patrimonial'[23] system of administration in the ideological guise of 'indirect rule' in order to enlist the dominant 'status groups'[24] in the service of colonial rule, and to contain the political consequences of changes in the class structure. Ideally, all relations within a patrimonial system are vertical ties of domination and dependence, with subordinate clients jostling for the favour of their patrons, and in this case, with the British Resident as the 'Great White Patron' at the apex of the system. Where an indigenous patrimonialism existed, as in the Muslim emirates, the British rapidly established their control over appointments, and rationalized the system of tax collection and

---

[22] T.L. Hodgkin, 'The African Middle Class', *Corona* 8 (1956), p. 88, reprinted in I. Wallerstein (ed.) *Social Change* (New York, 1966).

[23] M. Weber, *Economy and Society* vol. 1 ({1921} (New York, 1968), pp. 265-8. On-line at http://archive.org.

[24] On the distinction between classes and status groups (*Stände*, estates), see Weber, 'Class, Status, Party' ({1921} in H.H. Gerth and C. Wright Mills (eds) *From Max Weber: Essays in Sociology* (New York, 1946, London, 2008), pp. 186-8, and in *Economy and Society* vol. 2, ch. 9.6, see also vol. 1, ch1, IV.

administration. Where no indigenous patrimonialism existed, they transformed institutions of nobility to serve their purposes, raising rulers to authority over their fellows, subject to their retaining the favour of the Resident, and turned titled offices into a system of patronage. Where no indigenous nobility existed, or ruling houses appeared recalcitrant to British purposes, they simply appointed intermediaries with no royal or noble status, in some cases even strangers, to chieftaincies.

The very institution of chieftaincy is a colonial imposition, which standardises rank and function to the requirements of colonial administration. The purpose of all this was to carry out routine administration through subordinate intermediaries who were dependent on their colonial masters for their position, and to enable the colonial rulers to manipulate competition for office and status in their own interests. Rulers were judged initially by their loyalty to and dependence on the British. Considerations of legitimacy were always secondary. The system was most successful where indigenous rulers could claim some traditional entitlement to their office and prerogatives, and also where access to education and to commercial opportunities remained in the hands of the rulers, as in the emirates. Elsewhere, people resisted extortion and coercion by colonial agents with no recognized claims to their prerogatives. As the tasks of local administration became more complex, and commoners of education and wealth sought to play an active role in local affairs, the British administrators sought hesitantly to incorporate them into the system of Native Administration. In the thirties, British policy followed contradictory ends in the southern provinces: a return to the traditional, pre-colonial system to strengthen the legitimacy of indigenous rulers and the incorporation of educated and wealthy men with no traditional claims to office into the system.[25]

The material dominance of the culture of the colonial rulers, and the inculcation of its skills and values into the schools, mostly run by the missions, differentiated the subject population in terms of their access to certain economic opportunities, their claims to status honour, their style of life and patterns of social intercourse. Within local communities, it encouraged values opposed to those on which local and social and political institutions and claims to status were based. It gave rise to an elite of educated men, possessing the skills and knowledge necessary to operate in the world of the colonial administrators and thus able to challenge the position of local rulers, through whom the British sought to administer the country. The limitation of education in the emirates forestalled the subversive effects of education on the Native Authorities, but laid the foundation for the bitter and tragic conflicts between northerners and migrants from other communities over access to positions in the northern states and in the Federation.[26]

Colonialism created a peasantry in Nigeria.[27] It subordinated rural producers to the requirements of the

[25] M. Crowder and O. Ikime (eds), *West African Chiefs* (Ile-Ife, 1970); O. Ikime, 'Reconsidering Indirect Rule', *JHSN*, 4 (1968); O. Ikime and S.O. Osoba, 'Indirect Rule in British Africa', *Tarikh*, 3, 3 (New York, 1970); A. Afigbo, *The Warrant Chiefs* (London, 1972); J. A. Atanda, *The New Oyo Empire: Indirect Rule and Change in Western Nigeria, 1896-1034.* (London, 1975); R.K. Home 'Urban Growth and Urban Government', and J. Tseayo, 'The Emirate System and Tiv Reaction to Pagan Status in Northern Nigeria' in Williams (ed.), *Nigeria: Economy and Society* (London, 1976).

[26] See O. Nduka, *Western Education and the Nigerian Cultural Background* (Ibadan, 1964) and 'Colonial Education and Nigerian Society,' in Williams, *Nigeria*.

[27] My use of the term follows K.W.J. Post, ' "Peasantisation" and Rural Political Movements in Western Africa', *Archives Européennes de Sociologie, 13* (1972), and in Gutkind and Waterman (eds), *African Social Studies*.

metropolitan market and the colonial state which administered them through a culture to which they had no access. They depended for the realization of the value of their labour on the exchange of commodities in markets whose terms they could not control, which enabled mercantile companies, and subsequently the state and indigenous capitalists, to appropriate the surplus value of their labour. The prosperity, which the production of export crops and expansion of the market for food crops created, was bought at the expense of dependence and exploitation. This in turn made that prosperity precarious. Between the wars the terms of trade facing producers were considerably and at times drastically, worse than in the early years of the century. At various periods of low produce prices and increasing import prices, women and peasants resisted the imposition of coercive authority and the extension of taxation.[28]

In pre-colonial Nigeria, craftsmen produced to meet the requirements of the king or the community. The markets for commodities were limited by and largely to local demand, except where they had a very high value relative to weight and bulk. Within their communities, craftsmen had a recognized status, were effectively organized through guilds or even lineages, and were protected from the rigours of outside competition. Now they were required to compete with cheap imported manufacturers, and with craftsmen from other towns who could take advantage of improved transport facilities or even move to other towns. The extension of markets for craft products went together with more rigorous competition, and

---

[28] See J. van Allen, ' "Sitting on a Man": Colonialism and the Lost Political Institutions of Igbo Women,' *Canadian Journal of African Studies* 6, 2 (1972), Part **V** on the *Agbekoya* rebellion of 1968-1969.

increasing dependence on imported materials.[29] Polly Hill points out that rural crafts and trade were undermined during the colonial period, thus contributing to rural impoverishment,[30]

In some cases people turned to new opportunities in farming and trade. In Ibadan many members of weaving lineages took up other work. Outside the cocoa belt, where fewer alternative opportunities existed and imported cloths could not find a wide market, weaving expanded and became more specialized, serving the demand for quality cloths throughout the Yoruba towns and other regions of West Africa. In other cases, crafts were adapted to changing markets and to take advantage of imported tools and materials, in such activities as blacksmithing, shoemaking, or tailoring. New craft activities opened up opportunities for drivers, mechanics, or electricians. Older crafts looked to the 'Native Authority' to recognize and enforce the authority of their guilds, and protect them from outside competition. Newer crafts were often introduced by strangers, who could develop their own custom among their own communities and in the townships. Increasingly, craft activities were controlled by market competition, and dependence on the traders who supplied their materials and on the price of export crops which determined their markets, not the protective regulations of their guilds and the Native Authorities.

The development of the produce trade created opportunities for the intermediaries through whom the mercantile firms bought goods from and sold goods to its

---

[29] P.C. Lloyd, 'Craft Organization in Yoruba Towns', *Africa*, 23 (1953); M. Koll *Crafts and Co-operation in Western Nigeria* (Freiburg, 1969); J.M. Bray, 'The Industrial Structure of a Traditional Yoruba Town' (Ph.D thesis, University of Ibadan, 1966).
[30] P. Hill, *Population, Prosperity and Poverty: Kano 1900 and 1970* (Cambridge, 1977).

customers. The building of rural feeder roads created opportunities in transport for those entrepreneurs, mainly produce buyers, best able to take advantage of them. A complex hierarchy of traders developed, linked to one another and usually to the mercantile firms by ties of credit and clientage. Firms alternated between competition among themselves to capture the largest share of the market and tonnage of produce that they could and restrictive agreements to share the market among themselves. Competition and high produce prices, led to the expansion of credit and opportunities for independent traders; restriction, and low prices, led to the withdrawal of credit, the bankruptcy of traders, and exclusion of any competitors to the firms, other than a few Levantines with their international business contacts necessary to take on the companies.[31] In the 1930s the United Africa Company, formed in 1929 from an amalgamation of the major trading companies, controlled nearly half the market, and could dictate the policies of its major competitors. Independent African traders were virtually eliminated from the import-export business by the firms united in the Association of West African Merchants. Middlemen sought to use the 'Native Authorities' to protect their own spheres of operation from the extension of purchasing by the firms into the rural areas, and the increasing competition of Levantines. On a wider level, African traders from Nigeria and the Gold Coast attempted to export cocoa directly to America, and established banks, one of which survived the colonial period, to promote their own commercial activities. They could not compete with the superior resources,

---

[31] Hancock, *Survey*, 2, 2; Mars 'Extra-territorial Enterprises'; P.T. Bauer, *West African Trade* (Cambridge, 1954).

notably access to banking, shipping, and marketing facilities, and the favour of the Colonial Office, if not always of the local administrations, which the mercantile firms enjoyed.[32] There were conflicts of interests between farmers and traders and among the traders themselves. Poorer men were dependent on richer men, and richer men on the firms, so that the weaker often competed with one another for the favour of the stronger, and looked to the stronger to represent their interests to the Colonial Government.

Colonial rule did not require a large permanent wage-labour force. The tin mines recruited workers on a seasonal basis, and segregated them from the local population in mining camps. Wage labour replaced family, pawn and slave labour in agriculture to an increasing extent but on a seasonal or casual basis. Wage levels and the availability of labour tended to keep in line with produce prices, and thus the extent of alternative opportunities. The Government was the major employer of wage labour, notably in the railways, harbours, and coal mines, and in public works. Colonial wage policy was governed by the need to limit expenditure and to encourage people to seek opportunities in growing cash crops. Since government revenues were directly related to import and export levels, wage and salary earners shared with farmers and traders in their vulnerability to the price and levels of exports, even if the consequences were less direct. As early as 1897, a strike of labourers took place in Lagos in a situation where labour was scarce because of low government wage levels. Numerous other examples of workers combining to seek better wages and

---

[32] Hopkins, 'Economic Aspects of Political Movements in Nigeria and the Gold Coast, 1918-39', *Journal of African History*, 7 (1966); I. Duffield, 'The Business Activities of Duse Mohammed Ali', *JHSN*, 4 (1969).

conditions of work have been recorded.[33] Only with the Second World War, which led to a rapid increase in wage employment and a sharp increase in the cost of living, did workers' actions come to be politically significant.

Colonial administration and the activities of the missions required clerks, teachers, and clergymen, in limited numbers, and the development of education. Education not only provided opportunities for salaried employment, but also enabled people to develop formal accounting skills and come into contact with expatriate administrators and company managers. It could thus facilitate access to trade, and enable men to act in local political affairs as intermediaries between the administrators and the chiefs and people. In the emirates, the expansion of formal education was limited, and restricted largely to the family and retainers of the ruling lineages. In Southern Nigeria, it was often the sons of poor and commoner families who seized the opportunities that education and for that matter commerce offered. As the tasks of local administration became more complex, the Colonial Government sought to incorporate educated and wealthy men into the 'Native Authorities', which conflicted with their determination to maintain the authority of the indigenous rulers.[34] As successful traders found their further advancement blocked by the monopolistic practices of colonial firms, so educated Nigerians found themselves denied access to administrative office and the higher education which would

---

[33] A. Hughes and Cohen, 'An Emerging Nigerian Working Class: The Lagos Experience, 1897-1939', in P. Gutkind, R. Cohen and J, Copans (eds) *African Labour History* (Beverly Hills and London, 1979); Hopkins, 'The Lagos Strike of 1897', *Past and Present*, 35 (1966); J. Weeks, 'Wage Policy and the Colonial Legacy', *JMAS*, 9 (1971).

[34] See Home 'Urban Growth'. Cf. P.C. Lloyd, 'The Integration of New Economic Classes into Local Government in Western Nigeria', *African Affairs*, 53 (1953).

enable them to acquire qualifications equal to those of their colonial masters. The system of 'Native Administration' and the lack of representative political institutions excluded them from political office, except for appointees of the colonial rulers and three members elected to Lagos Town Council and four from Lagos and Calabar, to the Legislative Council. From the nineteenth century, nationalists fought for the chance to compete for rewards accorded to the criteria of merit and achievement, which colonial firms and rulers denied them. For example, the crucial issues raised by the Nigerian Youth Movement in the thirties were the status of Yaba Higher College, Nigeria's only institution of higher education which offered only sub-degree-level qualifications, and the 'cocoa pool' through which the firms restricted the share of Nigerian merchants in the cocoa trade.[35] Their failure led them to recognize that their goals could only be realized if they themselves controlled state power.[36]

Colonialism required African intermediaries in commerce and administration whose education and money made them privileged in relation to the peasants, craftsmen, and petty traders, but who were denied the opportunity to develop their skills and resources further by the exclusive practice of the firms and Government. They originally sought to gain equal opportunities within the framework of colonial rule, but increasingly came to use their skills and resources to oppose colonial rule itself. Under colonial rule, all classes were dependent for their livelihood on the fluctuating markets for export crops. In World War II, crop prices were drastically

---

[35] Hodgkin, 'The African Middle Class', and *Nationalism in Colonial Africa* (London, 1956); J.S. Coleman, *Nigeria: Background to Nationalism* (Berkeley, 1958).
[36] Hopkins, 'Economic Aspects'.

reduced by administrative regulation. Government controlled the wage levels of an expanded labour force, and recruited thousands of soldiers to its service. The price of goods on which consumers had come to depend increased sharply because of war-time inflation and restriction on imports. The relation between colonial rule and the economic deprivation of different classes was more nakedly exposed than under the *laissez faire* regime of the pre-war period.

The Transition to the Neo-Colonial Political Economy
The development of the colonial political economy established the material and institutional foundations for the transition to a neo-colonial political economy. The integration of Nigerian producers into the international exchange economy expanded the market to the point where the internal market could sustain the development of capitalist manufactures, given appropriate subsidies and protection by the state. The war-time establishment of the produce Marketing Boards established the institutional means for the state appropriation of the surplus value of peasant production. Initially Britain used the marketing Boards to subsidize the British consumer, and to shore up the reserves and balance the payments of the sterling bloc. Indigenous rulers could use them to finance party political activities, line their pockets, accumulate money capital, and finance industrial development, both directly and indirectly. Thus the marketing boards could be used to finance industrial investment and to establish an indigenous capitalist class.[37] The expansion of formal education, accentuated after

---

[37] There is an extensive literature on the Marketing Boards. See A. Aladejana, *The Marketing Board System: A Bibliography* (Ibadan, 1971); Bauer, West African Trade; H. C. Kriesel, *Marketing of Groundnuts in Nigeria, Cocoa Marketing in Nigeria, Cotton Marketing in Nigeria* (East Lansing and Ibadan, 1968-69); H.M.A. Onitiri and D. Olatunbosun (eds), *The Marketing*

World War II, produced the indigenous cadres to man the administration, direct the affairs of government, and provide middle-level management and semi-skilled manpower for international firms. Colonial rule thus gave rise to indigenous business and administrative classes, committed to a regulated market economy, and a strategy of development based on technologically advanced forms of production, and a complex and rationalized administration of government and productive enterprises which would ensure their continued dependence on metropolitan capitalism.

Decolonization was the sequel to rather than a condition of colonial development. It took place in the context of changes in the international political economy arising from the end of World War II. The United States emerged from the war as the dominant international power. It opposed the protective character of British economic policy in West Africa, in favour of the 'open door' policy which had long been imposed on China and Latin America, and self-determination for colonial people, as long as they determined in favour of an economy open to US penetration. The rhetoric of self-determination formed the basis for ideological competition between the United States and the Soviet Union, and for the demands of Asian and African nationalists.[38]

The war initiated a period of rapid technological development and economic growth. Strategic war materials remained important, but the market for simple manufactured goods, such as textiles, took second place to competition for markets for more expensive luxury goods, and for the sale of

---

Board System (Ibadan, 1972); G. Williams, 'Marketing without and with Marketing Boards in Nigeria,' *ROAPE* 34 (1985); J.-G. Deutsch, 'Educating the Middleman: Political and Economic History of Statutory Colonial Marketing in Nigeria', Ph. D. thesis, 1990 , Part VI.
[38] See Coleman, *Nigeria*, chapter 10.

intermediate and producer goods. The dominant mercantile firm in West Africa, the United Africa Company, was integrated into the multinational Unilever empire whose activities extended far beyond the West African export-import trade. In the 1930s, international competition to British manufactures had led to the imposition of discriminatory quotas against cheaper Japanese imports. It now led British firms to defend their imperial markets by establishing manufacturing industries on colonial soil. Other countries invested in manufacturing in Nigeria to gain access to the market. Thus the export of capital was used to promote the export of commodities.[39] It was thus in the interests of metropolitan capitalism to execute a strategic withdrawal from merchant trading, in favour of establishing manufacturing industries in Nigeria.[40] In turn, this would create a protected area for the development of African commercial activity and secure the domination of metropolitan firms over Nigeria through their control of the resources necessary for capitalist development, rather than through metropolitan control of the levers of state power.

In 1947, Britain's Labour Government extended its West African strategy of colonial development to political representation.[41] In 1948, the Foot Commission set in motion the Africanization of the civil service, and the Government announced the beginnings of constitutional reform which would give African politicians access to legislative and executive authority. Government agencies began to give more

---

[39] Lenin, *Imperialism. The Highest Stage of Capitalism* (1916) in *Selected Works* (in one vol.) (Moscow, 1968) p. 215.
[40] P. Kilby, *Industrialisation in an Open Economy: Nigeria 1945-66* (Cambridge, 1969).
[41] Cowen and Shenton, 'The Origins and Course of Fabian Colonialism in Africa,' *Journal of Historical Sociology* 4, 2 (1991), pp. 143-74.

sympathetic consideration to African businessmen in such matters as import licences and guarantees of bank credit. In the West, the administration sought to reform local government and give to the local bourgeoisie the leading position which it already enjoyed in the East.

The Colonial Government had acceded to the immediate demands of the Nigerian bourgeoisie, who responded by intensifying competition among themselves for the future spoils of office and preparing for electoral competition. Nationalist agitation by politicians gave way to their need to secure local bases of power. The Yoruba bourgeoisie organized the Egbe Omo Oduduwa, and then the Action Group, to promote Yoruba unity, and to press for a federal constitution which would give them control of the lucrative cocoa revenues and protect them against the Igbo challenge to their educational, economic, and political leadership. In the North, teachers, officials, and businessmen organized the Jam'iyyar Mutanen Arewa to reform and defend the institutions of the North and to protect Northern interests within the new constitutional dispensation. Leaders of the National Council of Nigeria and the Cameroons became increasingly involved in local issues and in the East, in the affairs of the Ibo State Union. The attempt by the Zikist movement to provoke the NCNC into militant confrontation with the authority and plans of the Colonial Government was firmly repudiated.[42]

Thus, from the very beginning, the crucial determinants of the process of decolonization were established. The first was

---

[42] Osoba, 'Ideological Trends in the Nigerian National Liberation Movement and the Problems of National Identity, Solidarity, Motivation, 1934-1965' *Ibadan*, 27 (1969); Coleman, *Nigeria*, chapters 14-17; R.L. Sklar, *Nigerian Political Parties* (Princeton, 1963), chapters 2-3; O. Awolowo, *Awo* (Cambridge, 1960); Ahmadu Bello, *My Life* (London, 1960); N. Azikiwe, *My Odyssey: an Autobiography* (London, 1971).

ultimate British control of political authority, backed by control of the armed forces and administrative service: political authority was conceded to Nigerian politicians in so far as they met the conditions set by the British. The second was the division among the Nigerian politicians, which enabled the British to play them off against one another, and broke down any attempt to oppose British plans and terms.[43] The third was the sustained expansion of the economy in the forties and fifties, and hence of the rate of increase of commercial and bureaucratic as well as political opportunities to satisfy the aspirations of the Nigerian bourgeoisie. The fourth was the weakness and divided state of the trade unions and the lack of other effective mass organizations, especially among the peasant farmers but also among the urban petty bourgeoisie, able to articulate the demands of the exploited classes, and provide mass support for the enforcement of radical nationalist demands. At the same time that they opened up new opportunities for political, administrative, and commercial activities to the Nigerian bourgeoisie, the British Government moved with severity against radical nationalists and trade unionists. Through their control of the political process of decolonization, the British promoted class and power relations which would ensure the continued domination of Nigeria by international capitalism.

The Development of the Neo-colonial Political Economy
The development of the neo-colonial economy required the transfer of state authority into indigenous hands. Neither the Colonial Government nor the colonial firms, secure in their

---

[43] See the account of the 1957 constitutional conference in K. Post and G. Jenkins, *The Price of Liberty: Personality and Politics in Colonial Nigeria* (Cambridge, 1973), chapter 13.

dominant commercial position, initiated the transition from trading to manufacturing. The pricing policies of the Marketing Board delayed the development of industry in Nigeria by limiting the expansion of the market, and the development of indigenous capitalism by denying African traders the opportunity to profit from the post-war boom in commodity prices. The surpluses accumulated by the Marketing Board were sent to Britain rather than invested in Nigeria.[44] Independence ended British control of public investment funds, of tariff and industrial policy, of fiscal policies and the allocation of foreign exchange. A central bank was established, able to regulate the money supply and currency exchange. State policy protected and subsidized industrial investment by protective tariffs, tariff rebates on imported machinery, tax holidays, and the provision of services and industrial estates.[45] The state controlled the allocation of profitable opportunities, which could be used to create protected niches for its clients, and enabled the Nigerian bourgeoisie to share in the spoils of the neo-colonial economy, and accumulate capital.

Markets and sources of investment and technology have been diversified among different metropolitan countries or, to put a different slant on the same thing, foreign exploitation has been multi-lateralized. The federal and the regional governments competed amongst themselves and with other neo-colonial states to attract foreign investment by a combination of subsidies and protection and by promising profit repatriation. Foreign investors responded in order to

[44] Akeredolu-Ale, 'The Competitive Threshold Hypothesis and Nigeria's Industrialisation Process', (review of Kilby, *Industrialisation*), *Nigerian Journal of Economic and Social Studies*, (NJESS) 14 (1972).
[45] See Weeks, 'Employment, Growth and Foreign Domination in Underdeveloped Countries' *Review of Radical Political Economics*, 4 (1972).

gain, extend, or protect their access to the Nigerian market, and to oligopolistic niches within it, and to take advantage of the bounties offered by the state.

As Philip C. Asiodu, the Permanent Secretary in the Federal Ministry of Mines and Power explained in 1969, 'Thus farmers, traders, and commercial firms came to be involved in a complex of market relations. The Nigerian system which is essentially pragmatic, has worked well in the past...Excepting (iron and steel) the whole field of industry remains open to private initiative. The usual tax and tariff incentives will be maintained.'[46] A striking 1975 example is the reintroduction of import licences for cars under 2000cc capacity to protect the newly established Volkswagen and Peugeot assembly plants. Peugeot would presumably need this measure of protection to pay the cost of airlifting bodies and engines from Lyon to Kaduna, where Nigerian-made batteries will be inserted.

The dominant institution of neo-colonial capitalism is the multinational corporation (multinational in its operations more than its ownership and control, which remain firmly outside underdeveloped countries). The productive, distributive and financial activities of the corporation are vertically integrated. They are able to control and diversify their sources of inputs, investments, and markets in such a way as to ensure their own profitability, security, and expansion. They have invested in capital-intensive and technologically-advanced industries in the import-substituting sector where state protection guarantees their markets.[47] These industries depend on foreign, or rather foreign-controlled, capital,

[46] See P.C. Asiodu, 'Industrial Policy and Incentives in Nigeria', (NJESS) 9 (1967), cited *Financial Times*, 4 August, 1969.
[47] *West Africa*, 7 April, 1975, p. 409.

supplies of intermediate goods, and technical and managerial skills. These investments do generate backward, and final demand, and sometimes forward linkages. But many of these linkages stimulate production in metropolitan rather than underdeveloped economies.

These industries generate a demand for the development of skills and learning, both for their own activities and for the public administration which serves them. But these are the skills which the highly educated middle class have acquired in metropolitan and colonial universities, which make them employable in capitalist firms and state administration and provide them with their economic privileges and political superiority over the poor. In this way they come to share with metropolitan capitalists a commitment to the development of capitalist production and the extension of state activity at the expense of peasant and petty commodity producers. The development of neo-colonial capitalism substituted imports of intermediate and producer goods for imports of consumer goods. This consolidates rather than undermines dependence on foreign suppliers, since production, as well as consumption, now depends on foreign imports.

The development of capitalism depends on the domination of capitalist production over peasant and petty commodity production, enforced by the state rather than produced by market competition. The monopoly purchasing power of the Marketing Boards enabled the state to increase the rate of exploitation of peasant labour to finance the emergence of a Nigerian capitalist class, and to finance the development of industrial investment, and the provision of urban services and amenities. Peasant and petty commodity producers provide inputs which capitalist firms cannot produce profitably. These include cheap food and consumer goods for the employees of capitalist firms and the state which services them, thereby reducing wage costs and inflating the salaries of managerial staff. Petty commodity production maintains the 'reserve army of labour', thus ensuring a flexible supply of labour to capitalist employers and limiting the bargaining strength of organized labour, thus again reducing wage costs. It provides opportunities for additional earnings to workers and gives them the hope of establishing themselves as independent men, [48] thus both subsidizing and encouraging wage employment. Capitalist production depends for its market firstly on the incomes of export-crop farmers, secondly on the incomes of workers and clerks employed by capitalist firms and the state, thirdly on the incomes derived by the bourgeoisie from the exploitation of the producers and more recently from their appropriation of a share in the oil revenues, and fourthly from the incomes on petty commodity producers, craftsmen and traders, and food-crop farmers generated by the spending of other classes.

At the same time, the development of capitalist production restricts the development of peasant and petty commodity production. The transfer by the state of resources from agriculture and the rural economy to itself and to capitalist production and the urban economy reduces the return on rural labour and investment, which impoverishes farmers and encourages the transfer of private resources, including skills, from the rural to the urban economy. Government loans and tax and tariff incentives subsidize capitalist firms at the expense of competition from petty commodity producers.

---

[48] Peace, 'Industrial Conflict'.

Petty commodity production depends on imported materials, whose prices are determined by capitalist distributors and their clients, and on materials produced or even discarded by capitalist firms. Ease of entry into production and thus mutual competition among producers restricts opportunities for capital accumulation from petty commodity production. These restrictions can only be overcome when producers, and more particularly distributors, can gain privileged access to supplies or markets, which in turn depends on their gaining the patronage of agents of the state or of capitalist firms. Thus capitalist development is parasitical on peasant and petty commodity production. Control of state policy and relations of exchange enables capitalists to determine the conditions of production of peasant and petty commodity producers.[49]

Decolonization altered the patterns of participation and influence in public affairs. Power was effectively devolved to the bourgeoisie who commanded the skills and resources necessary to determine public policy at the regional and national levels. The scale of the resources required to take advantage of the new opportunities for political participation was well beyond the reach of the petty traders and contractors who had previously been able to exercise some influence with the customary authorities at the local level. Allocation of resources at the local level was now determined by the interests of the ruling party at the regional, and ultimately the federal, level. Thus local influence depended on patronage relations with regional politicians, and the imposition of

---

[49] C. Gerry and O. Lebrun, 'Petty Producers and Capitalism', *ROAPE*, 3 (1975); cf. Weeks, 'Imbalance between the Centre and Periphery and the "Employment' Crisis" in Kenya', in Oxaal, *Beyond the Sociology*.

military rule deprived people of even these limited opportunities for patronage.[50]

Decolonization thus paved the way for capitalist development in Nigeria. But the development of capitalism consolidated rather than undermined foreign economic domination. It depended on the increasing exploitation of export-crop farmers, and restricted the development of peasant and petty commodity production.

Class Relations in the Neo-Political Economy

The transition from the colonial to the neo-colonial political economy both required and led to changes in class relations, and generated contradictions that could not be resolved within the framework of representative political institutions.

Expatriate domination of investment opportunities, thanks to their superior access to credit, supplies, and the technology and managerial skills necessary to industrial production, inhibits the accumulation and reinvestment of capital by indigenous entrepreneurs who lack the resources necessary to compete with vertically integrated multinational corporations. [51] Consequently indigenous entrepreneurs became 'compradores', i.e. intermediaries between foreign interests and the indigenous polity and economy, and/or turned to the state as a source of both capital and contracts. Lucrative profits have accrued to those able to establish control of monopolistic niches in the distribution of commodities, rather than to those who have organized their

[50] P.C. Lloyd, 'Integration', 'Local Government in Yoruba Towns' (D.Phil, University of Oxford, 1958); Post and Jenkins, *Price of Liberty*. Part **III**.
[51] See Akeredolu-Ale, *The Underdevelopment of Indigenous Entrepreneurship in Nigeria* (Ibadan, 1975), and 'Private Foreign Investment and the Underdevelopment of Indigenous Entrepreneurship in Nigeria', in Williams, *Nigeria*.

production most efficiently. Consequently, politics and the favour of foreign companies, itself a product of political influence, became the primary sources of capital accumulation by Nigerians. Initially, this capital was accumulated from the surplus value appropriated from the peasants by the Marketing Boards, Tariff protection and monopolistic distributive arrangements for imported and factory-produced goods increased profits at the expense of consumers. Professionals, bureaucrats, and merchants used state power to establish themselves as a bourgeoisie.[52]

Nigerian governments perpetuated the highly inegalitarian colonial administrative, salary, and tax structure, with its complex of fringe benefits (car and child allowances, health facilities and housing, subsidies available to the earners of high salaries). The state regulated expatriate quotas to encourage foreign companies to employ Nigerian managerial and professional staff. The lucrative salaries offered in the private sector and, by necessity, offered for professional and technical staff in the public sector led administrators, followed by academics, to demand equivalent salaries for themselves.[53] The 1971 Adebo Commission[54] was instructed 'to examine areas in which rationalisation and harmonisation of wages, salaries and other remuneration and conditions of employment are desirable and feasible as between the public and private

[52] Osoba, 'Ideological Trends'.
[53] Cf. Nigeria, *Report of the Advisory Committee on Aids to African Businessmen* (Lagos, 1959). The Memorandum of the Committee of Vice-Chancellors of Nigerian Universities, cited Waterman 'Conservatism amongst Nigerian workers' in Williams, *Nigeria*. See the demands of Nigerian academics for fringe benefits and a leading academic's description of their 'penury' *(West Africa*, 7 May, 1973) and the critique by Nduka, 'The Anatomy of Rationalization', *Nigerian Opinion*, 7, 1 (1971) and in Gutkind and Waterman, *African Social Studies*.
[54] Nigeria, *Second and Final Report of the Wages and Salaries Review Commission 1970-1971* (Chairman: S.O. Adebo), (Lagos, 1971) esp. pp. 13-15. 24-31; *White Paper on the Second and Final Report of the Wages and Salaries Commission 1970-1971* (Lagos, 1971), esp. pp. 8-10.

sectors of the economy'. In 1974, the Udoji Commission,[55] in carrying out similar instructions, repaid its bureaucratic sponsors handsomely. This provoked strikes by workers in the private sector but more particularly by professional staff and technical students who felt that they had fallen behind in the process, and were only pacified by a guaranteed increase on previous salaries of 30 to 40 per cent, still below the 100 per cent increases to daily paid workers earning ₦2.00 per day at the bottom, and senior officials earning 28 times as much at the top.

The bourgeoisie sought to establish areas of economic activity in which they would be protected from foreign competition, or in which foreign companies would have to operate through them. Initially this was provided by the withdrawal of foreign companies from produce and retail trading, by the exclusion of foreigners from land ownership, and by the established position of Nigerian entrepreneurs in such fields as passenger transport. This did not resolve the conflict between indigenous businessmen and multinational corporations over the terms of their relationship. The initial focus of African aspirations has been to exclude Lebanese merchants from their position in the distributive trades and certain assembly industries. The 1972 Nigerian Enterprise Promotions (Indigenization) Decree reserved large areas of economic activity for Indigenous businessmen, including advertising and public relations, pools, assembly of radios, record-players, etc., blending and bottling of alcoholic drinks, block and brick making, bread making, clearing and forwarding,

---

[55] Nigeria, Public Service Review Commission: *Main Report and Government Views on the Report of the Public Service Commission* (Chairman: J. Udoji)) (Lagos, 1974), summarized in *West Africa*, 13, 20, 27 January, 1975; and see 'Nigeria's Response to Udoji, *West Africa*, 3 March, 1975.

and retail trading. Multinational companies had only peripheral interests in these fields, in which Lebanese merchants were well represented. Local participation in equity shares and a minimum size are required for foreign firms operating in a wider range of activities, including beer brewing, tyre manufacture, construction, service and distribution of motor vehicles, manufacture of cement, paints, matches, metal containers and soaps, poultry farming, and wholesale trade. Finance for indigenous participation in foreign industries or takeover of them has been provided by banks, now 40 per cent government-owned, and required to allocate at least 40 per cent of their loans to Nigerian businessmen, by the legally and illegally gained wealth of the state-sponsored bourgeoisie, and by employees of foreign companies who have been lent money by firms to buy their shares at favourable prices. Civil servants are reported to be among the main recipients of bank loans for share purchases. Thus managers and bureaucrats have assimilated themselves to Nigeria's capitalist class. Nigeria has expanded and consolidated its capitalist class. Geographically, its own operations if not always the personal origins and of the businesses which have been taken over, are concentrated in Lagos and Kano, the major areas of industrial expansion. Increasing access to money and opportunities for the few will strengthen their ability to deny opportunities to the many. It may be, as a correspondent for *West Africa*[56] suggests, 'politically desirable that the transfer of ownership of foreign business should be spread both geographically and between social classes'; it is inconceivable that this should have been done. Multinational corporations have taken a leading role in

---

[56] *West Africa*, 11 February, 1974, p. 143.

sponsoring the acquisition of shares by Nigerians, and establishing on a firmer footing their alliance with Nigerian capitalism. This does not preclude future conflict over the relative share of foreign and indigenous capitalists in the profits of the neo-colonial economy.[57]

The ambiguous position of the bourgeoisie within the neo-colonial political economy is expressed in its ideological ambiguity.[58] Its nationalism is the outcome of its wish to appropriate resources back from the foreigner; its commitment to foreign investment is the outcome of its concrete dependence on the neo-colonial political economy. National unity and reconciliation express its ambition to act as a hegemonic class, providing moral and political leadership at the national level and within the international political arena; its tribalism is the outcome of its lack of control of the productive resources of the economy and hence of the competition among the bourgeoisie for favoured access to scarce resources and the need to manipulate particularistic interests and sentiments among the poor to maintain the bourgeoisie's political domination.

The bourgeoisie lacks the commitments of a religious, socialist, or nationalist character of the rationalizing, capital accumulating, surplus and expropriating classes, which directed the industrialization of Britain, Russia, Germany, and Japan. Perhaps it is this that lies behind the repeated call for a

[57] P. Collins, 'The Political Economy of Indigenization', *The African Review*, 4 (1975); Akeredolu-Ale, 'Private Foreign Investment'. A further Indigenization Decree was issued in 1976. In Kano, the major purchasers of shares, appointed as directors of foreign firms, have been merchants who have previously acted as distributors for them. The decrees institutionalized existing relations of dependence, Hoogvelt, 'Indigenization in Kano', *ROAPE*, 14 (1980). Part III.
[58] Cf. Osoba, 'Ideological Trends', and 'The Deepening Crisis of the Nigerian Bourgeoisie', *ROAPE*, 13 (1979).

'national ideology', which seeks to subordinate the energies of the people behind a single national goal. In fact, the Nigerian bourgeoisie do have an ideology, in the sense of a theoretical legitimation of the *status quo*. It is expressed in the concept of 'development',[59] which is 'that which we are all in favour of', and given statistical respectability in figures measuring the growth of commodity production, particularly production by capitalist mining and manufacturing industries. The demand for Nigerianization gives it a nationalist colouring. But this demand falls short of the demand for expropriation of foreign capitalists on whom the Nigerian bourgeoisie remains dependent. In this way, the ideology of 'national development' presents the bourgeoisie's image of itself as providing national leadership in the public interest, with its contradictions abolished and its immediate material interests preserved. What the bourgeoisie lacks, to use Mannheim's[60] terminology, is a Utopia, a set of ideas to inspire the transformation of the existing order and the liberation of human capacities.

The transition to a neo-colonial political economy changed the relationship between the classes who produce value and those that appropriate it.[61] State monopoly marketing boards introduced a new form of exploitation of the surplus value of peasant labour and increased the rate of exploitation to a point where the continued production and marketing of agricultural crops came to be threatened. The price of export crops came to be determined by political decisions rather than through the impersonal operations of the market. Consequently, the

---

[59] J.D.Y. Peel gave a more encompassing of the way in which Yoruba deploy the term '*Olaju*', which may be translated as 'enlightenment' (rather than 'development') in '*Olaju*: a Yoruba conception of development', *Journal of Development Studies*, 14 (1978). Parts **IV** and **V**.
[60] K. Mannheim, *Ideology and Utopia* (London, 1940).
[61] See Marx, *Capital*, vol. 1 p. 292 and ch. 6 & 7 (*CW* 35).

exploitation of export-crop farmers, as a class, sharing a common destiny which is determined by the Government's exercise of political decisions, has become clearly apparent to farmers. This has given rise to a specific peasant consciousness, at least among Yoruba cocoa farmers. Under conditions of falling crop prices, increasing taxes, and inflation, it gave rise to the *Agbekoya* rebellion of 1968-69, which forced the Government to reduce taxes and withdraw its officials from rural areas.[62]

Food-crop farmers and craftsmen and petty traders depend in large measure on the direct and multiplier effects of expenditure by cash-crop farmers for their incomes. Thus their own market situation is indirectly governed by the rate of exploitation of agricultural production, and by the terms of trade between export crops and manufactured goods. Even though oil has far surpassed agriculture's contribution to export and government revenue's, agricultural incomes still provide the major source of expenditure on items produced with local skills and resources. The consolidation of the intermediary position of merchant traders has excluded craftsmen and petty traders from direct access to expatriate firms for credit and supplies. The Nigerian merchants who

---

[62] The comprehensive account and analysis of the politics of farmers and farmers' organizations in Western Nigeria is C.E.F. Beer, 'The Farmers and the State in Western Nigeria', (Ph.D., University of Ibadan, (1971), published in a revised version as Beer, *The Politics of Peasant Groups in Western Nigeria* (Ibadan University Press, 1976); see also Beer and Williams, 'The Politics of the Ibadan Peasantry' in *The African Review*, 5 (1976) and in Williams, *Nigeria*; T. Adeniran, 'The Dynamics of Peasant Revolt in the Western State of Nigeria: a Conceptual Analysis', *Journal of Black Studies* (1974). Essay **V**. A film of the Agbekoya rising is available from *Yahoo Nolly* in Yoruba with English sub-titles. It captures the atmosphere of the time and relations among farmers and between farmers and their representatives and civil and military authorities and, allowing for some dramatic licence, is faithful to the historical narrative.
https://www.youtube.com/watch?v=7sj4B_sKH5Q (Part I) and
https://youtube/nngpwULP2gw (Part II).

displace expatriate trading firms, and more recently Levantine traders, tend to restrict the advance of credit to a limited network of dependents, and to take over many of the middlemen activities of petty traders themselves.

Craftsmen and petty traders find themselves competing in fields in which there are no effective formal and informal barriers to entry. Returns are therefore low, and required to meet subsistence and conventional expenditures. Expansion of output is limited by the craftsman's own labour time, and by his ability to attract, organize, and supervise apprentices. The more apprentices recruited, the greater the competition for clients in the future. Since craftsmen's prices are based on low marginal costs of labour and personal supervision, they cannot improve their relative position by organizing their labour force on capitalist lines and meeting the increased costs of paying and supervising waged labour. Co-operative arrangements allow the sharing of certain costs and risks, but only permit marginal extension of the limits to expansion.[63] Both craftsmen and petty traders know that higher profits are made by the merchants who sell them materials or buy commodities from them than they can make themselves. Tailors and petty cloth sellers thus aspire to become cloth merchants, mechanics plan to trade in motor parts, drivers to own their own taxis, yam sellers to trade in beans (requiring more working capital, and thus opportunities for profit). Access to these opportunities is controlled by the very merchants who exploit them. Thus craftsmen and petty traders, rather than combining to prevent their own exploitation, instead look to potential sponsors both for the supplies and credit necessary to carry out their

---

[63] See Koll, *Crafts and Co-operation*.

immediate activities and for assistance in surmounting the barriers to admission to the charmed circle of monopolistic advantage. During the colonial period, merchants from an earlier era were sometimes able to take advantage of new opportunities. In other cases, produce buyers and traders started their careers as clerks to or agents of mercantile companies, thus overcoming the initial hurdles of credit, working capital, and clientele. Since then, political influence, the favour of foreign companies, and lately influence with and marriage to army officers have become the best-trodden paths to commercial success. Personal skills, the taking up of opportunities for innovation, and the shrewd management of resources and personal relations all determine an individual's chance of commercial success, thus encouraging and sustaining an ethic of competition. But the situation of craftsmen and petty traders as a class is determined by the rate of exploitation of agricultural production on the one hand, and the expropriation of the resources and opportunities essential to their livelihood by manufacturers and merchants on the other. Relations with merchants and through them with the neo-colonial political economy as a whole are mediate through personal ties of clientage and patronage, and an ideology of entrepreneurial initiative, rather than through the impersonal ties of the market and an ideology of class conflict.

In more general terms, opportunities have been increased in capitalist enterprises and in state administration, to the advantage of those with education and formal qualifications, at the expense of the illiterate, and of people involved in craft and peasant production. This discriminates against women. They are less likely to be educated than men, and when they do acquire secondary and higher education, are more likely to be employed in lower status and worse-paid jobs than their male peers (as nurses, rather than doctors, secretaries rather than executives). In those activities in which women are most commonly engaged (craft production and petty trading), opportunities have been restricted by the requirements of capitalism. In these areas, the proportion of men employed increases as the returns to employment increase, and the success of women is often dependent on the favour of influential men.[64] While opportunities for access to education and formal employment qualifications have expanded dramatically so has the size of the bourgeoisie and the number of its children at school or university. By virtue of the financial, political, and cultural resources at its disposal, the bourgeoisie has been best placed to take advantage of publicly funded educational opportunities, thus putting these opportunities even further from the sons and daughters of the poor.[65]

The expansion of industry and administration has dramatically increased the number of people in industrial and clerical employment. The major attraction of wage and salary employment is the opportunity which can be used contemporaneously and subsequently in independent economic activity. This intensifies the wage or salary earner's determination to maintain and improve his real income, and thus his margin of savings, for both his immediate subsistence needs and family obligations, and his future trading or other opportunities depend on his maximizing his income from employment.[66]

---

[64] See D. Remy, 'Underdevelopment and the Experience of Women', in R. Reiter (ed.) *Towards an Anthropology of Women* (New York, 1975), and in Williams, *Nigeria*.
[65] See Nduka, 'Colonial Education'.
[66] Peace, *Choice, Class, and Conflict: A Study of Southern Nigerian Factory Workers* (Hassocks, 1979), pp. 49-79.

There are significant differences in the market situation of workers in different employment sectors. Wages are a relatively small proportion of total costs for capital-intensive foreign firms, usually operating in an oligopolistic market. Levantine and Nigerian firms tend to assemble consumer goods or process raw materials, or to be engaged in construction and transport, where they rely on cheap labour to maintain their position in more competitive markets. Trade union organizations tend to be promoted by the former, and severely repressed by the latter. Wage improvements in the latter firms tend to depend on a general increase in the wage level, which depends in turn on the industrial strength of workers in capital-intensive firms and government employ. During the colonial period, government was by far the most important employer of wage labour, and wage levels came to be determined by the decisions of a series of government commissions, concerned mainly to adjust wages upwards in line with trends in the cost of living. Industrial workers have been able to bargain for wage increases on a factory basis, but at the same time they have added their industrial strength to the periodic demands for overall wage increases in the face of inflation and have insisted on the extension of public sector awards to the private sector. A few manual workers with scarce skills and some employees with relatively high levels of formal education are able to sell their skills on a favourable labour market, or look to promotion within their firm for advancement. But for most factory workers, collective bargaining, supported where necessary by militant action, is their only weapon in protecting their real wages and their security of employment.[67]

The social organization of industrial production, the concentration of factories in a few centres and of their labour force in certain suburbs, the intractable problems of urban life, and the common involvement of wage earners in a national system of wage determination in the form of periodic government commissions, combine to produce among industrial workers recognition of a common fate arising from a common class situation. Militancy has been greater in industrial centres, such as Ikeja (on the outskirts of Lagos) and Kano, than in cities like Ibadan and Zaria, where there are few opportunities for wage employment, and limited opportunities for 'strangers' (who make up most of the wage labour force). At least at the factory level, workers have the organizational resources with which to defend their own interests under their own leadership. The national system of wage determination has provided the issues, such as the demand for publication of the Morgan Commission award in 1964, the implementation of the Adebo Commission interim award in 1971 and the extension of the Udoji Commission awards to the private sector in 1975, on which they have been able to force a confrontation with the Government and employers. The strike has provided them with the weapon for that confrontation, and has taken the form of a general strike, as in 1945 and in 1964, or waves of strikes in particular factories and industries as in 1950,

---

[67] See Waterman, 'Conservatism', on differences among workers. For a general overview of labour in Nigeria and a comprehensive bibliography, see Cohen, *Labour and Politics in Nigeria* (London, 1975). For subsequent developments see Waterman, *Industrial Relations and the Control of Labour Protest in Nigeria'* (The Hague, 1977).

1955, 1960, 1971, 1975, all coinciding with the preparation or publication of the reports of government commissions.[68]

Clerical and technical workers are concerned to increase the general level of wages. The system of regulating wage levels by periodic government awards has tied public to private and clerical to industrial wage levels. But the clerical workers and technical and professional staff are often more concerned with the regrading of posts than with general wage levels. Clerical workers' militancy has usually focused on demands for the implementation of various reports on grading in particular ministries; the dissatisfaction with the recommendations of the Udoji Commission was simply more general than earlier complaints.

Younger clerks seek advancement through further education, to the point where they are often accused of spending their working hours preparing for examinations. Since they have better opportunities for promotion than factory workers, they are more concerned to seek the favour of their seniors, which is usually alleged to be determined by kinship and ethnicity rather than merit. They also have greater security of tenure, and better prospects of a gratuity which can be invested on early retirement in commercial activities. Thus clerks, and professional and technical staff, may be militant in pressing wage demands, but they are more likely to be concerned with their relative grading than with raising wage levels as a whole.

---

[68] See the accounts of events in 1971 in Lagos, Kano and Zaria respectively in Peace, *Choice, Class and Conflict,* and 'Towards a Nigerian Working Class'; P. Lubeck, 'Unions, Workers and Consciousness in Kano', and 'Economic Security' in R. Sandbrook and R. Cohen (eds). *The Development of an African Working Class,* (London, 1976). For a list of government commissions on wage determination up to 1971 see Cohen, *Labour and Politics*, pp. 284-6.

What is the relation between the interest and actions of the workers and the self-employed? Economists of both left- and right wing inclinations have argued that wage and salary earners constitute a 'labour aristocracy', whose strategic economic position and bargaining ability enable them to gain a disproportionate share both of the social product, which enables them to engage in 'discretionary consumption' at the expense of peasants, and of employment opportunities. Politically, they are alleged to be conservative, protecting their own privileges rather than advancing the interests of the poor and exploited classes in general.[69]

Industrial workers are interested in raising wage levels, which tends to push up urban price levels to the advantage of craftsmen and petty traders who produce primarily for urban markets. Workers' immediate demands are thus distinct from the demands of farmers, and of those craftsmen and petty traders primarily dependent on rural markets and the multiplier effects of farmers' income, who are more concerned with favourable crop prices. Further, the dependence of clerks on government revenues for their incomes made them ultimately dependent on the state's ability to sustain its financial commitments by exploiting farmers. Even since the expansion of oil revenues, clerks do compete with other possible beneficiaries for a share in overall government expenditure. Factory employment was initially financed by exploiting the rural producers through Marketing Boards, and

---

[69] Cf. G. Arrighi and J. Saul, 'Socialism and Economic Development in Tropical Africa' *JMAS*, 6 (1968), and Arrighi, 'International Corporations, Labour Aristocracies and Economic Development in Tropical Africa', in R. Rhodes (ed.) *Imperialism and Underdevelopment* (New York, 1970), both reprinted in Arrighi and Saul, *The Political Economy of Tropical Africa* (New York, 1972); P. Kilby, *Industrialisation in an Open Economy, 1945-66* (Cambridge, 1969); and cf. Waterman, 'The 'Labour Aristocracy' in Africa', *Development and Change*, 7 (1975).

consumers through tariff protection and other devices for regulating markets. But, despite repeated assertions to the contrary, there is no empirical evidence that wage earners' households enjoy significantly greater levels or better quality of consumption than do rural households. It certainly stretches the meaning of words to regard the occasional evening's beer drinking with friends or the celebration of family occasions as 'discretionary consumption', on a par with the conspicuous emulation of the metropolitan bourgeoisie by their Nigerian counterparts.[70]

The 'labour aristocracy' thesis argues firstly that marginal increments in workers' wages are gained at the expense of the peasantry. This assumes that if wage increases were not forced on employers, at least part of the resources thus made available would be used to improve rural amenities or relieve the tax burden on the peasantry, or be passed on to the consumer in the form of lower prices. Reduction of taxes on the peasantry has usually resulted only from militant agitation by the peasants themselves, as in the case of the *Agbekoya* rebellion, or the state's need to maintain output levels, rather than the concern of the ruling classes for their welfare. In the non-competitive markets typical of the products of capitalist firms in underdeveloped countries, there is no reason on the most orthodox neo-classical assumptions to expect that consumers will benefit from relative reductions in production costs. In any case, in the capital-intensive industries in which

---

[70] The evidence on rural-income differentials is critically reviewed by C. H. Allen, 'Unions, Incomes and Development', *Developmental Trends in Kenya* (Centre for African Studies, Edinburgh, 1972), and in a careful case study of Kaduna by K. Hinchcliffe, 'Labour Aristocracy – A Northern Nigerian Case Study', *JMAS* 12 (1974). The long debate as to whether trade unions increased real wages in Nigeria is reviewed in Cohen, *Labour and Politics,* chapter 6, see p. 214, note 37 for sources. Peace, *Choice, Class and Conflict*, pp. 186-7 gives a more up to date index of real wages.

the alleged 'labour aristocracy' are employed, wages by definition make up a relatively small proportion of production costs, so that marginal changes in wages have little immediate effect on those costs.

It is further argued that 'development', whatever that means, depends on keeping down the incomes of the urban and rural poor in order to facilitate savings and investments by the state or by private capital.[71] This assumes that workers and farmers have a higher marginal propensity to consume, and specifically to consume imported goods or goods with high import content, than do the expropriators of the surplus. The assumption that the rich save and invest and the poor do not is inapplicable to peasants, whose incomes are not advanced by employers but dependent on their prior savings and investments.[72] Nor is it necessarily applicable to workers who seek to escape from wage slavery by saving up enough to establish their own business. When commercial profits depend on contacts and favours, the rich may be inclined to consumption rather than to savings and to investment in producer goods. And even investments in machinery are often oriented to gaining control of monopolistic distributive privileges, and depend for their profitability on the restriction of petty commodity production.

The interest in such theories is not in the validity of their assumptions but in their ideological import. The allegation that

[71] W.A. Lewis, *Reflections on Nigeria's Economic Growth* (Paris, 1967); Helleiner, *Peasant Agriculture*, p.140. See the critique by S.M. Essang and S.O. Olayide, 'Economic Development or Income Distribution?' A False Dilemma', *NJSA*, 1 (1974).

[72] Available empirical evidence consistently indicated high average and marginal rates of savings for Nigerian farmers though a wide range of incomes. See R. Galetti, K.D.S. Baldwin and I.O. Dina, *Nigerian Cocoa Farmers* (London, 1956), pp. 471-5, 596-7; M. Upton, *Agriculture in South-Western Nigeria* (University of Reading, 1967), p. 42; G. E. Okurume, *The Food Crop Economy in Nigerian Agricultural Policy* (East Lansing and Ibadan, 1969), pp. 91-2; Cf. Berry, 'Cocoa'; Hill, *Rural Capitalism*.

there is a conflict of interest between peasants and workers made by economists is a classic example of what Post[73] terms the 'displacement' of the 'primary contradiction' between the exploiters and the exploited on to a 'derived' contradiction between exploiting classes. But it is certainly not a contradiction that is widely recognized among the exploited classes themselves, tied to one another as they are through family, lineage, and mutual support.

The consolidation of the bourgeoisie, especially in so far as it has advanced through the command of formal education, has accentuated the difference between the bourgeoisie and the poor and illiterate in terms of life style, patterns of interaction, and patterns of residence. Interaction between rich and poor, even within the framework of kinship, is an interaction of unequals and thus of patron and supplicant, where the patron, while meeting the appropriate conventions, is in command of the situation. The poor share an ambiguous attitude to the rich. On the one hand they are admired as exemplars of the success to which the poor aspire, to whom they look for assistance with employment, credit, and other favours. On the other hand, they are berated for their selfishness in looking only to their own advantage and that of their immediate family, of monopolizing educational and other opportunities, rather than helping others to better themselves. On the one hand inequality is regarded as part of the natural order of things and privilege as a proper reward for investment, skill, and effort; on the other egalitarian values are expressed in such phrases as 'our wives shop in the same market [as the wives of the rich]'.[74]

---

[73] Post, *Arise Ye Starvelings*; Waterman, 'Conservatism'.
[74] See B. B. Lloyd, 'Education and Family Life'; and P.C. Lloyd, 'Class Consciousness'. Essay **IV**.

The social relations of production and distribution in which the urban petty bourgeoisie are involved preclude them from taking effective class action in their own interests. At times, they have followed populist leaders, to whom they have looked to favour them with a share of the resources appropriated by the bourgeoisie. Alternatively, they have sought individual advancement in relations of clientage to better placed patrons. By contrast, the social relations of production, distribution, and exchange in which the urban workers and cash-crop farmers are involved have produced significant class action on their part. In taking political action in support of their immediate class interests, both urban workers and peasant farmers have regarded themselves as fighting for their rights in general, and thus in opposing the unfairness of the existing order. In doing so, they provide a focus for the political consciousness of the urban petty bourgeoisie, and of food-crop farmers, who lack the resources to articulate and enforce their own demands of their own accord. Thus the proletariat has acted as a 'political élite', expressing the demands of the poor in general, and not as a 'labour aristocracy', maintaining their privileges at the expense of the poor.[75] On the other hand, we must recognize the limits to the political capacity, at least to date, even of urban workers and export-crop farmers. Workers have struck in defiance of government legislation, and cocoa farmers have expelled government agents from the countryside and forced down taxes. But workers have settled in the end for better wages, and cocoa farmers remain dependent on their rulers and the world market to determine the cocoa price. Neither of

---

[75] Peace, 'Towards a Nigerian Working Class'; cf. R. Jeffries, 'Labour Aristocracy? A Ghana Case Study', *ROAPE*, 3 (1975), and *Class, Power and Ideology in Ghana: The Railwaymen of Sekondi* (Cambridge, 1978).

them have the resources to intervene politically in the routine process of resource allocation. Nor have they the resources, including education and leadership, necessary to take over society and organize it in their own interests. It was the military, not the workers and peasants, who ended the life of the First Republic. It is the military regime which seeks to consolidate the development of capitalist society in Nigeria.

Politics, the State and Capitalist Development

During the colonial period, merchants, traders, and professionals sought political power as a condition of furthering their economic interests against their colonial masters. State power gave them access to a share in the profitable opportunities offered by the neo-colonial economy and the finance necessary to establish themselves as a bourgeoisie. Success in business enterprise depended on the favour of the state and foreign capitalists. Thus the bourgeoisie were forced to compete among themselves for access to profitable opportunities.[76] This took the form of rivalry for control of the spoils of political office. Politics became a zero-sum game, in which opposition was ruthlessly suppressed, modified only by cartel agreements among the regional barons, aimed at securing their own fiefs from outside subversion and sharing out Federal revenues which became increasingly important after independence and were to be decisive with the development of oil production.[77]

[76] See Frantz Fanon's incisive analysis of 'The Pitfalls of National Consciousness,' in *The Wretched of the Earth* ({1963} London, 1966).
[77] B. J. Dudley, 'Federalism and the Balance of Political Power in Nigeria,' *Journal of Commonwealth Political Studies*, 4 (1966); Sklar, 'Contradictions in the Nigerian Political System', *JMAS*, 3 (1965); K. Post and M. Vickers, *Structure and Conflict in Nigeria* (London, 1973).

The unequal political competition for resources at the Federal level, in which the Northern Region was able to dominate its competitors, ensured the instability of the successive compromises, which the bourgeoisie tried to patch up on successive occasions in order to save the game. No impersonal rules governing competition can be established to regulate it when the differences among regions and ethnic groups, and again within such groups, discriminate massively in favour of particular groups, and where access to office and its spoils is the object of politics. The ethics of business penetrated politics, the ethics of politics penetrated business; the ethics of the gangster penetrated both.[78]

In 1962, the crisis in Western Nigeria and the public enquiries which followed it established, for anyone who doubted it, that the Whitehall and Westminster rules for regulating competition for state power and the allocation of state resources had broken down. Regional governments established monopolies of political power and state patronage. Competition at the Federal level gave way to a ruthless cartel, determined to eliminate any opposition which could not be incorporated into the racket on its own terms. Crisis followed crisis: agreement could not be reached on census figures, the conduct of elections, the appointment of Vice-Chancellors and other public figures, and the siting of the iron and steel industry. The politicians had made it quite clear that their looting of public resources could not be challenged within the framework of electoral politics. Popular participation was limited to begging politicians to secure for individuals and communities a small slice of the national 'cake'. Broader values

---

[78] This is not to suggest that this process is typically Nigerian, or African. US and UK politics suggest that it is typically capitalist.

of equity and legitimacy had no place in the politics of wheeling and dealing; they could only be sought through direct resistance to exploitation and oppression, as in the 1964 general strike, or in the Tiv and Yoruba resistance to their respective regional governments.[79]

Between 1962 and 1967 the Nigerian state failed to resolve the contradictions inherent in the neo-colonial political economy. The state opened the economy to foreign exploitation and subjected itself to the political tutelage of the Western powers.[80] It failed to regulate relations between foreign capitalists and the indigenous bourgeoisie in such a way as to accommodate nationalist aspirations for Nigerian control of economic opportunities. The state was an instrument of private and sectional interests. Unlike its colonial predecessor, it was unable to lay down the rules for and arbitrate competition for political office and its spoils. It failed to weld the bourgeoisie into a coherent bloc,[81] able to institutionalize its rule over other classes. Successive threats of secession were made by offended Western, Northern, and Eastern interests who threatened to withdraw their own fiefdoms from the general arena of exploitation. In the crisis of 1966-67 the state could not protect the lives and property of its own officers and citizens. This led the Igbo bourgeoisie, with the support of most of the Igbo people, to reject the legitimacy

---

[79] Post, *The Nigerian Federal Elections of 1959: Politics and administration in a developing political system* (Oxford, 1963); Post and Vickers, *Structure and Conflict*; Sklar, *Nigerian Political Parties*; J.P. Mackintosh, *Nigerian Government and Politics* (London, 1966) p. 233; Federation of Nigeria, *Report of the Commission of Enquiry into the Affairs of Certain Statutory Corporations in Western Nigeria* (Chairman: Mr Justice Coker) (Lagos, 1962). On Tiv resistance, see M. Dent 'A Minority Party: The United Middle Belt Congress,' in Mackintosh, *Nigerian Government and Politics*. Tseayo, *The Emirate System*.

[80] Osoba, 'The Colonial Antecedents and Contemporary Development of Nigerian Foreign Policy' (PhD thesis, Moscow State University, 1967).

[81] Gramsci, *Selections from the Prison Notebooks* (London, 1971).

of the Nigerian state and the Nigerian nation, and follow the disastrous road to secession and defeat.[82] The state organized the exploitation by capitalists of peasant and petty commodity production. Farmers' living standards were reduced, opportunities for craftsmen and petty traders were restricted by politicians and their beneficiaries, and urban living standards were threatened by price inflation, particularly rents. Relations between capitalist and non-capitalist modes of production, and between the exploiting and exploited classes, could be maintained only by oppression. The state failed to retain the loyalty of the common men and women.

In 1966, the overthrow of the politicians' Government forced the new military rulers to turn to civil servants for advice and direction. In 1966 and 1967, Federal permanent secretaries intervened decisively to maintain Federal authority against successive Northern plans for secession, and Eastern plans for confederation.'[83] State policy was to be directed by the 'states-men',[84] committed in principle to the national interest, as institutionalized in the Federal Government. The dependence of the oil-producing states for their very existence

---

[82] A.M.H. Kirk-Greene (ed.), *Crisis and Conflict in Nigeria: a Documentary Sourcebook, 1966-70* (2 vols.) (London, 1971); R. Luckham, *The Nigerian Military* (Cambridge, 1971); R. Melson and H. Wolpe (eds) *Nigeria: Modernization and the Politics of Communalism* (East Lansing 1972); R. First, *The Barrel of a Gun: Power in Africa* (London, 1972); J. de St Jorre, *The Nigerian Civil War* (Hodder and Stoughton, London, 1972); Dudley, *Instability and Political Order* (Ibadan, 1973); J. J. Stremlau, *The International Politics of the Nigerian Civil War, 1967-1970* (Princeton, 1977); C. C. Aguolu, *Nigerian Civil War, 1967-70, An Annotated Bibliography* (Boston, 1973). See **Part IV** for more recent references to these events.

[83] First, *Barrel of a Gun*, pp. 320, 338, 354; M.O. Kayode and D. Otobo (eds), *Allison Akene Ayida: the Quintessential Public Servant* (Malthouse, Lagos, 1984) 'The Nigerian Revolution, 1966-76', Presidential Address to Nigerian Economic Society, 1971 (Ibadan, 1973). Mr Ayida was Permanent Secretary, Economic Development. General Gowon appointed Mr Ayida to be Head of Service and Federal Secretary to the Government in 1975.

[84] Philip Corrigan applies the term to civil servant reformers of nineteenth-century England in '"Appeals to Society": An Examination of how the Ideology of the State was Materialized in Britain before 1850' (BA dissertation, Department of Sociology, University of Durham, unpublished, 1973).

on Federal military power, and the defeat of Biafran claims to the oilfields, enable the Federal Government to appropriate an increasing share of the oil revenues and control the allocation of the remainder to the states. The dramatic multiplication of oil revenues since the war provides the fiscal base for the direction by the Federal state of the nation's affairs. The development of capitalist production in Nigeria requires the national regulation of the market and of production. It requires a state able to override particular capitalist interests, both domestic and foreign, in the interest of the overall development of a capitalist society. A strategy of developing capitalism under the overall direction of the Federal state has the support of employers' organizations, multinational corporations, and capitalist and socialist powers. It cannot succeed if the state surrenders itself to the dictation of any one of these interests. The development of capitalism is too serious a business to be left to the capitalists.[85]

Capitalism is more than a matter of just increasing manufactured output and establishing a capital goods sector.[86] Capitalist society requires the establishment of social and political institutions for reproducing and regulating the class relations necessary to capitalist production and domination. The institutional 'revolution', to use Allison Ayida's term, necessary for the maintenance and development of capitalism in Nigeria required:

1. The supremacy of the Federal state over both state governments and private and sectional interests, and the

---

[85] Cf. H. Alavi, 'The Post-Colonial State', *NLR*, 74 (1972). First, *Libya* (Harmondsworth, 1974).

[86] The failure to recognise this seems to me to be the major fault in Bill Warren's 'Imperialism and Capitalist Industrialisation', *New Left Review*, 81 (1973), and to have been missed in the outcry at his heresies against the orthodoxies of the theory of underdevelopment, *NLR*, 84 (1974).

regulation of competition among them for the allocation of state patronage.
2. Regulation and adjustments of the relation between Nigerian and foreign capitalists.
3. Regulations and adjustment of the relations between public and private economic activity.
4. Regulation and adjustment of relations between capitalist and non-capitalist modes of production, particularly between the need for surplus appropriation from, and for development of, peasant production.
5. Regulation and adjustment of relations between the exploiting class and the exploited classes, especially the proletariat and export-crop farmers.
6. The articulation of a 'national ideology' and the inculcation of commitments to the symbols of national authority.

Since 1966, a strategy was taking shape which intended to institutionalize state regulation of class relations and take class issues outside the realm of politics. Its aim was to make good General Gowon's claim that the Federal Government 'operates a system which knows no loyalty other than loyalty to the nation and people'.[87] 'Development objectives' were to be above politics. As Allison Ayida explained to the 1971 National Conference on Reconstruction and Development:

Those who would like to involve the representatives of the people and members of the political class who are not in office, in the planning process, should recognize the limitations of representative institutions in the formulation and maintenance of plan objectives. It is the executive, made up of Ministers, planners, administrators and other public officials, who are in a position to determine and maintain the objectives and targets of development policy. They should, however, ensure through regular intercourse and discussion with the spokesmen of the

[87] *Daily Times*, (Lagos), 2 May, 1973.

main economic groups in the society, that they are guided at all times in the discharge of their developmental responsibilities by the views and expressed and reasonable wants of the people and society at large.

Although the government should take the initiative for formulating national development objectives and targets, it is the people who alone can provide the necessary support for the realization of such goals. They should therefore be consulted at all stages and be made to feel a part of the planning and hence, the development process...[88]

In 1967, the four regions were replaced with twelve states, six from the former Northern Region and six from the three southern regions. This aimed to regulate political competition by ensuring to the bourgeoisie of each state an arena in which it is protected from outside competition, and by increasing the number of contenders so as to produce an equilibrium of diverse alliances at the centre rather than the domination of a single region and party. This would free the Federal Government from sectional domination, and help to relegate the struggle for patronage to the state level. Federal appropriation of the lion's share of the oil revenues and the right to allocate the remainder enabled it to act as arbitrator between state interests. It first took control of all off-shore royalties and rents, and then reduced the share of on-shore royalties and rents accruing to the state of origin to 45 per cent and now 20 per cent. The Federal state also benefitted directly from the increasing share of profits taxes (70 per cent in 1971-72) in total oil revenues. Philip Asiodu told the annual National

---

[88] 'Development Objectives' in Ayida and Onitiri (eds) *Reconstruction and Development in Nigeria*.

Management Conference in 1973[89] that 'The effect of all these is, in fact, to strengthen the principle of 'national' management of oil wealth or distribution of revenue on the basis of national wealth'.

Military support gave civil servants a wider degree of freedom from intervention in decision-making by private and sectional interests than was possible under the rule of politicians. And at a humbler level, since 1970, and despite arbitrary actions by some soldiers, individuals have been free to go about their business without being harassed by politicians and political thugs.[90]

On 1 October (Independence Day) 1970, General Gowon outlined a nine-point programme which would pave the way to the establishment of a civilian government, and in words he used four years later cancelling the promise to restore civilian government, 'lay the foundation of a self-sustaining political system which can stand the test of time in such a manner that a national political crisis does not become a threat to the nation's continued existence as a single entity and which will ensure a smooth and orderly transition from one government to another'.[91]

The programme required:[92]

1. The reorganization of the Armed Forces.

---

[89] *Daily Times*, 19, 20 March 1973; L. Rupley, 'Revenue Allocation Once Again' and 'The Next Revenue Allocation', *West Africa*, 1, 8 July 1974 and 6 January 1975. See Part **II**.

[90] Numerous people in Ibadan gave this reason to Gavin Williams in 1970 for preferring a continuation of military rule to any prospect of the return of politicians. By 1975, support for the Gowon regime had collapsed.

[91] Independence Day Speech, 1974, *West Africa*, 7 October, 1974.

[92] *Daily Times of Nigeria, The First Ten Years, Independent Nigeria* (Lagos, 1970), p. 4. Cf. A. Atta, 'The Development of Nigeria's Political Personality', *Quarterly Journal of Administration (QJA,)* 6 (1971). Mr Atta was head of the civil service until his death in 1972. Gowon's government failed to achieve any of these goals. The governments of Murtala Muhammed and Obasanjo implemented all of them, except the holding of a census, which they judged to be politically too sensitive, and the eradication of corruption.

2. The implementation of the National Development Plan.
3. The eradication of corruption in our national life.
4. The settlement of the question of the creation of further states.
5. The preparation and adoption of a new constitution.
6. The introduction of a new revenue allocation formula.
7. Conducting a national population census.
8. The organization of genuinely national political parties.
9. The organization of elections and installation of popularly elected governments in the states and at the centre.

The *Second National Development Plan 1970-74* [93] complemented these primarily political objectives with the promise to establish Nigeria as:
1. A united strong and self-reliant nation.
2. A great and dynamic economy;
3. A just and egalitarian society;
4. A land of bright and full opportunities for all citizens;
5. A free and democratic society.

A just and egalitarian society puts a premium on reducing inequalities in inter-personal incomes and promoting balanced development among the various communities in the different geographical areas in the country. It organizes its economic institutions in such a way that there is no oppression based on class, social status, ethnic group or state.

Although these pious declarations bore no resemblance to the expenditure and investment programmes listed in the Plan, they indicate a recognition of the necessity of a strategy for

---

[93] *The Second National Development Plan.* Lagos, 1970. The plan was critically reviewed in *QJA* 5, 3 (1971).

class and communal conciliation which is outlined explicitly in the *Guidelines for the Third National Development Plan, 1975-80*.[94]

The first item in the strategy was the extension of indigenous control of economic opportunities. The 1972 'Indigenization Decree', implemented by 1974, reserved specific economic opportunities for Nigerians and required Nigerian participation in firms engaged in a wide range of other activities. Major expatriate companies, even when not affected by the terms of the decree, have issued shares to the Nigerian public, as the bourgeoisie styles itself. The Government has taken a 40 per cent share in all commercial banks and 55 per cent shares in all oil companies. These measures are designed to enable it to regulate relations between foreign and indigenous capitalism within the neo-colonial economy.

Industries of 'strategic national importance' (oil, iron and steel) have been reserved to the state. Professor Aboyade has argued for the extension of the public sector as an instrument of 'decolonization', of plan fulfilment, and of financing long-term investment projects – and as a means of combating unemployment and bringing about distributive equity. Philip Asiodu has called for the strengthening of executive capacity and increasing operational autonomy for the public sector. Nigerian private capitalists have demanded curbs on the expansion of the state sector, particularly in such fields as distribution and insurance, and in taking over firms under the (1972) Indigenization Decree. They demand that 'the

---

[94] *The National Development Plan* Lagos, 1973. The plan was outlined in *The Times* (London) 4 March, 1975 (advertisement) and printed in *Africa* (1975), and in more detail in *West Africa*, 7 April, 1975.

government's role should be confined to drawing the rules of the economic game in the country and the provision of infrastructural facilities essential for productive economic operations'.[95] The *Guidelines* for the Third Plan note that the Indigenization Decree makes it necessary to 'delimit areas for private and state participation'. Thus the Federal Government plans to delimit the respective arenas of economic activity open to foreign and domestic capitalists, and to Federal and state governments, in order to regulate the relations among them.

The decline in the production of certain export crops, and the embarrassing failure of the Western State Government to handle the farmers' *Agbekoya*[96] rebellion in 1968-69, led the Federal Government to take over responsibility for fixing produce prices and taxes in January 1973. Henceforth, they declared, prices would be fixed in the light of 'trends in world prices and local production costs', 'with no trading surpluses in view', in order to provide adequate incentives to producers through the pursuit of a price policy which would substantially increase producers, income as an inducement to expansion'.[97] Prices would no longer be governed by the immediate revenue needs of individual states. The Federal Government is now in a position to regulate policy towards export-crop farmers and the rural economy in general in the light of broader

---

[95] Turi Muhammadu, 'Private Sector versus Public Sector', *New Nigerian* (Kaduna) 1 May, 1973. Prof. Aboyade was the Government's main adviser on economic policy. He was appointed Vice-Chancellor of the University of Ife in 1975. Chief Henry Fajemirokun and other spokesmen of the Chamber of Commerce were the leading spokesmen for the private sector. For Asiodu's views, see *Daily Times* 19, 20 March, 1973. See also *Daily Times*, 19, 22 January, 1973, 24 January, 4 February, 23 April, 1974; *Sunday Times* (Lagos) 18, 25 November, 1973; *West Africa*, 13 January, 1975.

[96] See Part V.

[97] *Daily Times*, 13 January 1973. *Guidelines*, p. 11. State marketing boards were subsequently replaced by (federal) commodity boards.

requirements of capitalist development, viz. development of the rural market, discouragement of rural-urban migration, encouragement of agricultural output, and the need to stem rural unrest.

The *Guidelines* place agriculture first, rather than among the also-rans as its predecessors did. But its diagnosis and remedies emphasize the importance of direct inputs by the state (credit, extension, and marketing facilities), relative to the need for price incentives and rural feeder roads to stimulate peasant production. The burden of state marketing will be imposed on food crops in the cause of stable prices. The Federal Government plans to acquire large areas of land 'to be leased out on uniform terms to farmers as in the case of industrial estates', on which it 'will be much easier to provide extension services, agricultural inputs, etc.'[98] The Nigerian Agricultural Bank's first loans went to the Co-operative Union of the North-Eastern State (₦3.7 million), and to twelve individual farmers, presumably one from each state, ₦900.000.[99] Neither North-East state co-operatives, with little experience in marketing let alone extension, nor private capitalist farmers in Nigeria have shown any capacity to use investments on this scale, and the money will probably be diverted to more lucrative commercial purposes, along with a large part of the rest of the ₦24 million thus far allocated by the Bank and the ₦40 million allocated for 1975-76.[100]

Over the last two years (1973-1975), peasant farmers have benefitted from a series of increases in the prices paid for export crops, which are three or four times as high as during

---

[98] *Guidelines*, p.14.
[99] General Gowon, 1974 Budget Speech, *Daily Times,* 2 April, 1974.
[100] *West Africa,* 27 January, 1975. See also 7 April, 1975. Cf. King, 'Cooperative'.

the period of low prices in the sixties.[101] But these increases follow the dramatic, if precarious, increases in world commodity prices in the seventies, and except in the case of groundnuts, the production of which has been drastically curtailed by the Sahel drought, do little more than catch up with the rate of inflation, and do not restore the real price levels of the fifties. For their part, food crop farmers are reported to have been incensed by demands for increased wages from their labourers, following the Udoji award, as well as because of inadequate transport facilities, and farmers attempted to prevent food from entering the towns.[102]

Prior to the development of oil production, Nigeria's prosperity was built on peasant agriculture. Ventures into capitalist farming and state settlement have proved disastrous, and state marketing arrangements burdensome. Yet Nigeria plans to develop agriculture by encouraging capitalist and state farming and distribution. Defence expenditure rather than agriculture will cycle the oil revenues into the economy – and recycle a substantial share back into the economies of metropolitan arms suppliers.[103]

The *Guidelines* combine the rhetoric commitment of the *Second Plan* to 'equitable income distribution' with hard headed proposals 'for the institutionalization of the incomes review process'. Previous *ad hoc* commissions had been 'appointed under strong pressure exerted in the form of

---

[101] In 1975 producer prices for cocoa were £330 (₦660), for groundnuts £ 125 (₦250), for special palm oil £140 (₦280), for palm kernels, £125 (₦150), and for cotton £154 (₦308) per ton. (₦2=£1) when the currencies were converted on 1 January 1973. See Olatunbosun and Olayide, 'Effects of the Marketing Boards on the Output and Income of Primary Producers' in Onitiri and Olatunbosun (eds) *The Marketing Board System*. See Part **IV** and Forrest, 'Agricultural Policies'.

[102] *West Africa*, 3 March, 1975.

[103] Nigeria's defence budget was ₦547 million of a total budget of ₦4890 million. For a critique of Nigeria's rural development strategy, see Part **V**.

industrial unrest caused by widespread dissatisfaction with the level, structure and alignment of incomes in the country'. It proposed an Income Analysis Agency which, apart from providing employment for economists, will keep the government informed of wage and salary trends in both private and public sectors, and of movements in the cost of living, and would 'inform and educate the public on the realities of the relationship among prices, wages, standards of living and economic growth', and calculate 'growth dividends' as a basis for determining a 'national incomes policy'. Minimum wage levels are to be determined by minimum wage committees, established in each state, under the overall aegis of a National Wages Board, which would also encourage 'employers and workers in an industry to establish a joint industrial council'. Considerations of hardship and equity, the main concern of previous commissions on wages and salaries, would be relegated to the committees, and balanced by a concern for what the *Guidelines* elegantly disguise as 'the inter-factoral distribution of national income'.

The implementation of these brave proposals requires restructuring of the patterns of wage determination and collective bargaining. In 1974 a Labour Decree was issued, with elaborate provision regarding wages, contracts of employment, recruitment, wage advances, and the right of workers to join or not to join trade unions.[104] Since 1948, the Nigerian trade union movement has been divided into two or more factions, dependent on the financial sponsorship and ideological guidance of competing trade union internationals, and their cold war sponsors. Unity has been achieved only for

---

[104] *Daily Times,* 11 June 1974, *New Nigerian,* 5, 12 July, 2, 9 August, 1974.

the duration of campaigns for government wage reviews (1964, 1971, 1975). The 1975 Apena Cemetery Declaration established a Nigerian Labour Council with two committees, one to examine Udoji and one to draft a constitution, and agreed to affiliate to and presumably draw funds from 'all international labour organizations', and to work towards the development of industrial unions.[105] Since trade union leadership is essentially an entrepreneurial activity, in which leaders compete for the custom of factory unions and the sponsorship of metropolitan powers, the institutionalization of class conflict through responsible trade unions will take more than a truce and a declaration of intent by labour leaders.[106]

Employers have long been anxious to break the link between government reviews of wages, usually based on the cost of living criteria, and wage demands in the private sector. In 1971, and again in 1975, they attempted without success to prevent government wage awards, which followed periods of wage freeze in the public sector, being extended to the private sector, where they argued that wage increases had already taken account of the cost of living. The Adebo and Udoji Commissions were both invited to propose rationalizations of the wage and salary structure. Adebo followed its predecessors in emphasizing hardship to low wage earners. After Udoji, the Government was forced by widespread unrest to concede a minimum increase of 30 per cent over the pre-Udoji levels for all employees. While employers and the Government seek to

---

[105] *West Africa,* 24 February, 1975.
[106] For a history of Nigeria's trade union centres, see Cohen, *Labour and Politics.* For a critique of the Marxist NTUC and SWAFP, see Waterman, 'Communist Theory in the Nigerian Trade Union Movement', *Politics and Society* (1973). In 1976, the Federal Military Government dissolved the NCL and reconstituted it, and established a number of industrial unions, under government sponsorship.

separate the question of minimum wages and overall wage determination, and break the link between wage reviews in the public sector and wage demands in the private sector, the workers themselves have not been willing to allow them to do so.

The Nigerian state has contained the opposition of workers and peasants by its control of the means of violence and by buying them off with wage and price increases, which tend to fuel rather than catch up with inflation. They have not been able to institutionalize procedures for regulating class conflict and determining income distribution. This in turn would require the establishment of constitutional arrangements supported by public sentiments, which legitimated and effected bourgeois domination, guaranteed national unity, and regulated competition among the bourgeoisie. The military state has been no more able to resolve this issue than the politicians who preceded it.

The Federal Government has taken over responsibility for higher education, exercised through the National Universities Commission, and has assumed shared jurisdiction over primary and secondary education. The National Youth Corps has posted young graduates to work in states away from home and sought to inculcate a commitment to national service – as well as guaranteeing a period of employment immediately after graduation. The state's declared aims are to rationalize and expand the provision of educational facilities at all levels, to meet the manpower needs of the economy, and to rectify the geographical imbalance in educational and thus employment opportunities. Its most ambitious undertaking is the commitment to implementing universal and compulsory primary education in all states by September 1979. Whether this will fulfil its declared aim of evening up educational opportunities in different regions is uncertain. Initially, relatively advantaged states will find it easier to recruit the teachers on who the success of the scheme depends. At best it may help the four most northern states to run faster in order to be able to stand still in relation to their southern rivals. There are ambitious plans for new universities, particularly in the North. This will not solve the problem of there being too few qualified applicants from certain states. At the state level, voluntary agency, primarily mission schools are being taken over in several states, in a bid to standardize the quality of schooling and inculcate national, rather than particularistic religious, sentiments. Neither of these moves prevents the rich from using private primary schools to ensure their offspring privileged access to state secondary schools and perpetuating class privilege.[107]

As *New Nigerian* declared, [108] complaining about the predominantly Yoruba composition of the census staff, 'even the man on the farm knows that – contrary to what he has been told – the census is a political exercise. It is in fact the joker in the FMG's 9-point programme'. The census figures reduced the returns for the West and South-East to below the inflated 1963 returns, and dramatically increased the figures of the northern states to almost double the 1963 figure, and nearly four times the 1951-2 figure in several cases. The four predominantly Hausa-Fulani-Kanuri states, which dominated the old North and through it the Federation, now claimed the 51 per cent controlling majority, which the six states making up the old

---

[107] See Nduka, 'Colonial Education'.
[108] 20 July, 1973. See the list of names of census officials, published in *New Nigerian* on 18 and again on 19 July. Of the 29, nineteen are recognizably Yoruba.

North had previously held. While the southern states, and particularly the West, cried foul and the Federal Government pleaded for restraint and declared the figures provisional, and presumably negotiable, the *New Nigerian* declared that 'it would be incredible and disastrous to reject the 1973 census'.[109] Governor Audu Bako of Kano State added insult to injury by declaring that the idea of disbanding the Interim Common Services Agency, managing former Northern Region institutions, would be 'dividing the indivisible'.[110] Clearly, the twelve-state system had failed to exorcise the spectre of Northern domination, and, for a second time, the census had failed to provide an agreed basis for electoral competition.

The recognition of aspirations among minorities in the old regions for their own states did not end the demands for new states. In most states, groups who felt themselves disadvantaged, threatened by competition from others, or merely out of power, have promoted campaigns for the further division of existing states to secure control of their own fiefs. State agitation and inter-state rivalries have been promoted by the new scheme for revenue allocation, and accentuated by the census figures. The Federal Government increased the share of revenues that it distributes among the state rather than retains for itself or returns to the state of origin. Half of these revenues were divided into equal shares for each state; the other half allocated according to population. Thus the census strengthened the claims of northern states for an increased share of Federal revenues, has justified the relative decline in

---

[109] Reported *West Africa*, 14 October 1974.
[110] Reported and criticized, *Daily Times*, 8 June 1974. Gen. Murtala's government declared the census null and void.

the revenues of the West, and has encouraged agitation for the creation of more states.[111]

Nor was the spectre of corruption exorcised. Serious allegations of corruption were made against Federal institutions, such as the Nigerian National Supply Company,[112] and against senior administrators and commissioners in the Federal and state governments. The Government's major concern was to take action against people who allege corruption 'against highly placed public officials within a view of discrediting the military régime.'[113] Detention of such people, and later of workers and trade unionists, led to student disturbances and the closure of university campuses. Corruption is an integral part of parasitical capitalism. It cannot be abolished by moral persuasion or administrative regulation. The Federal Government failed to keep corruption at bay and allowed itself to be subverted by corrupt practices. But then it commands the most lucrative spoils of all.

In other words, the Military Government failed to establish the conditions necessary for the establishment of bourgeois rule through a constitutional government. It failed to eradicate corruption, arrive at agreed census figures, or settle the question of new states. A counter-élite of businessmen, professionals, and academics see themselves as the rightful rulers of Nigeria, by virtue of their education, experience, and untested claims to popular support, and regard the military increasingly as usurpers. But it is clear that they were simply

---

[111] For census figures for 1952-3, 1963, 1973, see *West Africa*, 20 May 1974. Cf. Rupley, 'The Next Revenue Allocation'. General Murtala's government increased the number of states from 12 to nineteen. By 1996, successive military governments had raised the number to 36, plus the Federal Capital Territory of Kaduna.

[112] See *West Africa*, 18, 25 February, 1975.

[113] See *West Africa*, 5, 12, 19, 23 September, 1974, 13 January, 1975. Cf. letter by S. Oyovbaire, *West Africa*, 4 November, 1974.

preparing to resume the struggle for spoils and office once the military (themselves not unconcerned with spoils or office) had ceded political authority to them. As General Gowon declared, when he announced the indefinite postponement of the return of civilian rule on Independence Day 1974, four years after enunciating the nine-point plan, and two years before the vesting day for constitutional government:

There has already emerged such a high degree of sectional politicking intemperate utterances and writings, all designed to whip up ill-feeling within the country to the benefit of the few...We had thought that genuine demonstration of moderation and self-control in pursuing sectional ends in the overall interest of the country would have become the second nature of Nigerians.[114]

Nigeria has demonstrated its capacity to achieve a high rate of growth of manufactured output, and to establish certain producer goods industries. Neither the Military Government nor its political rivals have demonstrated their capacity to establish the social institutions necessary for a successful Nigerian 'capitalist revolution',[115] and the maintenance of a capitalist society.[116]

---

[114] Reported in *West Africa*, 4 October, 1974.
[115] Cf. Moore. 'The American Civil War: the Last Capitalist Revolution', *Social Origins of Dictatorship and Democracy* (Boston, 1966), chapter 3. Collins, Turner and Williams, 'Capitalism and the Coup', in Williams, *Nigeria*, 1st edition.

Part III

Politics in Nigeria[1]
(with Terisa Turner)

The Study of Politics

'Politics is a dirty business', as the *Concise Oxford Dictionary* reminds us. It is also 'the science and art of government'.[2] In its first aspect, politics is a particular, and discreditable activity, whose virtue is to be 'scheming, crafty', and which turns of the private advantage of its practitioners. In its second aspect, politics is concerned with the administration of the common affairs of the public, a matter of universal rather than particular concern, whose virtue is to be 'judicious, expedient' in both defining and promoting the common good. The contradiction between private interests and public interest gives rise to, but is not resolved by, the state.[3] The state is required both to mediate among competing interests, and to reconcile or subordinate them to the wider requirements of the public interest.[4]

Politics thus has two related dimensions, the competitive pursuit of private interests, and the determination of public policy. But the nature of both private and public interests is

---

[1] From John Dunn, ed., *West African States: Failure and Promise* (Cambridge University Press, 1978)

[2] J. B. Sykes (ed.), *Concise Oxford Dictionary*, 6th ed. (Oxford, 1976), pp. 854-5.

[3] Marx and Engels, *The German Ideology* ({1846}), (CW, 5 p. 46; MW, ch. 23, p. 185.

[4] 'The executive of the modern state is but an instrument for the management of the common affairs of the whole bourgeoisie' [*Die moderne Staatsgewalt ist nur ein Ausschluß, der die gemeinschaftlichen Geschäfte der ganzen Bourgeoisklasse verwaltet.*], Marx and Engels, *Manifesto. CW* 6, p. 486; *MW*, ch. 24, p. 247.

defined by class relations. Classes are groups which arise out of the division of labour in society. They are defined by their place in the process of production, their access to markets for commodities, including labour power, and their relation to the state. Where producers have access to their own means of production, surplus expropriation takes place through control of market and state relations. Class relations link together different groups within societies, and between societies.

Classes may be stabilized into accepting relations of domination and subordination, or organized into relations of patronage and clientage. Class relations may be contested, both in their particular forms, and in general. Both stabilization and contestation require references to values to justify claims and inspire actions. Politics comes to be a contest over values, and not simply over interests.

Thus any study of politics must examine:
a) the allocation of scarce resources;
b) the determination of public policy; and
c) the relations and conflict among classes.

These require an examination of production, market and state relations, and the ideologies through which these are defined, defended and challenged. Politics cannot be studied separately from political economy.[5]

Politics as the Allocation of Scarce Resources
Max Weber pointed out that profit-making may arise from several types of 'profit-making apart from 'the continuous buying and selling on the market with free exchange': 'trade and speculation in different currencies'; 'predatory profit from political organizations or persons connected with politics', 'a

---

[5] D. Ricardo, *On the Principles of Political Economy and Taxation* (Harmondsworth, 1971), p. 49.

position of power guaranteed by the political authority' which includes 'colonial profits', either through 'plantations with compulsory deliveries' or compulsory labour or through monopolistic and compulsory trade, and fiscal profits, through the farming of taxes and of offices, and 'profit opportunities in unusual transactions with political bodies'.[6] These all look familiar from Nigeria and do not mark 'petro-economies' out from other capitalist economies.

The production or the marketing of commodities requires the favour and co-operation of agencies of the state. Access to resources, including opportunities for profit making, requires the favour of those who control the resources, or who control the private and public institutions which allocate them. Consequently, politics turns, as the drafters of the current Nigerian constitutional proposals reminds us, on gaining the 'opportunity to acquire wealth and prestige, to be able to distribute benefits in the form of jobs, contracts, scholarships, and gifts of money and so on to one's relatives and political allies'.[7]

Politics thus comes to be the process of gaining control of public resources for the pursuit of private ends. This sort of politics can only take place within an appropriate framework. In Nigeria since the Second World War, several items constituted this framework. Nigeria continued to depend on foreign markets for the export of primary products, and on foreign imports of manufactured, intermediate and capital goods. The state gained control and influence over a significant share of strategic resources. A category of politicians and state

---

[6] Weber, *Economy and Society*, vol. 1, ch. 2.31, pp. 164-5.
[7] *Report of the Constitution Drafting Committee* (Lagos 1976), vol. 1, p. v. The central elements of the Draft Constitution can be attributed primarily to Billy J. Dudley.

functionaries, later joined by military commanders, was established, with the exclusive claim to allocate state resources. Specific constituencies were delineated, through which the resources were allocated, and to which politicians looked for loyalty and support in return for such rewards.

The competition for access to resources in Nigeria has taken place predominantly between ethnically defined constituencies. These constituencies were not simply given, but redefined in the process of political competition. Ethnic identities do not present themselves ready-made, determining in advance the lines of political conflict. They are socially constructed in relation to the exigencies of specific historical situations. Differences and similarities of language, custom, religion and historical experience are used selectively to define and legitimate particular claims to solidarity and exclusion. These constructed identities may use the language of kinship. But they are founded not on the primordial ties of close kin but on solidarities based variously on communities under a common political authority and with corporate claims to land, or on a common language or a common religion. These criteria are themselves ambiguous and may cut across one another. The definition of appropriate solidarities and the choice of political alliances are made according to calculations of relative advantage and political judgment. The conquest of Nigerian peoples led to the definition of provincial and divisional boundaries, based in part on pre-colonial polities, as modified and amalgamated to meet colonial administrative requirements. These boundaries defined the areas for which a distinctive status and administration would later be claimed, and claims for fair treatment in the allocation of funds and opportunities would in due course be made.

To maintain the system of allocation, the following conditions must be met. Formal and informal rules must be defined, which govern competition among politicians and other claimants to resources and opportunities. Political alliances must be formed which incorporate powerful contending interests, and sustain an adequate share of rewards to these, while enforcing the exclusion of other interests. Popular tolerance of the system of appropriating and allocating rewards must be secured, by coercion and by the spread of opportunities and rewards among constituents.

Politics as the Determination of Public Policy
The regulation of conflicts among contending private interests requires a state which is capable of enforcing decisions and legitimating its authority over various interests.[8] State power, which is seen consistently to favour particular interests at the expense of others not only forfeits the support of the excluded interests but also undermines the legitimacy of its own claims to authority. The state comes to depend only on force and on those who control the instruments of coercion.

The state itself organizes and engages in economic activity. It is responsible directly or indirectly, for the allocation of strategic opportunities and resources. Therefore, the state becomes an arena for political conflict rather than an institution capable of standing above and mediating such conflict. State authority is constrained, in principle, by impersonal rules which do not discriminate formally among competing interests. But state institutions themselves have particular interests which conflict with those of other public and private bodies. And different state agencies form links with

---

[8]   Weber, 'Politics as a Vocation', in *From Max Weber*.

private interests with which they are involved in their day-to-day business activities. Thus conflicts among private interests come to be repeated in, or even to penetrate and engulf, state institutions.

There is a basic contradiction within the state. On the one hand, the state and its agencies are required to regulate conflict among contending interests. On the other hand, the state serves as the instrument of these contending interests. As the introduction to the Nigerian draft constitution declares: 'Such is the pre-occupation with power and its material benefits that political ideals as to how society can be organized and ruled to the best advantage of all hardly enter into the calculation'.[9]

There is a need for political ideals, embodying public goals and values, which are above politics and define the framework within which political conflict is to take place. The drafting committee sought to embody such ideals in the Nigerian draft constitution. They are all the more necessary in Nigeria 'because of the heterogeneity of the society, the increasing gap between the rich and poor, the growing cleavage between the social groupings, all of which combine to confuse the nation and bedevil the march to orderly progress'.[10]

This reconciliation of the interest of 'rich and poor' requires a common 'collective conscience',[11] embodied in a universal value transcending particular interests. The draft constitution recognizes the need to define such a universal goal: 'What do we really want for the generality of Nigerians in the foreseeable future? The answer must surely be that we seek to

[9] Drafting Committee, vol. 1, p v.
[10] *Drafting Committee*, vol. 1, p. vi.
[11] E. Durkheim, *The Division of Labour in Society*, (New York, 1964).

enhance the welfare of the individual through providing better educational facilities, housing, health facilities, more jobs and a rising standard of living for the people as a whole'. This is to take place within the framework of Nigeria's established 'ideology, namely, Mixed Economy'.[12]

By assuming that growth precedes distribution,[13] the authors justify inequality as a means to the universal goal of 'development'. The common value of welfare, as the guiding value of public policy, has the virtue of overriding claims of sectional interests, and the 'confusion' these cause the nation. It offers an ideology under which all can contribute instead to 'the concerted march to orderly progress', and in which public objectives are taken out of political contention. As and Engels point out, each class which aspires to rule must present its particular interest as a universal interest.[14] Further, the universal interest of the bourgeoisie in creating and maintaining the most favourable conditions for capitalism conflicts with the competing interests in making their own profits of particular capitalists.

Politics as the Relations and Conflicts among Classes

The constitutional draft itself, true to the impersonal principles of constitutional liberalism, makes no reference to conflict between classes, either in its explicit provisions, or in devising its array of check and balances between the powers of the institution of state. But the very nature both of private interests, and of the public interest embodied, in principle, in the state and its national ideology, are defined by the relations among classes. The determination of class relations in practice

---

[12] *Drafting Committee*, vol. 1, p. xiii.
[13] The fallacy in this view is exposed by Weeks, 'Imbalance'.
[14] Marx and Engels, *German Ideology* *CW* 5 pp. 45, 47, *MW*, ch. 14, p. 185.

cannot be derived by *a priori* deduction from the functional requirements of the reproduction of capitalist social relations.[15] This not only grants the state, when it is defined as that institution which reproduces the social relations of production, an omniscience and an omnipotence which should properly be confined to theological discourse. It also fails to recognize the contradictory requirements of social relations within civil society, and between civil society and the state, and within the state itself. These contradictions are the basis for the social action of contending groups and are resolved and reproduced through a political process of conflict and contention.

'Class' relations, defined to include production, market and moral relations, do not only, or necessarily, take the form of the organization of 'parties', or political groups for collective action, on the basis of class affiliation and solidarity. Groups, defining themselves around criteria other than class, such as status or ethnic affiliation, will organize themselves to gain privileged access to means of production, and to appropriate market opportunities and state resources.[16]

Political conflicts may be based either around communal solidarities, or on solidarities based on identity of, or more often, an alliance of class interests more commonly, politics draws severally from both communal and class identities. A person's political identity is not unambiguously given, but is adopted in relation to particular contexts of action. In such

---

[15] As in N. Poulantzas, *Political Power and Social Classes* (London, 1973), but compare Poulantzas, 'The Capitalist State; a reply to Miliband and Laclau, *NLR*, 95 (1976), p. 74, which defines the state as a 'relation', but without appearing to grasp the implication that the state can only be specified empirically. See P.R.D. Corrigan, 'State Formation and Moral Regulation in 19th Century Britain' (PhD thesis, University of Durham, 1977); P.R.D. Corrigan, H. Ramsay and D. Sayer, *Socialist Construction and Marxist Theory* (London, 1978).
[16] M. Weber, 'Class, Status, Party' p. 189.

contexts, salient identities will be acted on, in accordance with criteria of practical rationality. In turn, the salience of alternative identities will be governed by the social relations which constitute the changing contexts of political action. Thus J.D.Y. Peel has pointed out that where the most strategic and lucrative sources of opportunity are controlled by the state, and distributed among communities, politics may be expected to continue to turn around competing communal loyalties.[17] This does not, of course, mean that class considerations are eliminated from politics. Class relations develop round the appropriation of resources by and from the state, and take the form of relations of patronage and clientage. Where patrons compete for clients, and clients seek opportunities to become patrons, such relations themselves become a focus for both resentment and contention.

Oil, Sheik Yamani reminds us, comes from God. Even when oil does provide a manna from heaven, or perhaps Hades, so that contention focuses on its distribution, rather than production, its revenues are invested in, and may provide a market for productive activities. These market and production relations remain a focus of class opposition. Conflict over the command of state power escalates because of the increasing concentration of resources in state hands.

Class conflicts may be regulated and reconciled by reference to considerations of mutual advantage and to shared values. But they may also raise questions as to the interpretation and implementation of particular values or lead to the counter-position of different sets of values. Thus, the demand for 'fairness', 'justice' and the 'rights' of the common

---

[17] Peel, *Ijeshas and Nigerians*, pp. 223-4, 262.

people may be, and has been put in opposition to the values and pursuit of personal advantage, and against those of progress and development.

The Political Economy of Neo-colonialism 1939-1966
Capitalism in Nigeria has always taken a primarily commercial form. Control of the terms of exchange of commodities has been the major source of profit. The state has regulated access to commercial opportunities. The import-export trade has held a strategic position in the hinterland of European commercial activities. The staple exports have changed from slaves to export crops to mineral oil. Imports of cheap cloth, liquor and guns have been replaced by more expensive versions, by cars and cement, by machines and semi-manufactures. But the trade has always required both foreign commercial firms on the one hand, and local intermediaries who organize foreign access to local supplies and markets on the other. The terms of these relations between imperialists and '*compradores*' have always been the source of competition among parties within each side, and of antagonism between the two sides.

The foundations of the neo-colonial political economy were established in five ways. In 1939 the British government set up state monopoly marketing boards. The state bought crops at well below world prices, so that it withheld income from producers and transferred it to the state and its beneficiaries. Initially these funds were used by the colonial government to finance Britain's sterling and trade balances. Nigerian politicians sought to gain control of these revenues to finance their political and commercial activities, the expansion of the state administration, and the development projects with which they would reward themselves and their constituents. The marketing boards established the fiscal basis for post-war Nigerian politics, and financed the creation and expansion of a commercial and a bureaucratic bourgeoisie.

In 1947, the British government moved first towards representative and then responsible government, on the model of the 'white' Dominions. Colonial government was to be replaced by government of politicians. Administrative and political office, state revenue, and state authority were ceded to Nigerian politicians and bureaucrats between 1947 and 1960. In this way, the British sought to create a new stratum of intermediaries through whom they could protect British strategic and commercial interests. Constitutional reforms created a stratum of professional politicians. Politics turned on the competition for the spoils of political office.

Between 1947 and 1966 foreign firms carried out a strategic shift in the nature of their operations in response to the opening of international competition for access to the Nigerian market, local commercial aspirations and protectionist legislation. They left the local trade in produce and the wholesaling of cheap, staple lines to Nigerian and Levantine traders, and imported more expensive and capital-intensive products, the market for which was expanded by the state's transfer of income from export crop farmers to wealthier consumers. They substituted the import of semi-manufactures, machines and raw materials for their factories, for the import of cheap manufactured goods, following the lead of the United Africa Company. Another Anglo-Dutch corporation, Shell, established its claims to and began production in the Nigerian oilfields. The dominant position of foreign firms was consolidated and opportunities were opened to Nigerian businessmen.

Between 1954 and 1966 state institutions such as the Central Bank were created for regulating the national economy and the terms of its relations to the international economy. The state extended its regulation of access to commercial opportunities, for both foreign and local businessmen, in the form of marketing board licences, tax reliefs, loans and contracts, and later import tariffs and exchange controls. Increasing state activity and Nigerianization dramatically expanded the opportunities for bureaucratic employment. Political and economic competition thus extended to the control of bureaucratic, as well as judicial offices despite the institutions designed to insulate them for 'political' influence.

Nigerian governments, politicians and businessmen competed amongst themselves for the rents and profits to be derived from foreign business activities and foreign state capital ('aid'). They acted as agents for foreign firms and foreign governments, wishing to establish themselves commercially and politically in Nigeria. This facilitated the diversification of foreign trade and investments.

The Politics of Resource Allocation 1946-1966
'Politics' was the competition among, and the alliances between, politicians and their clients and associates.[18] Its object was to control the resources of the state, and the rents and profits from foreign and local business activities. It was not limited to competition for electoral office. Academic, bureaucratic and judicial positions, and commercial opportunities were all equally 'politicized'. Politics was the

---

[18] Shehu Othman, 'Nigeria': Power for Profit: Class, corporatism and factionalism in the military', in D.C. O'Brien, J. Dunn, and R. Rathbone (eds) *Contemporary West African States.* (Cambridge, 1989). We collaborated later in S. Othman and G. Williams, 'Politics, Power and Democracy in Nigeria', in Jonathan Hyslop (ed.), *African Democratisation in an Era of Globalisation* (Johannesburg, 1999).

means of class formation, financing the accumulation of money by the Nigerian bourgeoisie. It was the means of class competition, through which resources and opportunities were distributed.

Conflicts firstly concerned the allocation of particular resources, such as jobs, public funds, foreign aid, and via the population census, voters and constituencies. Secondly, parties disputed more general questions regarding the constitutional framework within which competition takes place, such as revenue allocation, the creation of new states, and the proper relations between regional and federal governments. Although such issues were often argued in terms of general principles, disputes turned on the consequences which their application would have for particular groups, defined in regional or ethnic terms.

During the 1950s, the British government remained the arbiter in the constitutional conflict and electoral competition. It directed developments by playing Nigerian politicians off against one another, and by protecting the institutional base of northern conservatism in the Northern Region government and the Native Authorities. Politicians accepted compromise as the price of access to state office, and thus to the revenue of state.

Between 1948 and 1951 politicians sought office as spokesmen for their communities, within their regions. The AG (Action Group) and NPC (Northern People's Congress) were formed as regional parties in the West and the North in response to the nationalist challenge of the NCNC (National Council of Nigeria and the Cameroons) and NEPU (Northern Elements Progressive Union) and to the threat of Igbo and southern competition. In 1951, each party claimed the allegiance of a majority in one of the three regional assemblies, though in the 1954 federal election the NCNC would win a majority of Western as well as Eastern seats.

Regional government control of patronage was consolidated in 1954. The Macpherson Constitution of 1950 had not granted self-government, and thus Nigerian control of state funds. In 1953, both the AG and the NCNC demanded self-government by 1956. The NPC rejected this. They retired to the North and produced a plan for confederal government, which would give them autonomy from southern competition and protect their authoritarian social and political institutions. The promise of regional security won some AG sympathy for confederation. However, insults to northerners in Lagos were answered by attacks on Igbos in Kano, provoked by a southern (AG) political meeting. The ensuing constitutional conferences compromised by agreeing to self-government for those regions that desired it by 1956. The fiscal base for the three regional governments was established by regionalizing the commodity marketing boards and allocating revenue to the regions on the basis of 'derivation'. Lagos was made a separate federal territory, and the North was allocated half the seats in the federal legislature.

These decisions met the immediate demands of all three ruling parties. The AG's immediate concern was to gain for the Western Region government control of the lucrative marketing board and tax revenues derived from the export of cocoa. The NPC was primarily concerned to defend the 'unity' and 'traditions' of the North. This meant defending the authority of the Native Administrations, and excluding southern competitors from jobs and commercial opportunities controlled by local and regional governments and marketing boards. It required the incorporation of non-Muslim peoples into the 'northern system',[19] in which the NPC claimed a monopoly of political representation, with which they could protect northern interests at the federal level. Neither the NCNC's policies of new states and a stronger federal government, nor the East's interest in a different allocation of revenues were realized. Yet the NCNC agreed to the new constitution because it gave them access to state funds with which the party leaders could pursue their political and commercial ends.[20]

The first priority of Nigerian politicians was to establish control over their regional fiefs and eliminate opposition within them. Between 1956 and 1961 the party in power in each region consolidated its control of local government and its legislative majority. Parties combined appeals to ethnic and regional interests with the manipulation of patronage to individuals and communities, administrative coercion against opposition councils and simple repression of opponents. In each region, political minorities demanded new states which they would be able to dominate. In 1957, in the Yoruba West, the NCNC proposed a separate state for the colonial Oyo province in which they expected to win an electoral majority. In all three regions, ethnic minorities claimed new states, and allied with parties in power in other regions, the NCNC in the case of the Mid-West, and the AG in the case of certain northern and eastern minorities. But the established interests

[19] Tseayo, 'The Emirate System'.
[20] *Report of the Tribunal appointed to enquire into allegations on the Official Conduct of the Premier of, and certain persons holding Ministerial and other Public Offices in the Eastern Region of Nigeria*, Cmd. 51 (London 1957) (The Foster Sutton Report). Cf. Osoba, 'Ideological Trends'.

of regional governments and the colonial administration took precedence over the claims of minorities to separate status.

At the 1957 constitutional conference the colonial secretary, Alex Lennox-Boyd exposed the conflicts among the Nigerian delegations.[21] The North adamantly opposed new states in the North, which would end its majority of seats in the central legislature. The AG and NCNC proposals for new states varied according to their respective calculations of the political benefits. The colonial secretary insisted that the creation of new states would delay self-government and eventual independence. The issue was passed on to the Willink Commission[22] which duly recommended against change. The conference agreed to self-government for the West and East in 1957. The question of independence was postponed to conferences in 1958 and 1960 at which agreement to the Anglo-Nigerian Defence Pact was secured. In 1953-4 and 1957-8, constitutional issues were determined by the interests of each party vested in their control of regional governments.

However, the 1957-8 constitutional and fiscal provisions increased the economic and police powers of the federal government. Control of the federal government became a means of controlling, or protecting, regional governments. Between 1960 and 1964, two attempts were made to challenge the federal domination of the NPC and its dependent allies. But these were followed by compromises in which the politicians sought the protection and patronage of the established federal and regional governments.

---

[21] Post and Jenkins, *The Price of Liberty* (Cambridge 1973), pp. 351-93.
[22] *Report of the Commission Appointed to Enquire into the Fears of Minorities and the Means of Allaying Them* (Chairman: Henry Willink). Cmd, 505, 1958.

In 1959 the NPC and NCNC formed a federal coalition based on the numerical preponderance of the North and their shared antipathy to their regional rivals, the AG. The NPC resented AG 'interference' in the North in the form of support for the Middle-Belt State. The violent resistance of the Tiv to NPC rule in 1960 and 1964 failed to secure their new state, but angered the NPC. The NCNC hoped to use federal power to end AG control in the West, and to establish a separate Mid-West Region. The AG sought to develop a national opposition, adding an ideology of 'democratic socialism' to its base in the West and its support for new states.[23] The Western Region premier, Chief Akintola, and several of the party leaders saw no reason for the west to finance the national political ambitions of the party leader, Chief Awolowo. They sought access to federal patronage through a rapprochement with the NPC, and made no secret of their hostility to socialism, democratic or otherwise. In 1962, the AG persuaded the governor of the West to replace Chief Akintola before parliament met, to prevent him dissolving it before they could recoup their election expenses. His supporters and members of the NCNC provoked a fracas in the House of Assembly when it met to reinstate his successor. The federal government used the occasion to declare a state of emergency. By 1963 they had been able to reconstruct a new majority of AG defectors and the NCNC in support of Chief Akintola, and to charge Chief Awolowo and his close associates with treason for which they were duly convicted. In 1963 the Mid-West Region was duly established.

Shared antipathy to the AG was insufficient to sustain the NCNC's alliance with the NPC. The eastern NCNC resented the

---

[23] Action Group, *Democratic Socialism. Being the Manifesto of the Action Group of Nigeria* (Lagos 1960). Its 'socialism' was a matter of supporting local against foreign capitalism. See pp. 7-8.

NPC control of federal government policy, and its allocations of expenditures in favour of the North. This was sharpened by the rising share of 'eastern' oil in federal revenues. The mid-western NCNC was, by contrast, aware of the economic dependence of the new region, where oil production had yet to begin, on federal favour. The Eastern Region returns for the 1962 census clearly inflated the count. Together with a sharp increase in the West, this would have ended the North's numerical majority of the 'population', and thus of parliamentary constituencies. The North replied by 'verifying' their figures by adding 8½ million to the original 22½ million. A new census was arranged in 1963 in which all regions inflated the figures to retain the political status quo.

In 1964, Chief Akintola formed a new party, the NNDP (Nigerian National Democratic Party), taking most western NCNC parliamentarians with him. He tried to win Yoruba support by taking to a shrill extreme the old AG theme of Igbo favouritism, focusing on appointments to the federal universities and bureaucracies. This did not win the allegiance of his opponents in the Western Region. It did focus attention on the real rivalries between Yoruba and Igbo academics and administrators for preferment. Ethnic conflict was exacerbated in 1965 when Dr Njoku, the Igbo vice-chancellor of the federal University of Lagos was summarily replaced by Dr. Biobaku, a Yoruba. The politics of ethnic competition was far from a monopoly of politicians.

In 1964, the NCNC formed the UPGA (United Progressive Grand Alliance) with the rump of the AG and NEPU, though without abandoning their federal ministries. The NPC united with the NNDP and their minor allies in the NNA (Nigerian National Alliance) built on their common determination to control state power, and their common hostility to the Igbo. The decisive features of the campaign were administrative coercion and licensed thuggery, backed in the North by refusals to accept nominations. Clearly, no challenge to the ruling parties would be tolerated. UPGA declared an electoral boycott which was completely successful only in the east. UPGA candidates were elected throughout the mid-west and in twenty western seats but elsewhere the boycott only let in NNDP nominees. The president refused to recognize the results and reappoint the premier, but the military refused to accept his authority on judicial advice. A compromise was reached, under which the NPC-NCNC coalition was continued. New elections were held in areas where no polling had taken place, enabling the NCNC to recover its seats in the East, but abandoning the AG to NNDP predominance in the West. In April, federal ministerial offices were expanded to seventy-six, to accommodate eleven NNDP ministers. Yet again, politicians had demonstrated their solidarity with the holders of power and patronage.

This willingness to join the winning side under pressure was celebrated as the Nigerian ability to compromise. But the conditions for compromise no longer existed. British arbitration had been removed. Federal control of the rules of political competition was itself the object of conflict. The accumulation of wealth and the conspicuous consumption by politicians and their clients, and the cost of state administration could only be financed by exactions on export crop farmers, and control of urban wages. At the same time the prices of export crops were falling and the cost of living rising. In the October 1965 Western Region election, the NNDP could only retain power by blatant rigging. Victimization, intimidation and the distribution of largesse to NNDP supporters were insufficient. Fraudulent electoral victory was followed by a drastic cut in the price paid to the producer for cocoa. Arson and riots were directed against the NNDP and the local supporters, and in some places against local Hausa. The NNDP retaliated with thuggery and repression, creating opportunities for robbery of mayhem. As with the Tiv resistance to the NPC in 1964, the army was needed to impose order. Government by politicians could not sustain the conditions necessary for its existence.

The conflicts of the era of politicians were not resolved when the military assumed power in January 1966. Instead the army itself became the focus and source of such conflicts. The overthrow of politicians was popularly welcomed in the south and tolerated in the north. But the majors who initiated the coup failed to seize power, except briefly in Kaduna. The rump cabinet was forced to cede power to Major General Ironsi. The coup-makers, who were mainly Igbo, did succeed in killing the federal, northern and western premiers, and several senior army officers, mainly northerners. They failed to kill the two Igbo premiers and most Igbo officers, notably Ironsi himself. The killings undermined authority within the army and the solidarity of the soldiers. General Ironsi detained the coup-makers but failed to decide what to do with them. Northerners saw them as assassins of brother officers. Southern radicals saw them as deliverers of the people from oppression of politicians in general and the NPC in particular.

The new military rulers shared with the majors a contempt for politicians and a belief in the military virtues of discipline, hierarchy and central command. The country's ills would be corrected by applying these virtues to civil administration.

Ironsi relied for advice on a small circle of civil servants and officers, mainly Igbo, even on matters affecting the North. Like the British he preferred to deal with traditional rulers, and rebuffed the advances of northern opponents of the NPC. Chief Awolowo remained in prison. The sins of the era of politicians were blamed on regionalism, a view widely shared among radicals in the south. Northern fears of unitary government were ignored or treated as reactionary. The terms of reference of the Constitutional Review Group emphasized the evils of regionalism and party politics. In April, the Northern Region government announced that local courts prisons and police would be taken from the control of the Native Authorities, the organizational base of the NPC. In May, the Ironsi government announced that the 'former regions are abolished', the public services would be unified, and all political associations banned. Then, and again in June, they emphasized that this was an administrative measure, taken by a 'corrective' regime, without prejudice to the constitutional review. They refused to recognize the dire political consequences of their administrative measures. These measures threatened the power base of the NPC. But they also threatened the ability of all northern groups, including the 'minorities', to protect themselves from competition in education, employment and commerce. Some Igbo in the north blatantly proclaimed 'their' victory over the NPC. Army promotions appeared to create an Igbo hegemony. The killings of northern officers and political leaders in January remained unavenged. In May, northern students demonstrated against the unification decrees, proclaiming *'Araba'* ('let us secede'). More sinister forces, apparently organized by local merchants, contractors and other former NPC clients, attacked and killed Igbo in the major commercial cities of the North.

On 29 July, northern officers carried out a counter-coup. They killed General Ironsi and his host, Brigadier Fajuyi, military governor of the West, and Igbo commanders. Northern troops, both Hausa and 'minorities' like the Tiv, murdered Igbo soldiers and some civilians. Initially, northern officers and troops appear to have favoured secession and withdrawal to the North. They refused to accept the authority of the chief of staff, who resigned, but negotiated with Lt.-Col Gowon, a northerner. Gowon, advised by senior civil servants and judges, as well as the British high commissioner and US ambassador, persuaded them against secession and took power as Supreme Commander and Head of the Military Government, announcing that the 'basis for trust and confidence in our unitary system of government has not been able to stand the test of time', and that 'the base for unity is not there'.[24]

Northern secession had been checked, but national political authority no longer existed. For the coup had failed in the East, and the military governor Lt.-Col. Ojukwu, was unwilling to recognize the authority of Gowon and his government. From then on the East consistently demanded regional autonomy, both in the control of security forces and in constitutional matters. They would not concede to any proposals for new states in the minority areas of the East, where their major source of revenues, the oilfields, were largely situated. On 27 August, Ojukwu declared a day of mourning, and proclaimed that 'there is in fact no genuine basis for true unity'.[25]

---

[24] Kirk-Greene, *Crisis and Conflict*, vol. 1, p. 197.
[25] Kirk-Greene, *Crisis and Conflict*, vol. 1, p. 213.

Gowon sought a political solution to the problem. He released Chief Awolowo and other Action Group supporters. Regional meetings with 'leaders of thought' were convened, preparatory to a constitutional conference. The conference was formally constituted by representatives of the four regions and Lagos, each primarily concerned with its own security and interests. The East and the North both proposed a confederal arrangement, and accepted the right to secession. Only the Mid-West opposed it, though the West and Lagos preferred a federation with more states. Between 16 and 20 September 1966 the conference was adjourned and the northern delegation changed its position. They now accepted a strong central government, repudiated the right to secession and supported the creation of new states. This change was brought about by two influences. The first was the northern minorities, and northern minority troops in particular. The second was those northern army officers, bureaucrats and academics who saw the economic disadvantages of secession, and who recognized that only by creating new states could an effective central government and united army be retained. On 30 September, the government reported agreement that Nigeria should continue as a political entity, and 'substantial, but as yet not unanimous, agreement that more states should be created.[26]

While the conference deliberated, a series of attacks began on Igbos leaving the North. The governments denied the killings until the tragic broadcasts of 28 and 29 September, when Radio Kaduna relayed unsubstantiated reports of killings of northerners in the East. This seems to have sparked off the

---

[26] Kirk-Greene, *Crisis and Conflict*, vol. 1, p. 244.

appalling massacres of 28 September to 2 October. They were more widespread and better organized than they had been in May. Soldiers as well as Native Authority officials both instigated and participated in the slaughter. The pogrom appears to have resulted from the evident vulnerability of the Igbo refugees, and the political uncertainties of the period. It was encouraged by those northerners who feared the loss of regional security, and the protection and patronage of the regional government. On 3 October, the constitutional conference was adjourned. The East never returned to it. Non-easterners, other than Mid-West Igbos, were expelled from the East. Constitutional arrangements could no longer guarantee to the military government of Eastern Nigeria the protection of Igbo lives and property. The conditions for conciliation no longer existed. The politics of compromise and crisis had reached a bloody impasse.

The Determination of Public Policy, 1939-66

Competition for sectional advantage defined the politics of the era of politicians. Issues of public policy only came to be political when they were brought into the struggle for party and sectional advantage. As Dudley says, 'politics in Nigeria... is not about *alternative policies* but about the *control over men and resources*'.[27] The politicization of policy issues, and of public administration, was seen as a threat to sound policy and to good government.

Politicians, bureaucrats and the public at large shared a commitment to a common conception of development. They all welcomed the provision of more jobs, roads, schools and health services without questioning the character of the jobs, roads,

---

[27] Dudley, *Instability and Political Order*, p. 75.

schools and health services provided. Development would be promoted by increasing government spending and encouraging private investment, both local and foreign. The task of the state was to establish the conditions for the development of capitalism. The 1954 World Bank mission outlined a strategy of industrialization by invitation. [28] Government should finance infrastructure and encourage 'the free development of private initiative and private capital formation'.[29] Since the advantages of attracting foreign capital are self-evident, they must be secured by liberal incentives and 'assurance of free transferability of profits and repatriation of capital',[30] which all four governments duly gave in 1956. After independence, ministers in all four governments attacked any discussion of nationalization as irresponsible. The World Bank report does not mention protective tariffs. Individual firms secured from the government appropriate import duties, and exemption from import duties, to ensure their profits. What appeared to be a strategy of encouraging market competition in fact required the state to protect the accumulation of money capital.[31]

Nigerian businessmen depended on the favour of the state and foreign firms for their operations and profits.[32] Yet they also wished to expand the arena within which they had access to profitable opportunities. They expected the state to finance,

---

[28] For the label and a critique, see N. Girvan, 'The Development of Dependency Economics in the Caribbean and Latin America: Review and comparison', *Social and Economic Studies* 22, 1973.

[29] International Bank for Reconstruction and Development (IBRD), *The Economic Development of Nigeria* (Baltimore 1955), p. 27. Cf. Osoba, 'Ideology and Planning for National Economic Development 1946-72' in M. Tukur and T. Olagunju (eds), *Nigeria in Search of a Viable Polity* (Zaria, 1975).

[30] The Economic Development of Nigeria, p. 30.

[31] Weeks, 'Political Economy of Wage Transfer'.

[32] Weeks, 'Employment, Growth and Foreign Domination'.

subsidize and patronize them. Government contracts and produce licences backed by public credit created an arena of politically-protected profit making. Businessmen demanded that foreign firms act with local partners and through local agents who could thus interpose themselves between foreign importers and manufacturers and retailers and consumers to reap monopolistic profits and control the allocation of petty trading opportunities. They even asked to be relieved of taxes to free them to meet family responsibilities and accumulate savings. Only where Nigerian private business was unable to invest should the state set up firms whose shares could later be transferred to private owners. [33] An ethic of private entrepreneurship, assisted by the state, could be legitimated in the contending party slogans of 'pragmatic' or 'democratic' socialism, summed up as: socialism 'is the right of everyone to own his own business.'[34]

After 1957 the federal government acquired the fiscal and constitutional powers to regulate the national economy. It increased its share of tax revenues, and acquired powers over foreign loans and investment, banking and the money supply. Regions retained certain taxes, as well as the marketing board surpluses and half the royalties and rents on mining, but had to finance expanding expenditures, particularly education. The 1962-68 development plan was based on wishful thinking.[35] It relied on a level of foreign public and private investment which was simply not forthcoming. The growth of manufacturing and state employment increased the demand for imports. The

---

[33] *Report of the Advisory Committee on Aids to African Businessmen* (Lagos, 1959).
[34] Cited F. A. Baptiste, 'The Relations between the Western Region and the Federal Government of Nigeria' (M.A. thesis, University of Manchester, 1965).
[35] As recognized by the title of the book by its main author: W.F. Stolper, *Planning without Facts: Lessons in Resource Allocation from Nigeria's Development* (Cambridge, Mass., 1966).

consumption of the newly enriched accentuated this. Outflows of profits and interests had to be financed. The prices of export crops continued to fall. Only the expansion of oil production promised some relief. Strategic investment decisions were decided, or left undecided, according to considerations of sectional political advantage and the interests of specific foreign firms. The Kainji Dam hydro-electric project in the North was preferred to the development of natural gas in the East. The planned iron and steel complex was never built because of disagreements as to whether it should be sited in the North, or the East, or both. Regional governments directed industries to inappropriate locations to share out patronage and reward particular constituencies.

Colonial labour policy had been mainly concerned to keep wages down. Between 1938 and 1946 the government set up institutions for regulating industrial relations. Both the colonial government and its successors, wished to 'isolate industrial disputes from political agitation',[36] by encouraging 'responsible' trade unionism and voluntary collective bargaining. They failed to carry out the measures required to establish either.

Most Nigerian unions have been organized by professional trade union secretaries. They competed to accumulate unions in different firms and government departments, and to establish their rival claims to speak and negotiate for workers at a national level. Rivalries for members were exacerbated by their dependence on financial sponsorship from competing international trade union centres, in return for their protégé's allegiance to their ideological and diplomatic postures.

---

[36] *Report of the Commission of Enquiry into the Disorders in the Eastern Provinces of Nigeria*, Col. 256 (London, 1950) (The Fitzgerald Report).

Successive government commissions repeated the same recommendations for strengthening and rationalizing trade union organization, without effect. Trade unionism continued to be an entrepreneurial activity, financially dependent on foreign patronage.

Periodic wage increases have been the result of government awards usually following commissions of enquiry. Commissions have been set up, awards conceded, and then extended to the major private employers, in response to general and specific strikes, or to the threat of these, and to the electoral calculations of regional governments. NECA, the Nigerian Employers Consultative Association, advocates collective bargaining to free the private sector from being tied to government awards. But the combination of permissive legislation and occasionally repressive practice has understandably failed to institutionalize collective bargaining or to prevent periodic confrontations of workers against government and employers.

Colonial and mission schools educated people for subordinate clerical positions. The transfer of authority required the expansion of higher education to create the administrators and managers who would take over the offices, assumptions and indeed the privileges of colonial officers and managers. Regional governments competed to expand schools and to fund universities which provided the qualifications that governed access to employment and salary levels. Political controversy did not centre on the content and purposes of education, but on the uneven geographical distribution of schools and universities, and the ethnic distribution of academic appointments.

Nigeria's economic dependence on capitalist countries was matched by the government's commitment to the assumptions and objectives of western foreign policy. Issues of foreign policy provided a focus for popular nationalist and pan-African sentiments. Demonstrations against the Anglo-Nigerian Defence Pact and over the news of the murder of Lumumba both led to riots in Lagos. The All-Nigeria People's Congress, initiated by NCNC ministers, and the Nigerian Youth Congress attacked the policies of the government. The AG reversed Chief Awolowo's pro-Western stance to win nationalist sympathies for its programme of 'democratic socialism' to the alarm of AG conservatives. The 1964 UPGA manifesto took up the AG support for the principle of nationalizing foreign firms, for non-alignment and for Pan-Africanism. But politics was not realigned around ideological issues. It continued to turn on the mundane issues of office and patronage.

The basic lines of federal economic and foreign policy remained unchanged. Certain symbolic changes were made. The Anglo-Nigerian Defence Pact was formally rescinded. Nigeria broke off diplomatic relations with France over atomic tests in the Sahara. But Nigeria remained a pillar of African conservatism. It maintained a military contingent with the UN in the Congo. It supported a two-Chinas and one-Germany policy at the UN. It adopted a moderate approach to Southern African problems and a supportive stance towards Britain's Rhodesian dilemma. Calls for national independence in both economic and foreign policy were brushed aside.

Failed by the politicians, radical and nationalists looked to the military to use state power 'to establish a strong, united and prosperous nation, free from corruption and internal strife', as Major Nzeogwu, the January coup leader declared in his broadcast to the nation.[37] A strong centralized state was required to override sectional interests to establish national control over the economy, to determine and execute a rational development strategy, and to create a pride in national achievements. Immediately after the July 1966 coup, the tendencies to regional security and secession seemed to predominate. But they were countered by bureaucrats and officers who recognized the economic advantages of unity and saw a need for centralized direction of development policy, while conceding to the states the satisfaction of sectional aspirations. Oil revenue would not only win regional support for national unity, but would finance the predominance of the federal government. Both Britain and America recognized the need of international capital for a strong central government, to which the Soviet Union was to give unqualified support. The development of capitalist production required a centralized authority and rational administration. There was a clear contradiction between the politics of commercial capitalism in Nigeria and the policies required for the development of capitalist production.

Relations and Conflicts among Classes, 1939- 1966
Colonialism transformed the class relations and political institutions of Nigerian societies. Specific class groups challenged on occasion the terms of their relations to the capitalist market system and the colonial state. Merchants, professionals and clerks opposed the monopolistic and racist practices of government and foreign firms, which excluded them from access to opportunities. Their methods were

---

[37] Kirk-Greene, *Crisis and Conflict*, vol. 1, p. 125.

constitutional. They formed associations, wrote editorials, sent petitions and delegations, and sought legislative office.

Farmers and petty traders acted on other issues. The Iseyin-Okeiho Rising of 1916 the Egba Revolt of 1918, and of the *Maiyegun* League in 1948 had many features in common with the later *Agbekoya* in 1968-69: harassment and extortion by government officials, increased taxes, low export and high import prices and stagnant wages.[38] Farmers too sought to present their grievances to the town authorities, but were forced back onto direct resistance. They refused taxes, attacked sanitary inspectors, court clerks and tax collectors, destroyed and looted government offices, attacked chiefs associated with unpopular measures, and on the part of the *Maiyegun*, resisted the cutting out of cocoa trees affected by swollen shoot diseases.[39] Some politicians and journalists presented or explained popular grievances but until the appearance of Adegoke Adelabu[40] on the political scene, they did not a give a lead to popular action. They identified with the explicit values of their colonial rulers and shared the colonial disdain and distrust for the masses. Even in protest against colonial abuses, they acted as intermediaries.

The Second World War accentuated the grievances of each group, and post-war controls exacerbated resentments. The marketing boards and import controls lowered export prices, raised consumer prices, and limited commercial opportunities. Nigerian businessmen joined American and British commercial interests in defence of 'free trade' and the 'open door'.

---

[38] J.A. Atanda, 'The Iseyin-Okeiho Rising of 1916', *JHSN*, 4 (1969).

[39] Beer, *The Politics of Peasant Groups in Western Nigeria* ((Ibadan, 1976); Beer and Williams, 'Politics of the Ibadan peasantry', pp. 139-45.

[40] Adegoke Adelabu, *Africa in Ebullition: Being a handbook of freedom for Nigerian nationalists* (Lagos, 1952). For the biography of Adelabu, see Post and Jenkins, *The Price of Liberty*.

Merchants opposed the marketing boards. Petty traders opposed 'conditional sales' of controlled commodities by foreign firms. Farmers' unions opposed low crop prices, new taxes and agricultural regulations.

The expansion of wage-employment increased the number and bargaining power of the workers. Rising living costs and stagnant wages provoked demonstrations, and increased union membership. In 1942 a government commission conceded an increased cost of living allowance. In June 1945 government workers, defying the caution of their union leaders, sustained a forty-four day general strike. A further commission then awarded a 50 per cent wage increase. In 1949, the shooting of striking miners at Enugu led to attacks on foreign firms in the East. UNAMAG, representing United Africa Company workers, tried to sustain the offensive in 1950 with two strikes, the first successful, the second a disaster.

The grievances of different classes provided a popular basis for national politics. Nationalists rejected the limited reforms of the 1945 Richards Constitution. They used popular grievances to establish their own claims to state power with the authorities. Radical nationalists and labour leaders united in the Zikist movement, sought to force politicians into a confrontation with the authorities. In 1948, and again in 1950, the colonial government acted firmly to repress the Zikists, at the same time as they opened commercial and administrative opportunities to Nigerians and steered nationalist politics into responsible electoral competition. Dr Azikiwe and other party leaders carefully distanced themselves from nationalist and labour radicalism.

Decolonization devolved power to regional governments, controlled by a bourgeois *stand* (status group) of politicians, businessmen and professionals, whose social and commercial ties extended across the region. Petty traders and contractors, and artisans, who had previously been able to influence customary authorities at the local level, could not take advantage of the new opportunities for political participation except as clients to merchants and politicians. In several commercial centres, they supported populist opposition parties, such as NEPU in the North, and NCNC in the Yoruba West. They often organized locally, in defence of the prerogatives and honour of their communities, as with the Ibadan *Mabolaje* and the Kano People's Party. Adelabu built the *Mabolaje* around the political, occupational and convivial societies of the Ibadan commoners and the farmers' *Maiyegun* League, over the concrete issues of jobs, contracts, arbitrary grading of cocoa, taxes, the imposition of officialdom, and not, as Sklar [41] suggests, around the defence of communal sentiments by the heads of chieftaincy lineages. His supporters looked to him to work the system for their benefit. Class conflict was thus incorporated into local politics, which was subordinated to the regional government's control of the instruments of patronage and coercion. Farmers' unions depended on the patronage and purposes of politicians and bureaucrats, to the point of formally agreeing to reductions in the cocoa price. Unions and co-operatives were concerned with credit and commercial marketing rather than farmers' grievances. [42]

By 1960 it was clear that hopes for 'life more abundant' were only to be realised for the few. The ethics of entrepreneurial initiative and of patronage shared among all

[41] Sklar, *Nigerian Political Parties*, pp. 284-320, 474-80.
[42] Beer, *Politics of Peasant Groups*.

Nigerians, are double-edged. They legitimate the unequal gains of the rich, but demand that the rich provide opportunities and assistance to the poor.[43] Nigerians found that colonial rule had been replaced by politicians' rule. Politics itself became the focus of resentment. It was identified with the corrupt and blatant enrichment of the few at the expense of the many, and the nepotism, tribalism and repression with which the politicians kept themselves in power.

The 1964 General Strike articulated the class resistance of workers and the popular resentment against politicians. Workers' restiveness led the rival unions to form a Joint Action Committee in 1963, and sustain it through the strike. A brief general strike in September 1963 led the government to establish the Morgan Commission. The unions threatened and then called a general strike to force publication of the Morgan report, and implementation of its awards, which the government arrogantly rejected after the start of the strike. Some 750,000 workers, by no means all of them unionized, went on strike for thirteen days, in defiance of the arrests of leaders and threats of dismissal, and gained partial implementation of the Morgan awards. As in 1945, the strike was actively supported by market traders and the urban poor. Despite the declared support for the strike of AG and NCNC leaders, a demonstration of 30,000 people at Ibadan race course chanted, 'No AG, no NCNC'. Workers' defence of their 'rights' focused popular grievances against all politicians and their practices.

Trade union unity did not survive the 1964 elections. Labour parties made little impact, and a strike called against

---

43 Waterman, 'Conservatism' p.182.

the election results failed. People gave their support to the political parties they had renounced, acting according to the rules of electoral politics, of competition to control the allocation of state resources. The strike was not about 'politics', but about justice. It was in effect a strike *against* parliamentary politics.

In Tivland in 1960 and 1964, in Ibadan districts after Adelabu's death in 1958, and in Yorubaland in 1965, supporters of opposition parties resisted the forcible imposition of regional government power upon their communities. They attacked government buildings, tax clerks and police. They vented their wrath particularly against local supporters of the ruling party. Post[44] suggests that the violence took the specific form of punishing offences against their communities. The violence did not simply involve people in the politics of resource allocation. It was also a popular rejection of the rule of politicians.

The Political Economy of Crisis and Reconstruction, 1966-1975

The coup of 29 July 1966 created a crisis of state authority. It was finally resolved by the consolidation of the power of the federal government and military victory over Biafran secession. Between 1969 and 1974 the production and price of oil both increased dramatically. These led to significant changes in the forms of state authority, of state intervention in the economy, and of Nigeria's relations with foreign countries.

In 1966 and 1967 federal permanent secretaries acted decisively to maintain federal authority. The creation of states ended the power of the regions. The federal government

---

[44] Post and Jenkins, *The Price of Liberty*, p. 440; Post and Vickers, *Structure and Conflict* p. 233.

appropriated an increasing share of the rising oil revenues, and controlled the allocation of the remainder to the states. Military rulers depended on bureaucrats and particularly on the federal permanent secretaries, to define policies. The war and increasing oil revenues expanded state economic activities. The federal government extended its control over imports, banking, foreign exchange and the relations between foreign and indigenous capital. This accelerated the substitution of imports of machinery for imports of consumer goods, and expanded factory production, thus extending state control over access to private commercial opportunities. Military, and federal and state government spending increased rapidly with decreasing budgetary controls. Federal and state governments formed numerous parastatal corporations to spend government money and promote development activities. The federal government took shares in foreign oil companies and joined the Organization of Petroleum Exporting Countries (OPEC).

After the war, oil production and oil prices both increased dramatically. In 1971/72 oil revenues of ₦640 million provided half of government revenue. By 1975/76 they had risen to ₦4,600 million, out of a total revenue of ₦5,300 million. Oil then provided 93 per cent of export earnings. Yet the industry employed only some 6,000 people. The vertically integrated activities of oil companies stimulate production abroad rather than in Nigeria.[45] Oil income arrives as manna from foreign firms. Political competition centres on the distribution of oil rents, rather than on the appropriation and distribution of surplus value produced by export crop farmers. Foreign

---

[45] Part II.

corporations compete for access to Nigeria's oil supplies and lucrative markets. A secure market position requires not simply sales and purchases, but investment in and the provision of technology for manufacture and mining. 'The export of capital thus becomes a means for encouraging the export of commodities.' In Nigeria, as elsewhere, oligopolistic, transnational firms are reluctant to engage in price competition, and pay 'considerations' to gain access to market opportunities; 'monopolies introduce everywhere monopolist principles; the utilization of 'connections' for profitable transactions takes the place of competition on the open market'. [46] The expansion of state expenditure and state regulation of economic activities increases the scope for bribes. State officials increasingly take over the comprador role of organizing foreign access to local supplies and markets.

Production by foreign firms also requires an efficient administration and provision of services and the development of government and other institutions that mirror their corporate values and organization. Thus the shift of foreign capital from trading to production creates the need for local technocrats. They increase local productive capacities, which may alter the terms of the state's relations with foreign capital, enabling foreign firms to withdraw from direct investment to the international marketing of services and commodities to develop new lines of business in the provision of technical advice and support'. [47] Foreign firms have often trained technocrats, as in the case of the staff of NNOC (Nigerian National Oil Corporation). They 'produce' technocrats in

---

[46] Lenin, *Imperialism*, p. 108.
[47] Sir Frank McFadzean, Chairman of Shell, Preface to their 1976 *Annual Report, Financial Times*, 14 May 1976.

another sense. Just as comprador middlemen are the historical creation and local counterparts of foreign commerce, so technocrats are the historical creation and local counterparts of transnational capitalist production.

The 1975 Coup and the Politics of Capitalism

On 29 July 1975, field officers who had fought the civil war and in several cases executed the coup of 29 July 1966 removed Gowon and the military governors, who had exercised administrative power for eight or nine years. Colonels and majors organized the coup. Four brigadiers took over the key positions in the government and army: Murtala Muhammed, head of state; Obasanjo, chief of staff, Supreme Headquarters; Danjuma, chief of staff, army; Bisalla, commissioner of defence. All officers above that rank were retired. The head of state and the military governors, with small cliques of civil service advisers and business associates, had decided policies and allocated patronage with scant regard for their military peers, let alone anyone else. The indefinite postponement of civilian rule and the determined retention of office by the governors, perpetuated their personal appropriation of the spoils of office. The authority of the Federal Executive Council, which included Brigadier Muhammed and other officers, were flagrantly overridden by Gowon's appointment of a NNOC general manager. The Udoji payments and port congestion demonstrated the government's ineptness. The coup was arranged in such a way as to avoid any shedding of blood, and to attempt to ensure the solidarity of the officer corps and the army.

The new government realized that the economic development, social stability and international standing of

Nigeria required institutional reform and firm and disciplined government. They needed to create a constitutional framework within which conflicts among interests could be managed without threatening the authority of the state and the stability of society. They needed a central state authority capable of deciding on, and implementing, public policies. They needed a programme which could meet popular aspirations. The most obvious feature of the new government has been its capacity to use military authority to decide a number of intractable issues and to carry out its declared intentions.

Its first step was to establish federal military authority over state governors and civil servants. The new state governors are responsible as serving officers to the chief of staff, Supreme Headquarters. They may be, and have been, transferred or removed. They no longer sit on the Supreme Military Council. Permanent secretaries are excluded from meetings of the federal Executive Council unless specifically invited. Several top federal and state permanent secretaries, including Ayida and Asiodu, were retired.

Measures were taken to discipline the civil service. The government retired 10,000 employees, of whom a well-publicized minority held senior police, judicial, academic and administrative posts. Tribunals exposed some amazing abuses, the government suspended certain contracts, and re-appropriated certain assets. It set up a Permanent Corrupt Practices Investigation Bureau and a Public Complaints Commission. Such measures could scarcely end collusion between state officials and local and foreign capitalists, as long as the state continues to be the major avenue for private accumulation of money, and the leading allocator of opportunities for profit.

The Gowon regime had failed to reorganize the army after the civil war. As Lt.-Gen. Danjuma declared: '... since the civil war, the Nigerian Army has been run as a social service, maintaining and paying an exceedingly large body of men that we do not really need and whom we cannot equip'.[48] At the beginning of 1976, the army announced a cautious policy of demobilization. Senior officers were promoted to generals and brigadiers. In February 1976, an incompetent attempt at a coup failed, but the head of state was assassinated. The coup makers resented the recent promotions, feared demobilization, and allegedly planned to restore Gowon to power. Most of the participants were publicly executed, including Major General Bisalla. Popular support for the actions of the new government and fear of the consequences of any new round of killing within the army account for the bitterness and anger of both the army and the public. Nationalist resentment focused on Britain, where Gowon was exiled.

The new government took action to resolve the constitutional problems with which Gowon had failed to deal. A commission was set up to examine petitions for new states. Some 200 proposals were made to draw different boundaries for sharing out oil revenues, jobs and opportunities. The commission recommended the creation of twenty states. The government agreed to, and established, a total of nineteen, and declared that to be the limit. A government proposal for uniform local government throughout the country was turned down, and traditional rulers have been accorded new respect, and allowed an active role in local government. A new federal capital is to be built in Abuja, in the centre of the country. A

---

[48] January 1976, cited *The Times*, Nigeria Supplement, 22 August, 1976.

unitary state has been set up in federal disguise. But it leaves local institutions, patronage and appointments in state hands, and ensures protection at the federal level for the interests of the far north.

On 1 October 1975 a firm timetable was drawn up for a return to civilian rule. A draft constitution has been submitted, and local government elections held, without overt party politics. From the institutions of local government, a constituent assembly is to be elected to consider the draft constitution. Political parties will then be formed for successive state and federal elections, prior to the handover of power on 1 October 1979. The constituent assembly, with its basis in local, indirect elections, supplemented by government nominations, recalls the 1950 General Review of the Constitution. 'Demilitarization' of politics may prove no less final than its model, the 'decolonization' of political office.

The draft constitution seeks to combine an effective central executive, capable of directing state policy and arbitrating among conflicting interests, with effective representation for sectional interests. It thus recommends an executive president, whose appointment and powers are hedged with an array of checks and balances which would have pleased Montesquieu himself. Presidents must win a plurality of votes, and one quarter of the votes both nationally and in half of the states. Presidential authority thus requires the support of a broad coalition of state interests. The composition of federal and state governments and their agencies, and the conduct of their affairs, must give due representation to their constituent states and communities, defined as recognizing 'the federal character of Nigeria'. [49] A draft which would have outlawed discrimination by state of origin was dropped.[50] A series of statutory bodies, appointed by the president with legislative approval, will carry out politically sensitive tasks, such as running elections and reviewing revenue allocation, and making politically sensitive appointments. Appointments to defence, police and security councils will not require legislative approval. Nor will ministerial appointments. The draft constitution and the somewhat muted debate which has followed it have been, in the words of the dissenting Minority Report on the Constitution, primarily concerned with 'provisions for the formal and dubious accountability of one set of members of the bourgeois political class to another...'[51]

The Third Plan had announced that finance was no longer a constraint on development, and the Gowon government spent and planned accordingly. Its expenditures rose rapidly to meet its revenues, and its plans assumed a continued increase in oil production and prices, together with a moderate rate of inflation. In May 1976, oil production had fallen back from 2.3 million to 1.6 million barrels a day. Immediately after the coup, the Muhammed government cut prices as a 'gesture of goodwill'. Since then, with demand high, production has risen to 2 million b/d in 1976, and prices, royalties and taxes have been increased. But despite this the companies have but back on exploration and development. In October 1976 Lt.-Gen. Obasanjo promised incentives for exploration, and emphasized the need for good relations with the companies. In April 1976 a government memorandum proposed to merge NNOC and the

---

[49] *Drafting Committee*, 1, ix.
[50] *Drafting Committee*, 2, 158.
[51] *Minority Report* (Y. B. Usman and S. O. Osoba), (Zaria 1977).

Oil Ministry into a single Nigerian National Company. But no action was taken until twelve months later. Administrators objected to paying oil professionals salaries comparable to their counterparts in the companies, since this would raise the salaries of oil technocrats and hence their status above those of the administrators.

The government was committed to ambitious investments intended to transform oil revenues into productive industries. Long delayed plans for an iron and steel mill, oil refineries and oil pipelines are going ahead. Ambitious schemes for liquefied natural gas, direct reduction steel plants using gas, and a petrochemical industry are planned. The 1976 and 1977 budgets encouraged assembly industries with increased protection for vehicles and other manufacturers, and reduced duties on raw materials. Merchant and development banks have been directed, without immediate effect, to use their money for long-term loans at low interest for industrial investments. The 1976 Indigenization Decree further expands the scope of Nigerian ownership and shareholding. A new category of businesses requiring 60 per cent Nigerian ownership covers banks, trading companies and a number of industries.

The 1976 Indigenization Decree, like its predecessor, renegotiates the terms of the relations between foreign and local capital. Foreign firms can realize the value of past investments by selling shares, and take new profits from management contracts rather than direct investments. Increased industrial investment will expand their market opportunities. Its success will depend on the expansion of the state sector, and will require an increase in the number of local technocrats and a consequent strengthening of their position within the state. But commerce offers easier and more lucrative profits than production does to private capitalists with access to government favour. A strategy of state-directed industrial expansion may well be undermined by the resulting competition over the commercial opportunities created by state expenditure.

A strategy of industrial development requires control of the labour force. The realization of any ambition to export manufactured goods depends on 'competitive' labour costs. Attempts to establish control have taken three forms: industrial relations legislation, reform of trade unions, and wage controls. In 1976 two new labour decrees created a complex hierarchy of institutions, headed by a National Industrial Relations Court, for enforcing settlements, banned strikes in essential services, and enabled the government to proscribe unions which act to 'disrupt the economy'. This law was soon applied to the bank employees. In December 1975 a Nigerian Labour Congress had eventually been established by appointing 102 national officers and sharing the top positions among the rival centres. In 1976, the government banned foreign labour organizations and set up the Adebiyi Commission[52] to enquire into the activities of the trade unions. In September it appointed an administrator to form a single central labour organization, and in 1977 proposed to establish a single central body with 31 industrial affiliates. By April, thirty-four unions had been listed, and the administrator had drawn up a detailed list of regulations for union elections. In 1977, the government banned a number of leaders from further trade union activity. The White Paper on the Adebiyi

---

[52] *Report of the (Adebiyi) Tribunal of Inquiry into the Activities of Trade Unions* (Lagos 1977). See Waterman, *Industrial Relations*.

report promised to stamp out 'racketeering, abuse of office, personality cult, politicization, conflicts of interest, and similar malpractices', and to submit the power of trade union leaders to 'reasonable and civilized regulation'. A new code of conduct for union leaders prohibits conflicts of interest, 'chronic indebtedness', 'drunkenness', and initially banned participation in politics. A wage freeze was declared until 1 June 1977, after which wage increases were to be limited to 7 per cent in the coming year, despite inflation of over 60 per cent since 1975. In such circumstances, neither proscription, nor regulation, of unions is likely to prevent industrial action by workers.

Despite the need to reduce expenditure, the government has maintained its commitment to universal primary education, and to spending on health, housing and agriculture. Cheap fertilizers and credit are being made available to 'feed the nation'. They may well contribute more to private commerce and government employment than to agricultural production. The proposal of the constitutional committee to abolish the marketing boards, once the main source of state government income and patronage, was rejected. Instead these have been reorganized as federal boards for each commodity.

In international politics the Nigerian government has taken a strong nationalist lead. In October 1975, it was still deploring external encouragement of rivalries in Angola.[53] With the South African intervention, it committed itself decisively to the MPLA, praised Soviet support for African liberation and

---

[53] Col J. N. Garba, Commissioner for External Affairs, to the General Assembly of the United Nations, 7 October, 1975, *Nigerian Bulletin on Foreign Affairs*, 5, 3 and 4 (1975), p. 2.

dismissed the American 'directive'[54] to African heads of state to insist on Soviet and Cuban withdrawal as 'a most intolerable presumption and a flagrant insult on the intelligence of African rulers'.[55] Nigeria plainly intends to continue her leading role in negotiations between developed and underdeveloped countries for new terms of trade and investment.

The Nigerian military government aims to establish the institutional conditions for industrial development and political stability. State investments and state regulation of the economy are intended to promote the development of capitalist production and national independence. Its constitutional measures and proposals attempt to accommodate the politics of sectional competition to the need for central direction in public policy. As Petras and Morley argue, '...regulation of foreign capital and promotion of growth and expansion of national bureaucratic and private capital leads to a new historical bloc of classes – in which national and foreign industrial capital collaborate'.[56] However, the capacity of the Nigerian state to achieve this measure of realignment with foreign capital remains doubtful. Technocratic nationalism lacks a firm class base in Nigerian society. Profit making continues to depend on collaboration with foreign firms and on the favour of the state. The state continues to control access to money, contracts commercial opportunities. Politics is a struggle for the control of these resources. But these resources are also means by which politics is carried out.

---

[54] Federal Government, Statement of (sic!) Angola, 6 January. 1976, *Nigerian Bulletin on Foreign Affairs*, 6, 1 (1976), p. 2.

[55] Gen. Murtala Muhammed, to the Extraordinary Summit Conference of the Organization of African Unity, 11 January, 1976, in *Nigerian Bulletin on Foreign Affairs*, 6, 1 (1976), p. 10.

[56] J. Petras and M. Morley, 'The Venezuelan Development 'Model' and U.S. Policy, *Development and Change*, 7 (1976).

The constitutional proposals recognize and accommodate this sort of politics. Politics is assumed to be a business of reconciling divergent interests, pursued by competing elites. Questions of foreign domination, class power and state policy are ignored or evaded. Bourgeois domination, the purpose and foundation of such politics, is taken for granted.

Civilian constitutional rule requires a bourgeoisie in command of productive resources, capable of settling its own affairs peaceably, maintaining the authority of the state, and accommodating the participation in politics of subordinate classes. The production, market, state and moral relations of Nigerian society generate conflicts among competing interests for access to scarce resources, between commercial interests and technocrats over the direction of state policy, and between the state and the subordinate classes over the terms of their exploitation. Neither the policies of the military government, nor the proposals of the constitution-makers show either the will or the capacity to tackle these sources of political instability. Civilian rule is thus likely to repeat the 'failure of politics', and hence to invite in its turn a fresh demonstration from the military of the 'failure of administration'.

30 September 1977.

Part IV

Economics and Politics in Nigeria

Capitalism and Agriculture

To reject the goal of capitalist development does not solve the question of whether it is likely to be achieved in Nigeria. This question turns partly on matters of definition. Is capitalism identified with the extension, throughout society, of production for the market? In which case Nigeria is thoroughly capitalist; or does it depend on the extension of production by wage labour? In which that case no society, not least Nigeria, is completely capitalist.

Marxists have typically followed Lenin's analysis that the extension of production for the market would lead to the emergence of a class of capitalist farmers, employing a proletariat of 'allotment-holding wage workers'.[1] They have assumed that large-scale capitalist (and state) farming would be more efficient than peasant production. Regrettably, this is an assumption which they share with policy makers in Nigeria and World Bank project officials. Since it is evident that in Nigeria, as in most other countries, 'backward' peasant producers have not been displaced by more 'efficient' capitalist farmers, Marxists[2] have sought to explain why this apparently natural process had been diverted or blocked. The obvious answer, that peasants survive because they use resources

---

[1] V.I. Lenin, The Development of Capitalism in Russia {1899} (*Collected Works*, vol. 3, p. 177).
[2] Part IV. I was persuaded by Sara Berry's criticism to change my mind on this topic.

more effectively and therefore produce more cheaply, was rejected by assumption.

Capitalist farms have been established in Nigeria. They have only been successful in specialised forms of 'factory' farming, such as poultry. Elsewhere, they have only been made possible by privileged access to state subsidies of the costs of machinery, fertilizer and other means of production, particularly on schemes such as the World-Bank financed Funtua Agricultural Development Project, or the government's Kano River Irrigation project.[3]

The costly development of capitalist farming can only undermine peasant production, on which Nigeria depends. Until 1970, Nigerian peasants were able to expand production of cocoa, groundnuts, and palm produce for export to the point where Nigeria was the world's largest or second largest exporter of each of these products and, at the same time increase production of food for an expanding internal market. Since the increase in oil prices and in federal government spending on agricultural development in the 1970s, agricultural exports have declined, in the case of groundnut and palm oil (though not palm kernels) to nothing; imports, especially of wheat and rice, have shot up; and food prices have increased even more rapidly than the prices of imported and manufactured goods. Farmers may have been able to increase production to take advantage of higher prices in some areas where fertile land is available and urban markets are

---

[3] C. Jackson, 'Hausa Women on Strike', *ROAPE* 13, 1978; T. Wallace, *Rural Development through Irrigation* (Zaria, 1979), 'The Kano River Project, Nigeria: the Impact of an Irrigation Scheme on Productivity and Welfare', T. Forrest, 'Agricultural Policies in Nigeria, 1900-1978', R. King, Co-operative Policy and Village Development in Northern Nigeria', in Heyer *et al.*, *Rural Development*. Williams, 'Agriculture in Nigeria' in the first edition of this book.

accessible.[4] In many isolated or arid, or densely-populated areas, poverty and insecurity are widespread, and are probably getting worse.[5]

Capitalism and Industry

Capitalist relations of production have expanded in manufacturing, though without eliminating independent craftsmen. Since independence, there has been a rapid, if uneven increase in the output of Nigerian industry.[6] Does this provide evidence of development of capitalist production in Nigeria? Clearly, what matters is the share of final output that is produced in Nigeria – so-called 'value added'. Value added in manufacturing has increased overall in roughly the same proportions as increase in output. However these figures would look far less impressive if prices were calculated at world market levels, rather than using the inflated prices which Nigerian consumers pay foreign firms for highly protected products.

Manufacturing is still dominated by low technology, light consumer goods; textile production has increased more rapidly than the earliest import substituting industries – beer, mineral waters, processed food and tobacco. Engineering is almost non-existent and chemicals consist mainly of toiletries and household detergents. Value added is lower in the high

---

[4] Williams, 'Agriculture in Nigeria', and J. Derrick, 'Farming in Nigeria', *West Africa*, 16 and 23 July, 1979.

[5] E.J. Usoro, 'Observed Disparity in Nigerian Rural Poverty', *Poverty in Nigeria*, Proceedings of the 1975 Annual Conference, Bagauda Lake, Kano, Nigerian Economic Society (NES); R.W. Shenton and M. Watts, 'Capitalism and Hunger in Northern Nigeria', *ROAPE*, 15 (1980).

[6] The most useful source for statistics on the Nigerian economy in 1975 was the Central Bank of Nigeria's *Annual and Monthly Reports*. See Nigerian Economic Society, also International Monetary Fund, *Survey of African Economics*, vol. 6 (Washington D.C., 1975). I am grateful to John Carlsen of the Centre for Development Research, Copenhagen, who compiled many of the relevant figures in an unpublished paper. 'Industrial Co-operation in the Lomé Convention – the case of Nigeria'.

technology industries, and the opening up of a number of motor vehicle assembly plants and the expansion of chemical and metal products has led to an increase in the proportion of import costs in the output of industry. Manufacturing in Nigeria provides an expanding and remarkably profitable market for metropolitan capital. In turn, this market is financed by oil revenues, whose dramatic expansion since 1970 has meant that, despite the growth in manufacturing, its share in Nigeria's gross national product is lower than in Kenya and Tanzania.

Nigeria's 1975 development plan allocated vast sums of money to expanding and improving the roads, ports, airports, railways, telecommunications, water and electricity supplies and petrol refineries required by the expansion of industrial production and the import of commodities. Some improvements have been made at great cost, such as the movement of Lagos traffic and the expansion of port capacity, but generally the government has been unable to meet the expanding demand for these facilities and consequently shortages, breakdowns and high costs continue to hold back the expansion of industry. Current plans to build the iron and steel complex which was proposed two decades ago and to create several petroleum and gas-related industries are designed to lay the foundations for industrial development using local material. These projects are expensive and have been funded by huge Eurocurrency loans. They will be slow to recover their investment costs. They will not reduce dependence on foreign technology and will extend Nigeria's dependence on a single, and finite resource, oil. Indeed, it is hard to see how Nigeria will be able to meet the import costs of its industrial production, let alone of all the other commodities which are bought abroad, once its oil supplies are exhausted.

Nigeria has no prospects of exporting industrial products on any scale. The spending of oil revenues has generated high rates of inflation while at the same time, despite periodic lowering of exchange rates, the government has been able to maintain a relatively high exchange rate for the naira. Although Nigerian workers find it extremely difficult to make ends meet, their money wages (but not their purchasing power) are high in comparison with other African countries. Production costs are inflated by high managerial and especially expatriate salary costs and by the high cost and uncertain provision of transport facilities, electricity and water supply. This structure is sustained by protective tariffs and import licences. Nigeria can be expected to provide an export market for industries situated in the countries of the Economic Community of West African States rather than the other way round.

It is clear that industrial development continues to be dominated by the substitution of imports of producer goods and semi-finished products for the import of some consumer goods. Firms invest in Nigeria to gain access to a lucrative market. There is little evidence of the development in Nigeria of an independent capacity for civil industrial production and none of any prospects of exporting manufactured goods.

During the 1970s, the Nigerian Government has taken several measures to increase national control over mining and manufacturing (agriculture has been opened up to foreign investors). The federal government has taken a majority shareholding in the oil industry, among others, and in response to Britain's pusillanimous policies in Southern Africa has nationalized the assets of British Petroleum (but not Shell, its own partners in Nigeria). In 1972 and 1976, 'Indigenization' Decrees reserved some economic activities for Nigerians and required majority Nigerian shareholdings in others. These changes have institutionalized the collaboration of the Nigerian bourgeoisie with foreign capital. Government and foreign banks, and foreign firms financed the acquisition of shares by Nigerian managers and civil servants, as well as their purchase of properties for rent to foreign companies and diplomatic missions. In Kano, foreign firms sold shares to and appointed their Nigerian distributors as directors. [7] The Nigerian bourgeoisie was still a 'junior partner'[8] of international capital.

Military Rule and the Politics of Spoils

The creation of a capitalist society needs more than an increase in industrial production and the extension of commodity production and wage-labour. It requires the creation of a state bureaucracy, capable of directing public policy to serve 'national' interests, and the articulation of a body of moral doctrines which discipline the competition for private advantage.[9] During the Gowon regime, senior civil servants were able to direct public policy. At the same time, the federal government became the major arena of the conflict of private interests. Gowon's successors have not been successful in eliminating corruption and sectionalism. They have remained to some degree above 'politics' i.e. sectional conflicts, but only by committing themselves to return power to civilian politicians, the most experienced exponents of such conflicts.[10]

---

[7] P. Collins, 'Public Policy and the Development of Indigenous Capitalism', *Journal of Comparative and Commonwealth Studies*, 15, 2 (1977); A. Hoogvelt, 'Indigenization in Kano', *ROAPE*, 14 (1980).

[8] Williams, 'Social Stratification'.

[9] S.O. Osoba, 'Deepening Crisis'.

[10] See Part III.

The transfer of constitutional authority by the military paralleled, in a modified and abbreviated form, constitutional decolonisation by the British. Like the British, the military government controlled effective political power and used it to direct constitutional discussions towards the outcome they preferred. They insisted on the Presidential form of government, and by creating 19 states, defined the framework within which electoral alignments would be formed. In order to create 'national' rather than sectional political parties, they required that parties be organised in two-thirds of the 19 states and that the successful Presidential candidate win at least one-quarter of the votes cast in two-thirds of the states. This ensured that politicians formed alliances of state-based interests. In the 1950s the three major political parties based their political power and party finances on their respective control of the government of the three regions. The creation of new states created a more complex pattern of conflicts and loyalties and allowed the political minorities of the former regions the chance to control their own states and to act more independently in the federal arena. The former leaders of the Northern People's Congress could no longer rely on their control of regional and local government to maintain their domination of the northern states. The first concern of the politicians was to recruit supporters and form alliances. The main issue in contention at the Constituent Assembly was whether the highest appeal from Shari'a Courts should be to the Federal Supreme Court. It provided an opportunity for politicians to appeal for Islamic solidarity, as an alternative to the Northern solidarity whose constitutional base had now been eliminated. It also divided Muslim politicians from their potential Christian allies. The conflict was effectively defused by the military authorities and the Sultan of Sokoto, who got the politicians of both sides off their respective hooks.

The 1979 elections reproduced, with interesting modifications, the divisions of the 1950s. The National Party of Nigeria (NPN) whose candidate won the Presidential elections and which proved to be the most successful nationally, organised itself as an alliance of state-based interests. As Richard Joseph has put it, the NPN 'regards itself as Nigeria's natural party of government, and with good reason'.[11] It was led by the former leaders of the parties that made up the Nigerian National Alliance (NNA) in 1965, notably the NPC in the old Northern Region and the NNDP in the West, as well as politicians who regarded their states' and their own interests as best served by joining the winning side. They also recruited a number of people who had served in the army or administration under the military governments and had retired, or been retired, from office. The NPN won seven state governorships (Bauchi, Benue, Cross Rivers, Kwara, Niger, Rivers, Sokoto) and the largest share of the vote for each of these states and in Kaduna. It won the largest share of the Presidential votes in nine states, adding Gongola to the other eight. The NPN were first or second best in all but Lagos, in the Presidential and Senatorial elections, and elected National Assembly representatives from 16, and State Assembly representatives from 15 states. No other party approached this breadth of support.

Nevertheless, NPN politicians were beaten in areas they regarded as their strongholds. The former leaders of the discredited NNDP were beaten by their rivals, Chief Awolowo's

---

[11] R. Joseph, 'Political Parties and Ideology in Nigeria', *ROAPE*, 13 (1979).

UPN, throughout the former Western Region, losing Ibadan City, which they thought was theirs, and winning only in Ogbomoso, home town of the late Chief Akintola. Alhaji Aminu Kano's PRP won by a huge majority in Kano, and won the governorship of Kaduna State, two of the four predominantly Hausa-speaking states. At the same time, the NPN successfully brought the Tiv political leaders in Benue Street into their fold, and won Cross Rivers and Rivers, the non-Igbo speaking areas of the former Eastern Region. The attempt to build the Nigerian People's Party as a national alliance, in opposition both to the NPN and the UPN, failed because of political rivalries. The NPP, led by Dr Azikiwe, won Anambra, Imo and Plateau, the Greater Nigerian People's Party (GNPP) led by Alhaji Waziri Ibrahim won Bornu and except in the Presidential poll, Gongola. The UPN won Bendel, as well as Lagos, Ogun, Ondo and Oyo, and made a significant showing in Gongola. Perhaps the most significant result was the turn-out: a majority of Nigerians did not care to vote for any politicians, even after 13 years of military rule.[12]

In the event, Alhaji Shehu Shagari, the NPN Presidential candidate, won the required quarter of the vote in only 12 of the 19 states. The Federal Electoral Commission, FEDECO, thanks to some remarkable arithmetic supplied originally by Chief Akinjide of the NPN, declared that he had satisfied the two-thirds rule and was duly elected. The military authorities clearly preferred to leave the consequent wranglings to the legal procedures of the Supreme Court, which confirmed Alhaji Shagari's election, rather than to the bargaining of politicians in an electoral college. The NPN will need to form some sort of

---

[12] A version of the election results was printed, with errors, in *West Africa*, 27 August, 1979.

alliance with minor parties to ensure parliamentary support
for their legislation.

A narrow conception of politics reduces it to the contest for
political office and the competition for its spoils. Politics in
Nigeria often seems to be about just this.[13] The manoeuvres
which produced the 1979 electoral alignments are an obvious
example. In another sense, electoral competition depoliticizes
both public issues and the mass of workers, peasants,
craftsmen and petty traders. Although claims to socialism were
made by the UPN and the PRP there was little difference
among the policies of the parties. All were committed to a
combination of private enterprise, state spending on education,
welfare and development, and a 'fair' division of resources
within the federation. Socialists failed to create a united,
national party and were consequently excluded from the
elections by FEDECO. However, in the absence of a mass,
popular movement, socialist politicians could only have
recruited personal followings in order to compete with
bourgeois politicians for elected office and disposal of its spoils.
Only through a mass, socialist movement can they establish a
different form of politics.

There was one exception to the absence of class politics in
the 1979 election. Workers, farmers, craftsmen and traders in
Kano, and also in Kaduna State, identified the PRP as the party
of the poor (*talakawa*), or the common people, and in that
respect as the successor to the NEPU. The *talakawa* identified
the NPN as the party of the bloc of aristocrats, merchants and
bureaucrats who monopolise 'traditional' and 'modern' official
positions, buy up urban land for housing and irrigated rural

---

[13] Part III.

areas, control trading opportunities, and invest in industrial enterprises.[14] The *talakawa* will look to their governors to improve the conditions of the poor and open up economic opportunities for them. It is unclear how the PRP can satisfy these expectations when economic power is controlled by their opponents and by the federal government.

Class action by the poor and exploited classes requires that they organise themselves to act directly in their own cause. Workers' strikes in 1964 and 1971 successfully demanded increases in wages, generated a tradition of workers' action, and provided a focus for the sense of injustice of the urban poor. The general strikes of 1945 and 1964 were initiated by government workers and led by the established union leaders. In 1971, the demand for the extension of the Adebo award to the private sector produced widespread strikes in the factories of Ikeja (Lagos) and Kano. In Ikeja, they were organised by 'house' unions at the level of the factory. In Kano, in the absence of trade unions, *mallamai* often took the lead in organising action. In 1976 the government restructured the trade union movement into a single central body, the Nigerian Labour Congress (NLC), consisting of a number of industrial unions. These reforms were designed to end the squabbling between rival trade union centres, sponsored by rival international organisations. Nevertheless, factional rivalries and offers of scholarships and assistance by international bodies continue in a more muted form. However, an emphasis on central trade union organisations overlooks the focus of industrial conflict – the factory and the industrial estate, in which workers can organise themselves effectively. In Lagos,

---

[14] See Lubeck, 'Labour in Kano since the Petroleum Boom,' *ROAPE*, 13 (1979).

the new trade union structure has in several instances provided the military government with a means of disciplining striking workers. The formation of government-financed industrial unions has undermined the independence of workers' organisations at the factory level. In Kano, on the other hand, government support for the NLC strengthens trade unionists in their struggle to force employers to recognise and negotiate with them.[15]

Trade union officials find themselves in an ambiguous position which is not of their own choosing. Government expects them to cooperate with policies designed to prevent strikes and to control government spending and thus to restrain wage increases. Workers expect trade unions to press their demands on both management and government and to secure wage increases to meet the costs of inflation. The dilemma of trade union officials opens the way to conflicts among the trade union leadership itself.

In 1975, the 'Udoji' awards doubled minimum wages in government employment. By 1976, inflation had already caught up with minimum wage levels, which were lower, in real terms than they had been in 1960. Since then government wages have been kept back, and fallen far behind the cost of living. In the private sector, both urban and rural wages have continued to rise, particularly in the south, and despite government policy, as a consequence of price inflation and the construction boom. Nevertheless, the cost of food and other necessities has increased even further. The 1979 budget not only continued the wage freeze in the face of rampant inflation, but also withdrew loans and allowances for the purchase and

---

[15] See 'Preface' to A. Peace, *Choice, Class and Conflict*; Lubeck, 'Labor in Kano' and reports on strikes and sacking of strike leaders in the Nigerian press in 1978.

maintenance of private vehicles. The National President of the NLC, Hassan Sunmonu, accepted that the budget was in the best interests of the workers. He and the government's policy were challenged by the Deputy President, David Ojeli, who declared that the budget was a slap in the face of Nigerian workers. On 24 May the NLC issued an ultimatum which demanded that vehicle loans and allowances be restored, that a housing allowance be paid to every worker, that agreements between unions and employers which still await approval from the Ministry of Labour, and that all decrees which restrict the rights of workers should be repealed. After lengthy negotiations in June, the government agreed to consider workers' demands, bar the restoration of vehicle loans and allowances.[16] Clearly, the trade union leadership did not seek to challenge the authority of the military government in the period just before the elections, and preferred to await the return of civilian rule. One of the first demands on civilian government will be for a general increase in wages for government employees, to bring them into line with the private sector and catch up with increasing prices. This will produce demands for the extension of wage rises throughout the private sector, and strikes to enforce them. A civilian government will not be able to use the NLC to restrain workers' action. As in 1964 and 1971, the demand for the implementation of government wage awards can provide the issue on which workers throughout the country can unite in a common action. At the same time, this demand defines the

---

[16] *West Africa* 18 June, 1979 and 16 July, 1979. I am grateful to Peter Waterman for drawing the significance of these events to my attention.

limits of workers' action.[17] Both farmers and workers have demonstrated their capacity to resist exploitation and challenge state oppression.[18]

In drawing attention to the capacity of workers and farmers to take action in defence of their interests, Peace and I did not emphasise sufficiently the very limited nature of the gains which were achieved and the inability of workers and of farmers to challenge the system of income distribution and the distribution of political power in Nigerian society.[19] Although their actions have provided a focus for popular grievances, they have not produced any broader political organizations of the working class, or of the poor. There appears to be no immediate prospect of the emergence of a significant socialist party. The task for socialists seems to me to be to find ways to build on the resistance of the common people to exploitation, and to create a popular socialist movement which goes beyond the issues which concern workers alone, and articulates the grievances of all exploited classes,[20] in opposition to the current alternatives of bourgeois politics and authoritarian rule.

30 September 1979

---

[17] I owe this to Dafe Otobo, then at the University of Ibadan. See also D. Otobo, 'The Nigerian General Strike of 1981,' *Review of African Political Economy*, 1981, Vol. 22, pp.65-81; and 'The Political Clash in the Aftermath of the Nigerian General Strike of 1981,' *Review of African Political Economy*, 1982, Vol.25, pp. 104-112

[18] Jane Guyer politely suggests that this 'this description must be 'understood very broadly and in all its implications'. J. Guyer, 'Representation Without Taxation: An Essay on Democracy in Rural Nigeria' *African Studies Review* 36 (1992). With taxes 'came petty council officials, and sanitary inspectors, who embezzled money and exacted bribes from the farmers for the non-implementation of incomprehensible regulations, or just demanded the bribes.' Part V. One farmer said to me that 'we would have put up with the taxes, but the problem was those sanitary inspectors.'

[19] Peace, 'Industrial Conflict in Nigeria,' in E. de Kadt and Williams (eds) *Sociology and Development* (London, 1974, 2001).

[20] Lenin *What is to be Done?* ({1902}, Oxford 1962, and in *Collected Works*, vol. 5. (Moscow, 1970).

Part V

Political Consciousness Among the Ibadan Poor[1]

Colonial Capitalism and Social Differentiation

Colonial capitalism has transformed significant social relationships into commodity relationships. It has thereby differentiated the colonized society along new lines, so that people's life-chances are determined by their access to and exclusion from resources introduced by the colonial political economy. At the very simplest level of analysis, Ibadan, like other societies, divides into two, those who have, and those who have not. The distinction is given expression in the Yoruba word *mekunnu*, best rendered in English as 'an ordinary person', or in the plural as 'the common people'.[2] Depending on the context, the *mekunnu* may be distinguished from the *olowo* (wealthy), who constitute the most obvious antithesis, but also from the *omowe* (educated), *olola* (noble, in Ibadan implying chiefs), or *alagbara* (powerful).[3]

The *mekunnu* are a diverse, and vaguely demarcated category including people with such different 'class situations'[4]

---

[1] de Kadt and G. Williams, eds, *Sociology and Development* (Tavistock Press, 1974).

[2] The best definition of the *mekunnu* that I was given was 'those without money in the bank, those without money in the hand, those who had to work before they can eat', Conversation, Ibadan 1971.

[3] Adeboye distinguishes *olaju* as 'the educated elite' in his research, Peel only finds the term used to refer to 'enlightenment'; O. Adeboye, 'Reading the Diary of Akinpelu Obisesan in Colonial Africa', p. 84; Peel, ' "*Olaju*" ', pp. 142-144.

[4] Weber, 'Class, Status, Party', p. 181.

as traders, farmers, and industrial workers. This chapter will accordingly examine the differences among these groups with respect to their specific class situation, the demands they make, and the resources that they can use to realize these demands. But we must not lose sight of what they share with each other: a common awareness of being excluded from the significant opportunities for gaining rewards in society, and aspirations and values derived from interaction with one another in the compound, the town, and the market. We shall concern ourselves particularly with the ways in which different groups of people among the *mekunnu* – the wage-employed, the self-employed, and the farmers – seek to advance their own interests and 'end their suffering'.

The basis of the colonial economy of Ibadan was the cultivation of cocoa, which spread rapidly in the 1892 to 1912. This entailed a migration of people from the city to the rural areas and the emergence of a peasantry, which in recent years, has come to develop a distinct rural consciousness. The cultivation of cocoa created lucrative opportunities in the export-import trade for mercantile firms, and on a smaller scale, for the intermediaries whom they needed to buy the cocoa from the farmers and to sell the imports financed from cocoa to the farmers and others. The development of the produce trade and the expansion of feeder roads in the twenties opened up opportunities in road transport for those, notably produce buyers, best placed to take advantage of them. Further, the multiplier effects of the cash derived from cocoa provided a market for foodstuffs, for a variety of crafts, with pre-colonial crafts being eclipsed by those using imported tools and materials, and for a host of petty traders. The increasingly complex needs of administration and the educational efforts of the missionaries created a new stratum of clerks particularly significant with the increasing administrative importance of Ibadan from 1939 onwards. Colonial rule also required the emergence of a small wage-labour force in construction, on the docks, in the ports, and on the railways.

Those who made best use of the new opportunities in trade and education found their opportunities for further advancement blocked by the administrative, educational and commercial policies of the colonial administration and the mercantile firms. It was these groups who led the opposition to colonial rule and who, during the 1950s, negotiated the terms of the relationship between Nigeria and the colonial interests in such a way as to give themselves access to a large part of the surplus value exacted from the peasantry and from the exploitation of mineral resources. This labour laid the foundations for a 'neo-colonial' economy, characterized by the rapid growth of the capital-intensive, technologically advanced, import substitution sector, of direct state involvement in the economy, and thus by the expansion of opportunities for wage employment, government employment and for indigenous entrepreneurs as well as for foreign capital.[5]

Thus, in contemporary Nigeria the significant levers of economic power continue to be in foreign hands. But the activities of the state administration, now controlled by businessmen, bureaucrats, professionals, and army officers in their own interests, ensure their association with foreign interests in the expropriation of profits and public money enable them to carve out areas of economic activity where the rewards are reserved for them. These groups constitute the

---

[5] Williams, 'Social Stratification'.

'haves,' many of whom are, however, of humble origin and retain links with their lineages and townsmen. Our concern here is with the response of 'have nots' too the expropriation of resources, rewards, and opportunities at their expense by the 'haves'.

Values and Aspirations in Contemporary Ibadan (1972)
Ibadan was established as a war camp. It was a town where rewards went to the brave and enterprising. A man wishing to establish himself politically would gather a following that would follow him both in war and in the affairs of the town and be compensated by grants of land and the exercise of influence with the powerful. Thus both leaders and followers valued initiative, independence, and generosity very highly.[6] These are the same values that one would expect to arise from the opportunity and reward system of colonial western Nigeria. Thus the successful men were precisely those who best exemplified these values,[7] these values; in turn legitimated their rewards. Examples of men from humble origins who became successful traders lent credence to a picture of a society with open mobility. These men were thus an élite in Nadel's sense,[8] an inimitable reference group that provided a model for the aspirations of others.

Education provided an important channel of mobility in southern Nigeria, initially very often for those from the humblest homes. People thus look to the expansion of educational opportunities to provide their children with a

---

[6] (Rev) Samuel Johnson, *History of the Yoruba: from the Earliest Times to the Beginning of the British Protectorate* ({ed. O. Johnson, 1921}, London 2010).
[7] P. C. Lloyd, *Power and Independence: Urban Africans' Perceptions of Social Inequality* (London, 1974).
[8] S. F. Nadel, 'The Concept of Social Elites', *International Social Science Bulletin,* 8 (1956).

chance to make good. Education is closely associated with the techniques and products of modern technology with which the accepted goals of 'progress' and 'development' are associated. The indispensability of the educated for the achievement of a 'modern' and 'civilized' society legitimates their rewards and prevents the control of power by the educated from being questioned as such, however much their exercise of that power may be disliked.

Increasingly social status is associated with sheer wealth and with the status symbol of modern capitalism (expensive cars, large houses) as well as lavish expenditure on customary ceremonies (funerals, naming ceremonies). Recognition of wealth as the criterion for social status is, however, often grudgingly given. Ibadans (but not in my experience élite Yoruba) tend to distinguish sharply between the *olowo* (the rich man, pure and simple), and the *olola* (man of honour), defined by one respondent as 'those who had been installed as chiefs, had plenty of farm and town land, and had given it to their people', and, by implication, whose honour cannot be bought – even though people are well aware that chieftaincy titles usually go to the man with the longest purse. The distinction between sheer cash and pure honour[9] here, as elsewhere, reflects concern at the fact of wealth alone deciding a man's status (and even the allocation of titles). As a watch-repairer of an honourable lineage (*ile ola*) regretfully explained, 'the *olowo* is more respected than the *olola* because he can back it up with money'.[10]

We have seen that the values and goals in terms of which the success if the rich is defined are to a large extent shared by

---

[9] Weber, 'Class, Status, Party', p. 192.
[10] Conversation, Ibadan, 1971.

the poor and define their aspirations, thereby legitimating the rewards of the rich. But competitive individualism as a universal value has its own contradictions – it creates aspirations which, by their nature, can only be realized by the few. As long as the rate of expansion of opportunities can be maintained, its contradictions need not become apparent. But in time the 'haves' come to be seen as monopolizing opportunities. The 'haves' own struggle for themselves and their offspring to survive and prosper in a competitive world leads them to regulate their relations with the prefatory relatives by whom they regard themselves as being surrounded. The poor in turn find the door shut in their faces when they seek the help of a potential patron. As many people told me, 'Everyone has his own responsibilities now'.

The gulf between the 'haves' and the 'have-nots' becomes even more marked as the 'haves' develop a distinct style of life and circle of interaction,[11] based on the mutual esteem of their peers and, all to often, a scarcely disguised contempt for the poor and illiterate. Education is here the key ingredient. In many respects the poorly paid clerk's life-style may be more sharply distinct from that of his illiterate contemporaries than is the life-style of a wealthy but illiterate trader. But the wealthy, literate or illiterate, are busy ensuring their own children the best possible education, while the highly educated are well placed to provide the standard of living to which they believe themselves entitled. The ensuing 'convergence of elites' means an increasing divergence between the life-styles of the 'haves' and the 'have nots.'

---

[11] B. B, Lloyd, 'Education and Family Life'; P. C. Lloyd, 'Class Consciousness'.

Thus we find that attitudes towards the rich are ambiguous. They are admired for their success, but berated for their selfishness. The government are often accused of looking after the interests of the 'haves':

> The government looks after the interests of the privileged few. They help their people, and if it is not their people, it is the people of their people (middle-aged woman, primary school teacher).
> The government are looking after the progress of the rich people; they want people on top to remain there and the poor people to remain poor' (29 year old man, mechanic, primary six education)
> The rich get richer and the poor get poorer. The rich wanted it that way, because if the poor were better off they would have the power to oppose the rich (middle-aged man, labourer, illiterate).

On the other hand, the ambiguities in attitudes towards the rich were clearly expressed in a discussion with two petty contractors during which the first, when asked whom he respected most in Nigerian society replied: 'those who are rich people and who help the poor'. His friend later commented:

> When there are politicians, we don't want politicians and we ask for the military government. But the military government does worse than the politicians. What we must do is love [fé] one another. What I mean is that we must try to help all. If one is in a big position, then one must not think of oneself and just one's people, but all the other people who are poor.

While the poor put their hopes in the education of their children, they complain variously that the expansion of education has meant a decline in its quality so that free primary education is of little value, while the elite (and the politicians who introduced free primary education) send their children to better, fee-paying schools; that scholarships established for the benefit of the poor were being given to the sons of rich men; that the dull children of rich parents could bribe their way into secondary school at the expense of poor but brilliant students; that secondary school fees were beyond the means of many poor parents; and that even if their children do graduate from secondary school after much hardship for their parents, it is the children of the rich who get the jobs, irrespective of qualification.

The palpable corruption of political life, which extended beyond the politicians to the elite generally and beyond the period of 'political' rule to the present, brought the legitimacy of the elite's earnings, so often based on extortion sustained by violent repression, into question. Wasteful consumption by men who spend another man's annual and even life-time income in a few hours intensifies resentments by the 'have nots.' The ambiguity of status recognition according to wealth and power was cynically exemplified by one respondent: 'We respect politicians – like we respect murderers.'

In an uncertain and competitive world where fortunes are seen to be made and lost and one's own fortune often appears to be beyond one's control (but is at the mercy of the international cocoa market, or other more immediate contingencies), Allah, or God, fate and luck are common (and not unwarranted) categories for the explanation of scarce resources within the lineage, between lineages, and between ethnic groups, accusations of witchcraft, poisoning, and ethnic favouritism are rife. Thus the disparities between the rich and poor can be explained in terms of personal effort, magic or good fortune. But although Allah may decide whether a man will become rich, or win a contract or title, He comes in very secular guises, such as political patrons or ministry officials, for contracts, or the *Olubadan* and his senior chiefs, for titles. People are very well aware of the secular steps to be taken to achieve their goals. Thus fatalistic explanations, often of a theological sort, are complemented by secular ones, which often point to the illegitimacy of a man's means of advancement and, as we have already seen, refer increasingly to structured discrimination against the poor.

Ibadan Townsmen – Craft Producers and Traders

In 1970, Ibadan was a city of some eight hundred thousand people. It divides roughly into the indigenous quarters, the homes of the descendants of the nineteenth-century settlers of Ibadan, and the stranger and elite quarters, occupied largely by migrants attracted to Ibadan by commerce, administration, or professional employment. Our concern here is with the 'indigenous' Ibadans. They occupy distinct areas of the city, and live mainly in the compounds of their patrilineages. They tend to interact largely with one another and most particularly with those resident in their own compound, and with people of a similar gender, age and status or of a similar occupation. Chieftaincy titles are competed for among all the Ibadan lineages. Quarters are not clearly defined. The authority of lineage heads and of chiefs in their own quarters has long been largely displaced by that of courts and bureaucrats and local influence is often exercised by men of wealth (*olowo*) rather than by men of 'chiefly' lineage (*ile ola*).

Although cocoa production continues to be the base of Ibadan's economy, even its oldest quarters are distinctly urban in characters. Unlike Lagos and Kano, the city has had little industrial development. It remains a centre of administration and commerce rather than manufacture. The majority of its population are self-employed traders and craftsmen, with a minority of clerks and labourers employed by the government and various business houses and contractors.

In this chapter we shall examine the position of the craftsmen and petty traders in the urban economy of Ibadan and the cocoa farmers of the rural areas, with respect to their class situation, their aspirations and demands, and the resources at their disposal, with a view to explaining their respective abilities to undertake collective action to enforce their interests.[12]

Numerous craftsmen practice their trades in Ibadan. They include motor mechanics, tailors, watch-repairers, carpenters, bricklayers, iron-benders, plumbers, radio technicians, goldsmiths, electricians, barbers, shoemakers, and photographers. Craftsmen take on apprentices for a fee (often between five and ten pounds) and the use of some years of the apprentices' labour time (anything from two to seven years). Although some youngsters do become apprenticed to traders, success in trade often requires more capital and more experience than any youngster can manage. Thus trading is an aspiration (and an almost universal one) to be financed out of savings.

The market situations of craft producers are dependent on their ability to expand his clientele in the face of competition from the surplus of producers that exists in relation to the

---

[12] For a comparable study of industrial workers see Peace, 'Industrial Conflict'. Brevity prevents due consideration being given here to other significant groups among the *mekunnu*, viz. women traders and craft producers, labourers, clerks, soldiers. Nor do I consider here the pre-emption of opportunities from Nigerian businessmen by expatriate firms.

available demand. As Koll explains, 'In the craft sector...the only entry restriction is success; and since success can only be measured after some time, more shops are opened than can be kept running'. Craft producers and traders are

> discriminated against by the massive subsidization of capital intensive and often foreign enterprises, by the operation of bureaucratic controls (e.g. import licences) and by the criteria for government assistance that require them to meet bureaucratic regulations and associated costs that are beyond their means or cut into their narrow profit margins.[13]

All craft producers depend on the overall level of demand for their products, which in Ibadan was closely bound up ultimately with the level of the cocoa price and with government expenditure and their multiplier effects. The demand for their particular products also depended on the price of the tools and materials that they required for their work. Tailors want cheap, imported cloth, and mechanics cheaper imported cars to be available, thus creating more opportunities for themselves. But lacking control over the level of demand or government policies of import restrictions, craft producers can do nothing but compete as best they can with one another, and agree collectively to restrict cut-throat competition lest they undercut each other's standards of living. Competition from manufactured products (often highly subsidized) restricts the market for the output of craft production are discriminated against by the massive subsidization of capital intensive and often foreign enterprises, by the operation of bureaucratic controls (e.g. import licences)

---

[13] M. Koll, *Crafts and Co-operation in Western Nigeria* (Freiburg, 1969), p. 22.

and by the criteria for government assistance which require then to meet bureaucratic regulations and associated costs that are beyond their means or cut into their narrow profit margins.

Yoruba crafts have usually been organized into guilds (*egbe*). Guild heads are formally recognized by the ruler of the town and in the older crafts especially, a guild's officers will hold titles ranked and named according to the common Yoruba political titles. They are responsible for regulating their trade in their town, which includes settling disputes among craftsmen and customers, determining who is allowed to practice the trade (which includes regulating apprenticeships and the entry of strangers to practice in the town), representing their members to the town's authorities, and maintaining prices.

During the 1930s the Ibadan guilds were incorporated into the system of tax collection and assessment, which consolidated the position of their officers who were recognized by the authorities. Today, however, the craft guilds appear to be in disarray. Allegations of embezzlement of funds are common; attendance at meetings and payment of subscriptions is irregular; disputes over office and the establishments of rival guilds occur; and there is little evidence of guilds being able to enforce their own regulations, particularly among the stranger community, but also among Ibadan sons. On the other hand, even their most disgruntled members are not happy to go it alone, recognizing the importance of combining with one another, and new guilds are formed almost as rapidly as the old ones fall apart.

Craft organizations have suffered from the replacement of the colonial system of native administration, in which they had a recognized place supported ultimately by the colonial administrations, by the system of elected councils and subsequently of appointed administrations in which even recognition of guild officers by the *Olubadan* could not ensure their effective authority over their members. Ibadan's attractions as the administrative capital and commercial centre of western Nigeria have drawn to it large numbers of non-Ibadan craftsmen who cannot easily be brought under the authority of the local guilds. Most crucially, the guilds have been unable to control entry to their crafts. The apprenticeship system is designed to slow down the rate of entry into the craft and lengthen their period of free service to the master. But as apprentices provide labour for their masters and are thus crucial to the success and expansion of their businesses, each master has an interest in taking on as many apprentices as he can handle and therefore, in the long term, enhance the oversupply of entrants to his trade. Thus we have conditions which dictate the need for collective organization to restrict competition, but which undermine effective collective action at the same time. Again, prices can often be maintained – but only by virtue of an inflationary situation, or by the price being sufficiently near to what the equilibrium price would be under free-market conditions to limit any temptation to undercut. As we shall see in the case of traders, restrictions on trade can be effected by the stronger against the weaker. But in the case of numerous individual producers who compete against one another, collective action is unlikely to provide an effective weapon for the weak against the strong.

This being the case, craftsmen must look to their own individual resources for advancement. This means finding the money to purchase the necessary equipment, which may require a generous sponsor, expanding one's clientele, which depends ultimately on satisfied customers spreading the word, and which can be assisted by a wide circle of friends, and, through these successes, attracting sufficient apprentices to increase turnover. The expansion of any craft business faces severe problems. The competition among craftsmen limits their rate of return on labour and capital and thus the resources available for reinvestment. Demand tends to be seasonal in many crafts, and is uncertain in nearly all. Although a producers may save rapidly in order to pay the initial fees and equipment costs necessary to establish themselves in trade, once established a variety of demands (for school fees, ceremonial expenses, house building) all limit their capacity to save. But even when they can save, their expansion is limited by their own labour time and if they can employ several apprentices, their ability to organize and supervise them. Since prices are calculated on the basis of low labour costs, both their own and that of unpaid apprentices, they are not in a position to reorganize their business on capitalist lines.

There are some opportunities to be gained from various sorts of cooperative arrangements. These usually involve the sharing of certain material resources (e.g. a shop site, expensive equipment, bulk buying of materials), informal arrangements for mutual assistance (including credits), and sharing of customers (e.g. between craftsmen in related trades – welders, battery chargers, and mechanics, for example, so that if A cannot take on work immediately, B will be available to do so in order to prevent the customer being lost outsiders). But such arrangements do not enable craftsmen to overcome the barriers to expansion: they only allow them to improve their competitive position and perhaps to extend the barriers a little.[14] Consequently craft producers aspire to reinvest their profits in trading concerns where the same limitations do not apply and where opportunities for expansion are indefinite, at least in principle. Further, they recognize that much higher profit margins (and far higher returns to labour time) are enjoyed by the traders who sell them materials than by themselves. Thus we find that tailors aspire to become cloth traders, mechanics to trade in motor parts, drivers to own their own taxis. In each case, their craft experience should enable them to build up to a circle of potential clients and to learn many of the ways of the trade they seek to enter. The crucial barrier is usually capital so that advancement lies in the hands of potential sponsors in whose eventual generosity craftsmen must put their fate, however disappointing their current experience might be.

An illustration of the weak position of craftsmen was provided by an officer of the Ibadan Bricklayers' Association. One of their aims is to regulate relationships with their clients, so that the association will intervene when house owners complain about shoddy or incomplete work and when bricklayers complain about debts being unpaid. But, he said, 'if the house owner is a lawyer or a big man [*enia pataki*], then there is nothing we can do...The law has died completely in Nigeria'. He complained that the high price of (hoarded) cement was cutting the demand for houses, that the Price Control Board officials 'have friends who are (distributive) agents', and that the bricklayers themselves could do nothing about this 'because we have no power and no money'. Non-bricklayers use their influence to get (government) contracts,

---

[14] Koll, *Crafts and Co-operation*.

which they then farm out to bricklayers, taking huge profits for themselves. The bricklayers (and other craftsmen in the building trade) 'can do nothing about this either, because the people who have the contracts have more power.' Why do the bricklayers not refuse to carry out the work? 'It is a case of hunger. If they do so, they will not have any food. Those without a penny will not have a chance and they will take the work when offered it.'

For most clerks and craft producers, hopes for the future lie in trading and in contracting. Traders and contractors are involved in a series of hierarchical distributive networks. As might be expected, profits are highest and competition least where monopolistic profits may be made by privileged suppliers/buyers at the top end of the selling/purchasing system, where prices can be artificially inflated and profits guaranteed. Men and women who entered the distributive hierarchy lower down have rarely prospered to any great extent.

During the colonial period, most successful produce buyers and traders started their careers as clerks to or agents with mercantile companies, thereby overcoming the initial needs for capital and clientele. After the Second World War, produce buying licences conferred exclusive advantages to middlemen in the sale of export crops. Since the advent of the 'years of the politicians' (l'aiye oselu), political influence and subsequently military connections have become the most effective way of entering a commercial career. Beneficiaries included 'army contractors' and 'army wives', government officials; distributive agents for imported or manufactured goods; and people with family or other assistance to provide the capital in order to start at a higher point in the distributive hierarchy.

Politics and political parties may have been prohibited but networks continued to be politically and economically active, ready to align and realign when 'politics' returned in 1978.

Licences and contracts are the most lucrative routes to the accumulation of wealth. Among all the commodities produced and consumed in Nigeria, food and clothing are the most important. Commodities – and people - are transported on an enormous scale for short and for very long distances, opening profitable space for entrepreneurs with the commercial skills, the financial resources, and the means to pay police for 'protection' (and to buy off armed robbers).[15] Entrepreneurial skills are aimed at or depend on securing a corner on the market rather than at innovations or at increases in efficiency and this requires the influence or financial assistance of a better placed sponsor. Politics can work both ways. Political connections may be a consequence of entrepreneurial success rather than just a route to commercial wealth.

There is considerable resentment of the richer by the poorer in such a set-up. Several respondents who traded in cocoa and cotton bitterly regretted the passing of the expatriate companies who provided the credit with which they financed their operations. They argued that the 'Europeans' had been chased away by those who 'want to take the European's money for themselves', and berated the selfishness of those who had replaced the European companies. These men, they complained, operate through a much smaller number of middlemen than their predecessors (who had operated a monopoly of six companies!), taking many of the middlemen's functions over for themselves or have secured a

---

[15] Peace, 'The politics of transporting', *Africa* 58, 1 (1988), drawing on ethnographic research conducted in 1970-1971.

place as privileged agents to foreign importers or manufacturers, thus closing off opportunities for those further down the distribution hierarchy.

On the other hand, the petty traders aspired to gain entry to the closed circle of privileged distributors, and they had to look to the established traders to provide the help that might enable them to do so, while, more immediately, relying on these same traders for suppliers and credit. One produce buyer complained to me bitterly that the licensed buyers (to whom he now sold, having previously sold to an expatriate firm) did not help buyers like himself to get licences, nor did they provide them with adequate credit. But when I suggested that the system of Marketing Board licences should be abolished (as in any case, buyers like himself often delivered their produce straight to the Board's store with only a chit from the licensed buyer to enable them to do so), he opposed this, as that would 'spoil the trade'!

While at the top, traders are primarily concerned to gain a share of monopolistic advantage, at the bottom they seek to regulate the trade in order to prevent ruination by cut-throat competition. Thus attempts to eliminate one of the stages in the bulking process (e.g. farmers selling directly to urban retailers; wholesalers buying from farmers instead of through farm-gate middlemen; Hausa ram sellers or Ijebu palm-oil sellers or women cloth traders selling directly to customers rather than through Ibadan middlemen) will be fiercely opposed as depriving someone else of their rightful living. But where capital requirements for entry are low, *egbe* are in the same position as the craftsmen and can do no more than try to recruit new entrants to the trade and to their association. As with craftsmen, price maintenance is only likely to be successful in an inflationary situation or when the price is set near to what the equilibrium price would be under free market conditions. Cooperation is important to enable groups of traders to share certain costs (e.g. through bulk-buying arrangements, joint chartering of transport) and arrangements for mutual assistance, but does not enable them to manipulate prices to their own advantage in the long term or to form a united front against the wealthier traders.

The introduction of the price control regulations revealed the weakness of the petty trader and the strength of the monopolist wholesaler only too well. First, it led to immediate restriction of output by producers and to immediate hoarding by wholesalers, who were able to sell at massively inflated prices (cement prices went up to twenty-five shillings per cwt.), as against the control price of twelve shillings and sixpence) and by 'conditional sales'. Enforcement of price control regulations, which included bans on hoarding, would be difficult in any case in a country with as many small retail outlets as Nigeria has. Many traders reported that price control inspectors simply took their 'dash' and left. Most prosecutions were of petty traders who were buying their supplies at more than the retail control price. The one 'big' wholesaler in Ibadan to be prosecuted was fined £150, a derisory sum to him, while other flagrant hoarders went ahead untouched.

Petty traders in controlled commodities such as beer, cement and tinned milk were unable to get many supplies and were charged extortionate prices for them. Unlike the wholesale distributors, they could not increase profit margins sufficiently to compensate for their reduced turnover. Hence they demanded that they be allowed to buy directly from the factories instead of through the recognized agents. Ibadan beer retailers held a series of public meetings at which they formed an association with the help of the United Labour Congress (ULC), Nigeria's largest trade-union centre, and demanded that half the supply for Ibadan be sold to them through the association, allowing the agents the other half (it was, it appears, felt to be unfair to deprive the agents of their means of livelihood entirely). Despite the optimism of the traders, nothing ever came of the negotiations, the breweries reputedly answering that they could only supply the association when their established customers' needs were met (!).[16] This left the beer sellers' only hope lying in the increase of supply as a result of the ending of import restrictions on beer.

Why were the beer sellers, a substantial number of traders, with the sympathy – even in a largely Muslim city - of the (large) drinking public unable to force the employers (and/or the government) to accede to their demands? After the first meeting, one middle-aged woman expressed scepticism at the association's chances of success. There had been meetings before, but it was the 'big men' (and women) who came to lead the association. They could always get others to follow them by offering to supply them beer at a cheaper price. It was difficult to get any clear evidence of profiteering on the part of the officers of this particular association. What is clear was that they failed, and never thought of using the one weapon that *prima facie* was available, viz. a boycott of the distributors, and thus of sales, until prices were reduced. This was because the distributors themselves owned large retail outlets and could break the boycott and induce others to do so. Undoubtedly the

---

[16] On the advantages of 'agency' arrangements to the manufacturers, see O. Olakanpo, 'A Preliminary Report on Indigenous Enterprise in Distributive Trades in Nigeria', NISER, mimeo, (Ibadan, c. 1967).

expatriate brewing company would have been sensitive to any pressure put on it by the government, but one could hardly expect anything from the government when its leading figures, or their wives, were themselves agents, or else friendly with them. Here, as in so many other instances, the dependence of the small man on the favour of the big man prevents any action (short perhaps of firing the hoarders' shops) to stop his being exploited along with the consumer, even though he is perfectly aware of being exploited, and of who the exploiters are.

The ability of a trade association to represent and enforce its members' interests effectively depends on the resources that it can command. Most craft producers and petty traders have few resources. What is more, they are only marginally involved in crucial relations of exploitation (the exaction of Marketing Board surpluses and the allocation and theft of state funds) characteristic of neo-colonial Nigeria. So they do little more than appeal hopelessly for the favour of the authorities. By contrast, organizations such as the Motor Transport Union can and do exercise influence with leading government and political figures and exercise sanctions as they see fit. ' To them that hath, it shall be given'; those who are able to organize effectively in defence of their interests prove to be those whose individual resources are considerable.

Any individual craft producer's or petty trader's chances of success depend upon their personal skills and contacts and their ability to take advantage of new opportunities, especially of possibilities for innovation. But in 1970 as a class, their situation was determined on the one hand, by the rate of exploitation of agricultural production and the (real) world price of agricultural exports and on the other, by the expropriation of resources and opportunities essential to their livelihood by merchant traders and manufacturers, foreign and local.

Undoubtedly, a certain populist consciousness exists among them. It is exemplified in the very use of the term *mekunnu*. In 1970, it had its economic roots in common dependence on the proceeds of cocoa cultivation and common exclusion from significant opportunities, and its social framework is embedded in the networks of mutual interaction and communication that link the *mekunnu* into coherent communities. But the social relations of production and distribution in which Ibadan craft producers and petty traders are involved, and the forms of social organization to which these relations give rise, do not bring them into solidaristic relations with one another in opposition to their exploiters. Their relations with the merchant traders and the 'haves' generally are mediated through relations of patronage and clientage rather than through impersonal market relations, or corporate forms of social organization.

In the 1950s in Ibadan, craft producers, and, most particularly, petty traders and contractors, were the key supporters of Alhaji Adegoke Adelabu, the populist leader of the Ibadan *mekunnu*. They looked to him to secure for the small man the favours that were monopolized by the (predominantly educated) 'big men' who dominated Ibadan affairs in the post-war period and continued to dominate regional politics throughout the fifties and right up to the present period. Long after his death, people in Ibadan told me that 'Adelabu, he loved the poor (*fe mekunnu)'*.[17] Today, in the absence of conditions enabling such a leadership to emerge,

---

[17] Williams, Review of Post and Jenkins, *The Price of Liberty*, in *African Affairs,* 73, 265 (1974).

the urban *mekunnu* tend to adopt individualist stratagems, such as the search for patronage, in order to advance their interests. They lack the means to act collectively, of their own accord, on their own behalf, and in their own interests. They cannot act as a 'class for themselves'. In Marx's words, 'They cannot represent themselves. They must be represented. Their representative must at the same time appear as their master.'[18]

Ibadan Farmers and the Agbekoya Rebellion

The spread of the money economy under colonial auspices, the attractions of cocoa as a profitable crop, and the existence of demobilized warriors seeking a new source of income at the end of the Yoruba wars in 1893, led fairly rapidly to the occupation of uncultivated land to the south, east, and north of the city beyond the existing farmlands, and in turn to the planting of cocoa trees.[19] The commitment of farmers' scarce resources to cocoa, however profitable, subordinated them to the changing requirements of the world market, over which they could exercise no control, and to the lesser exactions of the intermediaries on whom the farmers relied for the marketing of their crop.

Ibadan, unlike other Yoruba towns of importance, had no *oba* (king) and thus no conception of all lands being held for allocation to the town's lineages. As the demands for cocoa land gave it a monetary value, hunter-warriors who had camped beyond the outlying farmlands, and chieftaincy families who claimed and contended for authority over farmlands nearer to the city, asserted their right to allocate these lands and establish tenants on them. Despite conflicts

---

[18] Marx, *The Eighteenth Brumaire of Louis Bonaparte*, ({1852}, *CW* 11, p. 187,), ch. 25, p. 327.
[19] Berry, *Cocoa, Custom and Socio-Economic Change*.

between the chiefs and the hunter families,[20] and resistance by the farmers to the claims of the 'landlords', these rights were recognized by the colonial authorities whose main concern was to stabilize claims to land and to establish some kind of intermediate authority in the rural areas.

As Galetti *et al.* showed,[21] landholdings, particularly of cocoa land, were very unequal. However, a wealthy cocoa farmer was likely to invest his profits in education for his sons rather than in expanding his sons' landholdings, or to seek more lucrative gains from produce-building and from other trading activities returns than are offered by farming. This does not mean that there is no market in land - money has been passing hands in exchange for land since the early years of the century. But it does mean that there is a drift of people and resources from rural to more urban occupations, which inhibits the development of a '*kulak*' stratum capable of rationalizing agricultural production and dominating rural society through their *economic* superiority over other farmers.[22] The close relationship between country and town where all Ibadan farmers will have claims to residence and citizenship through their urban-based lineages means too that unsuccessful farmers with insufficient land to make a living will seek urban employment, or ensure that their sons do so, returning to the farm only at weekends, if at all to meet a part of their needs.

Consequently the backbone of rural society in Ibadan is the independent small holding peasant. He is permanently resident in a rural hamlet (or perhaps a village). He may owe nominal

---

[20] Chief A. O. Obisesan, Diaries, *passim,* Kenneth Dike Library, University of Ibadan.

[21] R. Galletti, K.D.S. Baldwin and I. Dina, *Nigerian Cocoa Farmers* (Oxford, 1956).

[22] Williams, 'Why is there no agrarian capitalism in Nigeria?' *Journal of Historical Sociology,*1, 4 (1988).

allegiance to an 'overlord' from whom his own family gained their land and will, if he can, employ some labour (usually Igbirra or Hausa migrants) on a seasonal basis. In the terms used by Mao[23] and sociologically established by Alavi,[24] he is a 'middle peasant'. His land will have been sufficient for him to make a living, but as he and his trees have aged together, his cocoa acreage and his labour power, and the family and other labour at his disposal) will have declined. He is middle-aged or elderly. Few youngsters do not seek a more promising future in the towns.

This is not to suggest an absence of stratification in the rural areas but rather that the most significant basis of stratification sociologically lies in people's occupations (e.g. produce buying against farming); in the contentious meanings attributed to custom and practice; and in their relation to urban sources of significant political and economic power. In Ibadan divisions, this was particularly true of the relation between 'landlord' or 'overlord' families (*onile*), and their 'tenants'. The payment was small. It was £2 to £3 *per annum* per village. But under the system of native administration,[25] the 'overlords' were the essential intermediaries between rulers and ruled. They often had access to urban sources of patronage. The tenant's claims to land depended to some extent on their overlord's prior claims, as well as on his recognition of them. The dependence of the tenant on his 'overlord' facilitated the exploitation of the tenants through practices, such as *isakole* (tribute in cash and kind), and *owe* (communal labour, here used as a tributary service) that

[23] Mao Zedong (Tse-tung), 'Analysis of Classes in Chinese Society', *Selected Works*, vol. 1 (Peking, 1965).
[24] H. Alavi, 'Peasants and Revolution'. *Socialist Register* (1965).
[25] Atanda, *The New Oyo Empire*. Crowder and Ikime, *West African Chiefs*.

claimed the legitimacy of custom, and through irregular exactions to meet the cost of the overlord's litigation and contests for titles, the celebration of his festivals or, in some cases, the mere lining of his pockets. Farmers in the Ibadan district, who regarded themselves as *omo'Ibadan* (sons of Ibadan) and had been established on their land for a generation or more, were disinclined to accept the legitimacy of claims to *isakole* whether as land rent, or as tribute.[26] With the end of the system of Native Administration and of colonial rule, the fortunes of the 'overlords' depended increasingly on their electoral fortunes and the favour of the regional government, while the passing of time confirmed their erstwhile tenants in their rights to land.[27]

One economic factor stratifying rural society is access to labour, where only a limited supply is available at a price equivalent to its marginal product, and the value of which was

---

[26] On Ibadan land tenure, see H. Ward-Price, *Land Tenure among the Yoruba* (Lagos, 1933); National Archives Ibadan, Oyoprof, 3/1881; Diaries and Correspondence of Chief Obisesan, *passim*. The meanings and practices of *isakole, iwisin/ isinba, and owe* (communal labour as tribute, in Ibadan), depend on the nature of the relationships, and on their political, geographical, and historical contexts. J.D.Y. Peel distinguishes in Ilesa between *'isakole'* as land rent from *'iwisin'* as 'tribute, which was always paid in food.' He writes: 'The initial novelty of *isakole* was not as an 'economic' rent' paid by the user to the owner of land as a scarce resource, but as a material recognition, through a payment which was obligatory, but not necessarily large, of the lack of permanent rights by a user, who was a *stranger*.' (Peel, *Ijeshas and Nigerian* pp. 43, 293n 28). The obligations of Ibadan cocoa farmers, who were not ' strangers', did not fit into either of the categories. The continuing political conflicts between Ife and Modakeke fitted both. Ife landlords claimed an 'economic rent' and a 'tribute' from Modakeke cocoa farmers on Ife land of one to three cwt. of cocoa per farmer, which at 1971 prices, could amount to £7.10s per cwt. per acre. (O. Famoriyo, 'An appraisal of Farm Tenancy Problems in Ife Division', M. A. Thesis University of Ibadan, 1969). Asiyanbola identifies one source of dispute as 'issues relating to landlord/ tenant relationship or indigene/non-indigene and by extension the problem of the citizenship issue.' (I. Albert, 'Ife-Modakeke Crisis', in O. Otite and I. Albert (eds) *Community Conflict in Nigeria: Management, Resolution, and Transformation* (Ibadan, 1999), cited in R.A. Asiyanbola, 'Ethnic Conflict in Nigeria: a Case of Ife-Modakeke in Historical Perspective', *ASSET: An International Journal of Agricultural Sciences, Sciences, Environment and Technology*, 4 1 (2010). See the account of the origins of the unresolved conflict in the nineteenth century by Samuel Johnson, *History of the Yoruba*, pp. 230-3, 525, 646-8.

[27] Peel, *Ijeshas and Nigerians*, p. 244.

in turn fixed for the farmer by the Marketing Board. Wealthy farmers, village *baale* and their close kin and associates were able to arrange the migration of sufficient seasonal labour to meet their own needs; these labourers are only available to the poorer men when the needs of the wealthier have been met. In Ibadan, this tended to overlap with the distinction between 'tenant' lineages and the 'overlord' lineages.

Agitations against the exploitative and oppressive practices of mercantile firms, middlemen, and government officials have long been a feature of political life in Ibadan.[28] However, leadership usually came from urban produce-buyers, as in the opposition to the 'cocoa-pool' in the thirties,[29] educated farmers such as Akinpelu Obisesan, once a mercantile clerk and for thirty years president of the Ibadan Co-operative Produce Union,[30] and populist politicians. The most successful of these was Adegoke Adelabu, to whom the farmers gave their support in the fifties. The *mekunnu* looked to him to wrest favours for them away from the educated elite who had come to dominate both civic and regional affairs. He opposed the rationalizing reforms of the last colonial administration and the new Action Group Government. These reforms included the replacement of the chiefs by literate customary court presidents; the reform of tax, so that assessment was in the hands of local committees and collection in the hands of tax clerks and *akoda* (native administration officials), instead of the chiefs and family heads; the introduction of a town-planning authority, the introduction of a town-planning

---

[28] Beer, *Politics of Peasant Groups*; Beer and Williams, 'Politics of the Ibadan Peasantry', p. 137.
[29] Beer, *Politics of Peasant Groups*.
[30] For the ICPMU, which was supported by the Registrar of Co-operative Societies, the development of the co-operative movement, and independent organisations of produce merchants and farmers, see Beer, 'Farmer and State', and *Politics of Peasant Groups, passim*.

authority and the capitation taxes to finance the introduction of free primary education. Each found its echo in the *Agbekoya*[31] rebellion and in the attacks in the rural areas on Action Group supporters (often *baale* and their kin and associates) that followed Adelabu's death.[32] But NCNC[33] leadership, down to the nomination of councillors for rural areas, remained firmly in urban hands, while the leading NCNC councillors and committee members in the Akanran area (Ibadan South East) were invariably men with a secondary occupation (crafts, or petty trading) in addition to farming.[34]

The introduction of the marketing-board system meant that the farmer could be exploited much more effectively by the government and the (urban) beneficiaries of its policies. It also made the process of exploitation direct and clear and was effected through a specifically political decision about the price rather than mediated through the incomprehensible fluctuations of market prices.

Nigerian governments sought to exploit the cocoa-marketing surpluses for development purposes, including infrastructural investment, public utilities and amenities (roads, education, medical services, water and electricity schemes), and for direct contributions to the progress of industrial investment. These amounted to a massive, and disproportionate, fiscal contribution by the farmers who were never, in return, been compensated by a producer price for

---

[31] *Agbe-ko-ya* (farmers renounce suffering).
[32] Post and Jenkins, *The Price of Liberty*.
[33] National Council of Nigeria and the Cameroons (later National Convention of Nigerian Citizens): governing party in the Eastern Region, 1951-66; members of Federal coalition governments 1954-66; and the main opposition party in the Western Region, 1951-62. It was banned with all other political parties from 1966.
[34] For the interesting similarities and differences between the support of Ibadan and of Ilesa for the NCNC, see Peel, *Ijeshas*, pp. 219-54.

cocoa in excess of the world price. [35] In addition, the government sought additional revenue by increasing direct taxation and various levies, promising the farmers various benefits and forms of assistance in return. The taxes certainly materialized, rising from the 'colonial' figure of 7s. *per capita per annum* to a *minimum* tax liability of £5. 10s in 1968; but the benefits did not. Government investments in agriculture were concentrated on expensive and wasteful government directed programmes such as the farm settlements. Direct assistance to peasant farmers was small, was usually publicized for electoral advantage, and given to the urban hangers-on of political leaders and the politically manipulated and urban-led Farmers' Union. Utilities and amenities in the rural areas were rare and their allocation determined by the electoral interests of particular politicians.

With taxes came tax collectors and a variety of petty council officials, such as town-planning officials, clerks, and sanitary inspectors, who embezzled money, exacted bribes from the farmers for the non-implementation of incomprehensible regulations, or just demanded the bribes. Accounts of the oppression of politicians and officials in the rural areas up to the *Agbekoya* rebellion make them sound more like the activities of an army of occupation than an indigenous administration. [36]

The farmers' rebellion took place at a time of continued political bitterness among the Yoruba political elite, and

---

[35] Kriesel, *Cocoa Marketing in Nigeria*, Consortium for the Study of Nigerian Rural Development, East Lancing and Ibadan, 1969. On the uses to which at least part of these surpluses were put see *Report of the Commission of Enquiry into the Affairs of Certain Statutory Corporations in Western Nigeria* (Chairman, Justice Coker) (Lagos, 1962).

[36] *Report of the Commission of Enquiry into the Civil Disturbances which occurred in certain parts of the Western State of Nigeria in the month of December, 1968* (Chairman: Justice Ayoola) (Ibadan, 1969).

particularly supporters of the NNDP[37] who, having been ousted by the military coup of 1966, regarded themselves as underrepresented in the State Government of the Western Region, and thus put their hopes behind the agitation for an Oyo state (which would include Ibadan), which they could expect to dominate'. Adeniran attributes the 'prelude to farmers 'meetings' with 'some of these middle-class elites.' The timing and engagement of local politicians and how cohesive the movement and its leaders is unclear. The language attributed to farmers and some of its substance was obviously produced by local political elites.[38]

The *Agbekoya* arose in the wake of political, and consequently economic disruption, a cocoa price consistently lower than they had obtained in the halcyon years of the fifties, cut-backs in government expenditure, increases in prices, and in a series of taxes consequent upon the Nigerian Civil War, which had begun in 1967.[39] In Egba and Ibadan and other divisions, specifically those where unrest was concentrated in 1968-9, cocoa production has long been in decline. Farmers have lacked the resources and/or incentives to cut out old trees and replant, so that the old trees have been leaching away the soil fertility and their output has been declining

---

[37] Nigerian National Democratic Party (NNDP) was formed in 1964 from dissident Action Groupers of the United Peoples Party and western members of the NCNC who had made up a coalition government in 1963 in the wake of a split in the Action Group, which ruled the west from 1951-1962. The blatant rigging of the 1965 elections led to widespread rioting that was ended only by the military coup of 1966. Although ideological differences were relevant, the conflict was also interpreted in ethnic terms, the Action Group being labeled an 'Ijebu' party (especially in Ibadan) while the NNDP was particularly associated with the people of the Oyo province (including Ibadan). See Dudley, 'Western Nigeria and the Nigerian Crisis' in Panter-Brick (ed.), *Nigerian Politics and Military Rule: Prelude to the Civil War* (London, 1969). The leadership of both the AG and NNDP were to be prominent in the United Party of Nigeria and the National Party of Nigeria, formed in 1978. The UPN swept all of the former Western State, including Oyo State, formed in 1976, in the 1979 elections.
[38] Adeniran, 'Dynamics'.
[39] Beer and Williams, 'Politics of the Ibadan peasantry.' Essay III.

steadily. Swollen shoot too, had killed many trees in Ibadan Division.[40] Thus in 1968 the farmers saw themselves as exploited and oppressed by a government that refused to pay fair prices for their cocoa, sent corrupt officials to persecute them, denied them the benefits and amenities that they had been promised, demanded higher and higher taxes, and now added a series of further tax demands when the farmers simply did not earn enough to meet their existing obligations.

Agitation began in September 1968 in Oyo against the wrongful use of community educational rates. New increases in the water rate and increased tax assessments fuelled resentments and agitation spread rapidly to Ibadan, Egba, Remo, Ijebu, and the Osun Divisions. The arrest of tax defaulters was the main spark for attacks in the authorities. In several towns, *oba*'s palaces were attacked and burnt down because they had allegedly called for the soldiers to assist tax collections, and in some cases, they had embezzled public funds. Attempts at intercession by the Governor and the *Olubadan* proved fruitless; Ibadan farmers shouted them down as *ole* (thieves).[41]

Relative calm reigned between January and June 1969 during which time the Ayoola Commission conducted an inquiry into the rioting. This produced some concessions, but did not meet the farmers' central demands, viz. a reduction of taxes to 30s. *per annum* and the withdrawal of all council officials from the rural areas. In late June, farmers' representatives in Ibadan agreed to pay 65s. tax, but clearly

---

[40] Beer, *Politics of Peasant Groups.*
[41] This account is based on *The Ayoola Report*, and *Daily Times, Nigerian Tribune* and *Daily Service* for 1969. It is consistent with Beer, *Politics of Peasant Groups*; Beer and Williams, 'Politics of the Ibadan Peasantry'; and with Adeniran, 'Dynamics', which provides more detail on local politics.

did not carry the farmers with them. On 25 June, Folarin Idowu, a farmers' leader, declared at a public meeting at Akanran that the farmers would pay only 30 shillings tax. When the government finally began its long delayed tax raids on 1 July, the police were ambushed at Olorunda corner, near Akanran; agitation spread throughout Ibadan division and to Ogbomoso, where the *Soun* was mercilessly hacked to pieces. In the small rural town, village heads (*baale*) bore much of the brunt of the farmers' anger and in Ibadan Division the *baale* of virtually every town and village of any size fled hurriedly to Ibadan.

Mass arrests could not force the farmers to acquiesce to the government's demands. After reports of the deaths of prisoners in jail, farmers invaded Ibadan on 16 September and released 464 prisoners from Agodi jail (opposite the State House and garrison). The police and army pursued the farmers again into their rural strongholds. After six days of fighting, the government forces took Egbeda and sacked Fada, which had become the headquarters of *Agbekoya* leader, Tafa Adeoye, while elsewhere coping with co-ordinated attacks from farmers on the Akanran road and in Egba Division. Despite brave words from the Governor,[42] peace proposals were in the air. A secret meeting with Chief Awolowo, former Action Group leader and Federal Finance Commissioner, forestalled the farmers' final plan, allegedly the firing of Ibadan City itself by setting the petrol pumps ablaze. Tax raids were halted and most of the farmers' demands were accepted in an announcement on 15 October.

---

[42] See Adeniran, 'Dynamics', p. 365.

The announcement of 15 October, 1969 (*Daily Times*) made the following concessions: tax was reduced to £2 *per capita, per annum*; there was an amnesty for all farmers arrested except for those charged with murder; all local government staff would be withdrawn from the villages and the rural district councils would be administered from Ibadan; motor park and market fees would be suspended and could only be introduced if councils showed evidence of capital expenditure on them; no special rates would be levied without the express permission of the people concerned; the jurisdiction of the town-planning authorities would be restricted to modern lay-outs; non-farmers would be excluded from the farmers union; the government would appoint representative advisory committees; the assets of local government staff would be investigated, and there would be an end to tax raids and to army and police patrols. Two significant demands were not met. The first was the demand for a Yoruba-Central (in effect, to-day's Oyo) State, put to loud cheers at the meeting at the *Olubadan's* palace on 9 October by two farmers' representatives but elsewhere denounced by Tafa Adeoye at his meeting with Awolowo as being the concern of politicians and not of farmers against whom the demands for such a state were being raised (*Daily Times*, 10 and 14 October, 1969). The second was the demand for an increase in the cocoa price to £250 per ton. Adeoye had declared to Awolowo on 5 October (*Daily Times*, 14 October 1969) that if this was not met the farmers would organize a hold-up of cocoa (as farmers had done in 1931 and 1937). For the moment, however, the government replied that an increase in mid-season would only benefit the middlemen and not the farmers.

Immediately after the settlement, Tafa Adeoye was installed in the offices of the Farmers' Union in Ibadan. It was widely rumoured that he had been bribed by the government and by Chief Awolowo. He got the aged Cadillac in which Adelabu has his elated supporters driven around Ibadan when he was elected as a Federal Minister in 1954. (By 1971, when I saw it, it could no longer be driven.)

Without its driving objective, the *Agbekoya* was riven by factionalism. According to Tunde Adeniran, from 1968 the *Agbekoya Parapo* had Mojeed Agbaje's fine house at Ayeye. The rival *Mekunnu Parapo* met at the residence of the NNDP-aligned Alhaji Busari Obisesan at Oke Foko. In an attempt to revive his waning fortunes Tafa Adeoye demanded a cocoa price of £250 per ton, which was then below the prevailing world price. There were unconfirmed rumours of plans to hold up cocoa and to burn it in the stores and of the rapid spread of *Agbekoya* activities into the prosperous cocoa-growing area of Ondo Division, whose farmers were far more concerned with the issue of the cocoa price than with the level of taxes.

After the announcement that the cocoa price would be the £150 per ton, rumours of impending unrest and reports of farmers' meetings led Governor Adebayo to issue a scarcely veiled warning against 'saboteurs'. On 16 September, 1970, Tafa Adeoye was arrested, and subsequently imprisoned in Jos in Northern Nigeria, and about forty farmers were arrested on charges of breach of the peace and membership of the banned *Agbekoya*. The unrest which the government feared never materialized and Tafa Adeoye was released after six months. But in 1972, the government sought to re-establish their officials in the villages, which lead to armed resistance and attacks on police posts.[43] Adeoye and a number of farmers were arrested by Gowon's government in 1975 for opposing the introduction of tenement rating in Ibadan. They were released when Gowon was overthrown.

An assessment of the *Agbekoya* rebellion must start by asking who were the *Agbekoya*, who led them, and for whose issues were they fighting. In the rural areas of Ibadan and Egba Division, where the most bitter fighting took place in 1969, there is no doubt that it was farmers resident in the rural areas who carried out the fighting. Elsewhere too, most reports refer to farmers, and most court charges were preferred against farmers, though in these cases the conflicts took place in the towns (Oyo, Ogbomoso, Isara, Ijebu-Igbo, all of which have many farmers resident). Throughout 1968-9 the conflicts took place in areas of declining cocoa production, most particularly in Ibadan and Egba Divisions and in Southern Osun Division, from where hunters were recruited to fight in Ibadan in September, 1969. Christopher Beer has shown the parallels between the areas where disturbances took place during the cutting out of swollen shoot and during the *Agbekoya* rebellion.[44]

The ambushes themselves were carried out largely by hunters, who had the necessary skills and equipment (*ju-ju* charms and dane guns), supported by farmers armed with machetes. Military units were organized separately in each area, with messengers linking farmers with one another in a ring in each of the Ibadan districts. Co-ordination between Egba and Ibadan farmers was obvious in the aftermath of the

---

[43] *West Africa*, 25 February, 1972.
[44] Beer 'Farmer and State', App. V, pp. 585-602 gives a chronology of main events, biographical information on Agbekoya members in Ibadan Division, and the text of a recorded *apala* song 'Tafa Adeoye'.

Agodi prison break in September. Farmers from Southern Osun Division supported the resistance of Egbeda.[45] During the final stage of the rebellion, at least, resistance appears to have been directed from Tafa Adeoye's own village, which lies within the arc formed by the Ibadan-Ife road (which passes Egbeda) and the road from Ibadan through Akanran. From here units were deployed with apparent sophistication to various parts of Ibadan Division, and contact was maintained with *Agbekoya* elsewhere.

Hunters are themselves farmers and unlikely to be wealthy farmers. With individual exceptions, it was the tenants who took part in the rebellion of June to September, and the 'overlords' (among whom are, of course, the village heads, the *baale*) and their families who did not. Although Akanran, for example, was regarded as the centre of the rebellion, a few of its residents (mostly, some of the Obisesans and their close followers), supported the rebellion, while support was almost universal in the surrounding hamlet. The *baale* and their families were opposed for supporting the government on whom their local authority ultimately depended. Many farmers also reported that their oppressive 'landlords' had been put in their place and would no longer attempt to exploit their tenants. A prominent opponent of the rebellion from Ibadan North declared to me that 'they are not the sons of the owners of the land. Their fathers have no farm land. But they gather themselves together to destroy a man's property...and chased away the sons of those people who had given their father's land.'

---

[45] For maps of the towns in Ibadan Division where the *Maiyegun* was active (1947-1949), riots took place after the death of Adegoke Adelabu (1958), and the *Agbekoya* rebellion took place (1968-1969), see Beer and Williams, 'Politics of the Ibadan Peasantry', p. 149, from Beer, *The Politics of Peasant Groups.*

I have already suggested that the backbone of rural society in Ibadan Division is independent smallholders, or 'middle peasants'. The limited information I have on participants tends to confirm that they formed the basis of the *Agbekoya*. One issue which the farmers raised to explain their plight, their inability to recruit labour, tends to confirm this. 'Poor peasants' by definition are liable to be employed as seasonal labourers rather than be employers themselves. The wealthiest farmers, while concerned about recruiting labour, are still able to outbid others for the available supply. The few wealthy farmers in the Akanran area, and those whose local influence is derived from their association with the urban sources of authority, either fled the area or were chased out when the fighting took place – at least as fast as I could judge. Finally, the ideas expressed by the participants are those typical of an independent (middle) peasantry. They emphasize that those who took part were the 'real farmers' (*agbe gidi*), a concept which implies rural residence and farming as one's primary occupation, but also a reasonable holding of land and cocoa. A man without enough land to support himself is despised by such farmers as 'riff-raff'.

Thus the rebellion grew out of the crisis faced by the 'middle peasants' in areas of declining cocoa production, who were caught between low prices for their produce, increased prices for the goods they need to purchase in the towns, and a sharp rise in direct taxation already at a disproportionate level in relation to their incomes.

The rebellion partly arose out of, and was partly encouraged by, the development of a specifically rural or peasant consciousness. The basis of this consciousness is expressed in the concept of *agbe gidi*, Together with this concept goes an emphasis on the ultimate dependence of the whole society, indeed of all societies, on the farmer who provides people with their food. The sharp drift of population from the rural areas to the towns and the post-war inflation of food prices, accentuated by two seasons of inadequate rains, give a particular sharpness to this point in Nigeria today. Farmers emphasised the virtues of hard work and back-breaking labour, especially their own, and refer contemptuously to the 'semi-literates who roam about the town doing nothing' (when they could be providing the farmers with much-needed labour).

This peasant consciousness included, too, an awareness that resources are being expropriated from the peasantry through taxes, through the exactions of corrupt officials, through 'cheating by produce buyers', and, most particularly, through the marketing board surpluses, and that they were being used to benefit the people, and especially the wealthy people, of the urban areas. Little of this money was used to provide them from the modest amenities that they need. As Akufo (Ibadan West) villagers declared to a *Nigerian Tribune* reporter on 6 July, 1969 at the height of the conflict: 'We do not know the reason why we should pay tax because we do not know how the money collected in the past was spent. We pay our taxes but we have no good road to transport our farm products to the city for sale'.

The resources that are allocated to the farmers by the government were seen to be appropriated by corrupt officials, politicians, and the so-called representatives of the farmers. It was to distinguish themselves from the recipients of this assistance. 'who claim to be farmers but are not', that the farmers emphasized that *they* are the *real* farmers as can be seen by the fact that they *live on the farms* (*agbe l'oko*) and *not* in the town.[46]

As we have seen, tax was the central issue in the conflict, amidst a large number of other issues. Several farmers in fact told me that it was not so much the tax that had led the farmers to go to fighting, but the tax collectors, town-planning, officials, and sanitary inspectors. But tax had to be central because, as Kanmi Isola Osobu wrote, tax collection 'is the occasion when the all-powerful government has for once to "come down" to the people and ask for funds'.[47] Thus, just as the interim Adebo Award provided the issue, and the ability to strike provided the means for the wage earners to give vent to a more general dissatisfaction with the existing social order and the deprivation of their 'rights',[48] so tax provided the farmers with the necessary issue and sanction with which to confront the authorities.

Prior to the *Agbekoya* rebellion, peasants had always been represented politically by others: produce buyers, chiefs, and politicians.[49] They provided the crucial link between the peasants and their rulers. At the beginning of the anti-tax agitation, men with political experience (and ambitions) seem to have played a leading role in many instances. In Akanran, the farmers who got together to discuss what they could do about extortionate tax demands first went to the leading figures in the village for advice, who included a wealthy farmer and a trader in kola nuts. These men, with Tafa Adeoye, were

---

[46] Interviews, Akanran village and district, 1971. See Adeniran, 'Dynamics' p. 365, who describes the farmers as 'peasants because they live *very* close to the ground'.

[47] *Nigerian Tribune*, 27 September, 1969; Beer, *The Politics of Peasant Groups*.

[48] Tax rebellions have been common in Southern Nigeria since taxes were introduced. They were especially widespread in various parts of the old Oyo province, which had opposed the tax increases by the Action Group Government in the mid-fifties.

[49] See Peace, 'Industrial Conflict'.

among those who negotiated with the civic authorities in December, 1968, agree to the return of the officials to the rural areas.

Tafa Adeoye had come to prominence when Governor Adebayo addressed the farmers on 15 November, when he reportedly declared that they would have to kill him before he paid his tax. Unlike any previous farmers' leaders, he had no education whatsoever (not even Koranic education), had never had any occupation but farming and no record of previous political activity. He came from a tenant family (although not tenants to the 'overlords', the Aperin, 'elephant-hunters' a.k.a. the Obisesan), whose urban lineage had never aspired to a title. He had a reasonable holding of cocoa but would never have been described as prosperous. He was a typical 'middle peasant' who articulated the farmers' determination to resist further exactions and displayed the courage necessary for such resistance.

The other initial leaders of the Akanran farmers are alleged to have tried to bargain with their position in order to gain government recognition on local courts and councils. They were the sort of men who saw themselves as negotiating a reasonable compromise with the government to the benefit of their members. It was they who first negotiated an abortive agreement that the council officials should be allowed to return, after they had presented the farmers' grievances to the authorities in December, 1968 and it was they who accepted the government's compromise of a £3. 10s (70 shillings) tax in May, 1969. They reckoned without the new determination on the part of the farmers and the uncompromising leadership which the crisis had thrown up. Consequently they were discarded and fled to the town in July. It was from this point that the 'middle peasants' in the persons of Tafa Adeoye and his associates took over their own leadership.

The 'natural rulers' (*oba* and chiefs) became as central an object of the farmers' hostility as the crisis developed as were the council officials. Caught in the classic predicament of the colonial African chief, the *oba*, *baale*, and chiefs appealed for conciliation, but asked the farmers to pay their taxes and desist from violence. The farmers saw 'their fathers' as betraying 'their sons'. Six senior Ibadan chiefs were coupled with two commissioners (Mr Adisa and Prince Lamuye) and Alhaji Busari Obisesan (chairman of several government bodies) as those whom Tafa Adeoye blamed for the conflict when he met Governor Adebayo on 6 November.[50] The links between the peasantry and their rulers, which Moore and Wolf[51] regard as a crucial constraint on peasant rebellion had snapped. [52]

The farmers are also approached prominent Ibadan politicians in October. They were told that the Ibadan (NCNC) politicians could do nothing (Chief Mojeed Agbaje[53] was the prominent exception here) as they were now in opposition. Only if they, Ibadan people, had a state of their own would they be able to look after the farmers' interests. From this arose the farmers' demand for a Yoruba Central State, which even in early October, 1969, was seen as so important that both

---

[50] *Nigerian Tribune*, 7 November 1969.

[51] Moore, *The Social Origins of Dictatorship and Democracy* (New York, 1966); E. Wolf, 'On Peasant Rebellions', *International Social Science Journal*, 21 (1969).

[52] This was less true of the *Maiyegun* than of the other farmers' associations. It emerged in 1947 in opposition to the cutting out of cocoa trees affected by 'swollen shoot' disease. It split, and its peasant core was incorporated into Adelabu's NCNC. Post and Jenkins, *The Price of Liberty*; Beer, *The Politics of Peasant Groups*.

[53] Chief Mojeed Agbaje was a lawyer and politician who represented the N.C.N.C.-Mabolaje Grand Alliance in Ibadan. He was a son of Chief Salami Agbaje who was the wealthiest merchant in Ibadan and a staunch supporter of the Action Group. On the *Maiyegun*, and the *Mabolaje/NCNC Grand Alliance*, see Sklar, *Nigerian Political Parties*; Beer, *Politics of Peasant Groups*: Beer, *Peasant Groups*; Adeniran, 'Dynamics'.

General Gowon himself and Chief Awolowo made conciliatory noises on the subject.[54] As we have seen, this was a demand which the farmers sacrificed in order to reach a settlement. Tafa Adeoye declared to the *Daily Times* on 5 November, 1969: 'State or no state, we are not interested. All we want is better prices for our cocoa. It is politicians who are crying for the creation of states and that has nothing to do with us.'

The rebellion went beyond the selective allocation of resources at the disposal of urban politicians. Consequently, the farmers were unable to manipulate the rebellion to their own ends (at least on this key issue). Political violence did not, on this occasion, involve arranging to employ thugs to attack others, but demanded leaders who would risk their own lives to resist oppression and exploitation. The politicians, whatever encouragement they might have given to the farmers in the hope of political reward, stayed on the side lines. And that is where the farmers want to keep them. Quoting Tafa Adeoye's *Daily Times* interview again:

> They caused all the trouble but when the police and army attacked us, none of them, except Chief Awolowo, intervened for us...From now on there shall be no more elections as far as we are concerned. We have all decided not to support any political party any more and we shall not vote for anyone any longer. We have had enough.

Like the industrial workers described by Adrian Peace[55] and unlike the self-employed craftsmen and traders, the farmers have organized themselves, under their own leadership, to enforce their interests collectively. Their

---

[54] *Daily Times*, 2 October, 1969; *Daily Service*, 8 October, 1969; *Sunday Times*, 12 October, 1969.
[55] Peace, 'Industrial Conflict'.

common dependence on the cocoa price and common experience of deprivation and oppression as rural-dwellers led to a recognition of a common fate. They showed that they have the consciousness and determination to resist oppressive and forcible exactions.

But at the same time, they remain dependent on the educated, urban elite for the provision of amenities. They know that the educated have failed them, and have indeed used farmers' organizations and money to cheat the farmers. But even Tafa Adeoye himself looked to the educated to turn the government away from its evil ways and save the farmers from their suffering.[56] And on the key issue, the cocoa price, the farmers remain at the mercy of their rulers (and the foreign consumers and manufacturers of chocolate). They lack the means to intervene effectively in the routine process of resource allocation. They are unable to withdraw from the colonial political economy to which eighty years of cocoa cultivation have subordinated them. They lack the resources and the education (or the outside leadership) necessary to take over the economy and see that it is organized in their interests.

March 1972

---

[56] Gavin Williams, Interview with Tafa Adeoye, October, 1971.

Part VI

Ideologies and Strategies for Rural Development: a Critique[1]

.

Ideologies are sets of assumptions which govern our interpretations of the world. They determine the selection and arrangement of facts and our evaluations of them. Consequently, they determine our selection of strategies. The task of a critique is to lay bare the assumptions of ideologies and the strategies which follow them.[2]

---

[1] First presented to a Conference convened in 1975 at the *Nigerian Institute of Economic Research (NISER)* by the Director, Dr Ekundayo Akeredolu-Ale.

[2] The include references to research undertaken in the 1970s, The starting-points for research on rural Hausa society are Hill, *Rural Hausa,* and *Population, Prosperity and Poverty* culminating in Paul Clough, *Morality and Economic Growth in Rural West Africa: Indigenous Accumulation in Hausaland* (Oxford, 2014), For Western (south-western) Nigeria, see Berry, *Cocoa, Custom and Socio-Economic Change,* and *Fathers Work for their Sons: Accumulation, Mobility, and Class Formation in an Extended Yoruba Community* (Berkeley, 1985); J. Guyer, 'An African Niche Economy: An Essay on Democracy in Rural Nigeria, 1952-1990,' *African Studies Review,* 36 (1997); and *Farming to Feed Ibadan* (Oxford 1997); and P. Roberts, 'The Sexual Politics of Labour: Rural Women in Western Nigeria and Hausa Niger', in K. Young, *et al., Serving Two Masters,* (New Delhi, 1988); For northern states see C. Jackson, 'Hausa women on strike', in *ROAPE* 13 (1979); R. Shenton and L. Lennihan, 'Capital and Class: Peasant Differentiation in Northern Nigeria', *Journal of Peasant Studies,* 9, 1 (1981); M. Watts, *Silent Violence: Food, Family and Peasantry in Northern Nigeria* (Berkeley 1983); See further B. Beckman, 'Bakalori: Peasants versus State and Capital', *Nigerian Journal of Political Science,* 4, 1-2 (1985).; and more generally G. Williams, 'Why Is there no Agrarian Capitalism in Nigeria?'. For collected essays, see G. Williams, 'The World Bank and the Peasant Problem', T. Forrest, 'Agricultural Policies in Nigeria', and T. Wallace, 'The Kano River Project, Nigeria: The Impact of an Irrigation Scheme on Productivity and Welfare,' in Heyer *et al,* (eds) *Rural Development* and M. Watts (ed.), *State, Oil and Agriculture.* For the consequences of subsidized U.S. imports, see B. Beckman and G. Andrae, *The Wheat Trap: Bread and Underdevelopment in Nigeria* (London 1985). Publications by D.W. Norman and his colleagues appear below. See note 4.

The Problem

The 1970s were a period of intensive agricultural policy research and debates, which were shaped by the USAID-funded Consortium for the Study of Nigerian Rural Development (CSNRD), with its U.S. centre at Michigan State University, working with Nigerian universities and international research institutes.

The Report and its recommendations are outdated. They have been modernized but its assumptions – that agricultural progress is to be brought about by the transformation of subsistence farmers by technological innovations remain. They incorporate the (hybrid) seeds-irrigation-fertilizer (and pesticide) 'revolution', whose suitability to any of Nigeria's ecologies and economic feasibility without very high subsidies - and to the preference of Nigerian consumers, is limited. Many of them were implanted in stereotypes of farmers, traders and herders and their kin. The Report lacked an understanding of how they lived their lives, of how and why they made their production decisions and of the working of many of the credit, commodity, and land markets in which they engaged. Gender, generation, marriage and kin relations were not mentioned. The document proposed that government provide her agricultural producers with favourable price relationships (though government could hardly do this other than in markets for which it set the prices). Government would engage in 'production campaigns' for (in order) 'export crops', 'important import substitution crops', 'superior foods that could contribute to superior nutritional levels' and 'the great staple carbohydrate food' (the separation of the last two shows an ignorance of Nigerian diet and cooking).[3]

There appeared to be widespread but by no means unquestioned agreement among agricultural economists, consistent with the CSNRD framework, on the nature of Nigeria's rural development problem.

The agricultural sector at present is characterised by very small production units. The most prominent feature is one of small holders cultivating two or three acres each. Techniques of production are not advanced. There is little mechanization. The seeds are low yielding. The use of fertilizers and pesticides is not widespread. Prices are low and this reduces incentives to modernize. The land tenure system encourages fragmentation. Storage and marketing facilities are not well organized. Credit facilities are not adequate. Finally, social amenities are generally at a low level when compared with the urban areas of the country.[4]

We are also told that rural communities are characterized by under-employment (meaning low productivity per worker, or

---

[3] G.L. Johnson and others, CSNRD, *Strategies and Recommendations for Nigerian Rural Development,* 1969-1986, CSNRD (Lagos and East Lansing, 1969) http://pdf.usaid.gov/pdf docs/PNAAE469.pdf

[4] D. W. Norman, 'Initiating Change in Traditional Agriculture', *Samaru Research Bulletin,* 7 (1970); S. A. Oni, 'Increased Food production through Agricultural Innovations in Nigeria', *West African Journal of Agricultural Economics,* WAJAE 1, 1 (1972); I. J. Ebong, 'Nigerian Social Objectives and the Rural Sector', *Rural Development in Nigeria* (Proceedings of the 1972 Annual Conference of the Nigerian Economic Society (NES), Ibadan, 1973, p. 18; A. A. Fayemi, 'Problems of Agricultural Production in Nigeria and How to Solve them', Inaugural Lecture, (University of Ibadan, 1972–73); S. K. T. Williams, 'Rural Poverty to Rural Prosperity: a Strategy for Development in Nigeria', Inaugural Lecture, (University of Ife, 1973); O. Ogunfowora, 'Farm Survey as a Data Base for Analysis and Planning', Nigerian Rural Development Study, Rural Development Papers, Department of Agricultural Economics, University of Ibadan (NRDS) 14 (1974), pp. 1-2. For critiques of these assumptions, see J. C. Fine, 'A Re-appraisal of Some Common Assumptions about Agricultural Development in Nigeria', *Samaru Agricultural Newsletter* (SAN), 10, 5 (1968); Comrade O. Oni and B. Onimade, *Economic Development of Nigeria: The Socialist Alternative* (Ibadan. 1975), pp. 187-188.

perhaps just poverty?) and unemployment,[5] though we also learn
that shortage of labour is the main constraint on increasing output.[6]
Despite this, the CSNRD insists that family planning is essential to
curb the rate of population growth.[7] Further, it is often assumed
that at low levels of income, typical of peasant farmers 'increases
in earnings tend to be consumed; an increase in consumption
taking the form of a relative cut in marketable surplus, a shift to the
consumption of superior foods, or an increase in the import content
of rural expenditure.'[8]

There also appears to have been agreement on solutions. As
Ogunfowora writes:

> In recent years, there seems to be a growing theoretical
> consensus that a combination of increased supply of credit and
> improved biological and chemical technologies is a measure
> which has high potential for increasing firm productivity,
> income and employment.[9]

More generally,

> abundant land, availability of capital, the existence of an
> untapped reserve of technological knowledge and the present
> of a large and growing market for Nigeria's agricultural

[5] Essang. 'Agricultural Development and Employment Generation in Nigeria', NRDS, 2 (1972), p. 2.
[6] See also J. K. Olayemi, 'Some Economic Characteristics of Peasant Agriculture in the Cocoa Belt of Western Nigeria', Bulletin of Rural Economics and Sociology, (BRES), 7, 2 (1972), NISER Reprint, no. 85; Essang 'The Land "Surplus" Notion and Nigerian Agricultural Development Policy', WAJAE, 2, 1 (1973); Norman, 'Economic Analysis of Agricultural Production and Labour Utilization among the Hausa in the North of Nigeria', African Rural Employment Papers, Michigan State University, (AREP), 5 (1973).
[7] Johnson, (CSNRD), p. 133.
[8] O. Teriba, 'Rural Credit and Rural Development in Nigeria', NES. p. 173. See also Ogunfowora, Essang and Olayide, 'Capital and Credit in Nigerian Agricultural Development', NRDS, 6 (1972); Norman, 'Interdisciplinary Research on Rural Development. The Experience of the Rural Economy Research Unit in Northern Nigeria', Overseas Liaison Committee, American Council on Education, ACE, 6 (1974).
[9] Ogunfowora, 'Income and Employment Potential of Credit and Technology in Peasant Farming', NRDS, 9 (1973).

products,[10] creates possibilities for increasing rural output if rural production can be reorganized appropriately.

The problem then is to organize the social relations of production in such a way as to facilitate the application of these new technologies, and this is widely thought to be incompatible with the predominance of 'an inefficient peasant agriculture that is incapable of adequately supplying the food and fibre needs of the country'.[11]

This diagnosis is remarkably similar to one from an earlier era of commodity shortage – 1946: 'The peasantry's principal occupation is, and must continue to be, subsistence farming, and there is consequently no reasonable expectation of any rapid or substantial growth of production from this, the main source of world oilseed production.'[12]

The problem is defined from the urban or metropolitan standpoint of the ruling classes.'[13] Peasant poverty is not problematic in itself – it is almost assumed to be the natural state of peasants. It is only a problem in that it inhibits the output of marketed crops, in that increasing food prices may reduce the incomes of urban dwellers and increase the discontent of urban workers, and in that it may even provoke farmers to resist their exploitation and oppression.

---

[10] Essang, 'Land "Surplus" Notion', NRDS 2, p. 3.

[11] Olayide *et al., A Quantitative Analysis of Food Requirements, Supplies and Demands in Nigeria, 1968-1985*, (Federal Department of Agriculture, Lagos 1972), pp. 68-69; see also O. Oni and Onimade, *Economic Development*, p. 93; but cf. E. M. Abasiekong, 'Peasants and the Economic Man Model: Are Nigerian Peasants Economic Men?' SAN 17, (1975); Essang, 'The Land Surplus Notion' *WAJAE*, 2, 1, pp. 63-64.

[12] Mr. Samuel, of the United African Company, proposing a scheme for the mechanized clearing of land and production of groundnuts, cited A. Wood, *The Groundnut Affair*, (London, 1950).

[13] As pointed out by R. O. Adegboye, 'Redemption of Pledged Property through Rural Credit', NES, pp. 181-182.

Alternative ideologies, while sharing some common ground with others, offer different diagnoses of the sources of the problem, and recommend different solutions.

Capitalist Ideologies and Strategies

Capitalist ideologies rest on two general assumptions. The distinction between them is obscured as both are brought under the rubric of the 'division of labour.'[14] The first assumption is that scarce resources are optimally allocated when they are exchanged through the sale and purchase of commodities by firms and consumers in unrestricted competitive markets. Ideally, there should be no barriers to entry into any productive or distributive enterprise and, logically, free access of all producers to the means of production. The second assumption is that the most efficient productive units are not individual producers who exchange the product of their own labour in the market, but capitalist firms in which wage labourers co-operate under the direction of management to produce commodities which are sold for the profit of the firm. This socialization of labour enables the firm to operate on a scale large enough to apply advanced technologies to production, which increases the productivity of labour. This mode of production presupposes the separation of capital and labour, and the exclusion of the producer from control of the means of production and from disposal of the product of his labour.[15]

The assumption of capitalist rural development strategies is that capitalist firms can finance the application of biological, chemical and mechanical technologies, and that the profit

---

[14] K. Marx, *Capital,* 1976, vols. 1, 14; MW, ch. 32A, pp. 513-515; ch. 32; and *passim*
[15] Marx, *Capital,* vol. 1, esp. ch. 7, 26 ch. 9, 28; *MW,* ch. 32, App. 521-523.

motive will ensure that they manage these resources and market their produce profitably. This contrasts with peasants who are thought to be unwilling or unable to take advantage of market opportunities to the same extent. They must therefore be by-passed, or even eliminated, in favour of capitalist farms.[16]

Capitalist farmers must control money, land, labour and markets. As Marx pointed out, the 'so-called primitive accumulation of capital' was not achieved by abstinence and thrift on the part of the virtuous but by slavery, plunder and the forcible expropriation of the peasants.[17] It is not a matter of saving and investment by private entrepreneurs, but of the imposition of a process of class formation by the state. For capitalist farming to flourish in Nigeria, it will be necessary for the state to finance investments,[18] and to acquire land for private firms.'[19] The state can pay wages to labourers on private farms, otherwise a regular supply of cheap labour can only be provided if peasants are denied alternative sources of land. This requires expropriation of peasant land, restrictions on the movement of labour or various forms of forced labour, as practised on plantations and settler farms in the Americas, in East and South Africa, and in colonies in Asia.

Thus, during the colonial period, Lord Lever did not seek permission to establish plantations in competition with peasant producers but a monopoly over the purchase of palm products and a government guarantee of his labour supply, and

---

[16] As required by Olayide *et al,*. Quantitative Analysis of Food Requirements, pp. 81-82, 86; E. O. Idusogie, Olayide and Olatunbosun, 'Implications of Agricultural Wastes on Nigerian Nutrition and Economy', *BRES* 8, 2 (1973) pp. 258-259; *Guidelines to the Third National Development Plan, 1975-80* (Lagos, 1973), pp. 68-73.

[17] Marx, *Capital*, vol. 1, Part 8, p. 873, CW MW, ch. 32A, pp. 521-3.

[18] Olayide *et. al.,* Quantitative Analysis, pp. 82, 86.

[19] Third Plan, p. 14.

his profits. In 1907, he asked for land to plant oil palms and to establish oil mills. By 1925, he demanded freehold concessions for planting, a labour supply guaranteed by the government, and the exclusive right of buying and processing fruit from producers. In 1944, the U.A.C. proposed for Nigeria a scheme similar to the ill-fated Tanganyikan groundnut scheme, in which the government would provide land and capital, the African would provide labour, and the company would manage both plantation and mill for a guaranteed profit.[20] It was not the efficiency of plantation management, nor even the improved quality of oil, which enabled plantations in Sumatra, supplemented by Lever's plantation in the Belgian Congo, to outstrip Nigerian oil palm output. It was the willingness of the colonial regimes to ensure the supply of cheap labour which guaranteed the profitability of their operations.

Alternatively, capitalist farmers may be recruited from rural communities. They are usually identified by their large holdings of land, off-farm employment, particularly in trading or government service, political influence, profit-orientation and amenability to the advice of extension officers. They are well placed to take advantage of subsidized inputs and services, to apply recommended cultivation techniques, and to market their output.[21] Such 'rural capitalists' are identified as the sources of agricultural innovation and development, setting an example to the backward peasants. Indeed, business-like management of agricultural production is taken to be the very

[20] R. K. Udo, 'Sixty Years of Plantation Agriculture in Southern Nigeria, 1902-62,' *Economic Geography*, 41, 4 (1965); cf. Hancock, Survey vol. 2, part 2; Usoro, *The Nigerian Oil Palm Industry* (Ibadan, 1974), pp. 36-50.
[21] Essang, 'Institutional Arrangements and Income Distribution in a Primary Export Economy,' *BRES* 6, 2 (1971) pp. 210-211.

essence of capitalism.[22] Governments are consequently advised to concentrate resources on these paragons of Progress.[23]

Since the costs of subsidizing capitalist farms are high, and the public, and sometimes even private gains meagre, and since peasants resist their own elimination, a capitalist state may choose to leave the bulk of agricultural production in peasant hands. Peasants may then be directed to cultivate crops required by capitalist interests and state policy, and to adopt officially approved practices. The forcible imposition of agricultural regulations provokes peasant resistance in the absence of adequate incentives and compensation. Incentives, of course, are always relative, if administrators, public or private, control the supply of means of production (such as irrigated land)[24] or the purchase of crops (such as flue-cured tobacco)[25] they can use their monopoly power to reduce the cost of enforcing compliance with their directives. Peasants are thus able to increase their incomes, but on the terms dictated to them by state officials or capitalist firms. Monopoly purchasing power enables capitalists or the state to appropriate the surplus value of the product of peasant labour. In this way peasants can be forced to deliver a tribute to finance the accumulation of money capital by capitalists and the state. Thus they are exploited in aid of the development of

---

[22] P. Hill, 'Ghanaian Capitalist Cocoa Farmers,' in *Studies in Rural Capitalism.*

[23] E. M. Rodgers, J. R. Ashcroft and N. Roling, *Diffusion of Innovation in Brazil, India and Nigeria,* (1970). *Third Plan,* p. 82; cf. C. Hutton and R. Cohen, 'African Peasants and the Resistance to Change' in Oxaal, *et al., Beyond the Sociology.*

[24] T. Barnett, *The Gezira*; cf. T. Wallace, Rural Development; cf Barnett, 'Evaluating the Gezira Scheme'; T. Wallace, 'The Kano River Project', in Heyer *et al. Rural Development.*

[25] Q. B. O. Antonio, in 'Nigerian Social Objectives and the Rural Sector'; with 'Comments' by F. O. Fajana, NES, pp. 29, 43; Cf. A. A. Adesimi, 'An Econometric Study of Air-cured Tobacco Supply in Western Nigeria, 1945-64', *Nigerian Journal of Economic and Social Studies,* (*NJESS*) 12, 3 (1970) p. 315; Cf. D. Feldman, 'The Economics of Ideology', in C. Leys (ed.), *Politics and Change in Developing Countries* (Cambridge, 1969).

urban and industrial capitalism, and denied the resources necessary for the development of the rural economy.[26]

State Socialist Ideologies and Strategies

State socialist ideology, like capitalism, identifies productive powers with technology.[27] The application of technology to raise the productivity of labour and land depends on the socialization of labour into large units under managerial direction. This task is originally undertaken by capitalism, which progressively eliminates backward, pre-capitalist modes of production, and lays the material basis for the transition to socialist relations of production.[28] Thus Engels argued that peasant production could not and should not be protected from the encroachment of capitalism on agriculture;[29] Kautsky showed, to the satisfaction of both Mensheviks and Bolsheviks, that the development of productive powers in agriculture required large-scale operations.[30]

Capitalism increases the productive capacity of agriculture in order to realize profits rather than produce for human needs. It exploits the worker, underutilizes land and labour and wastes a large part of its output. State socialists consequently argue that the 'anarchy of the market cannot

---

[26] G.K. Helleiner, The Fiscal Role of the Marketing Boards in Nigerian Economic Development 1947-1961, *Economic Journal*, 74, 295 (1964); and in *Peasant Agriculture, Government and Economic Growth in Nigeria* (Homewood, Ill, 1966), pp. 183-184. cf. Olatunbosun, 'Trends and Prospects of Nigeria's Agricultural Exports', in Onitiri and Olatunbosun, ed. NISER (1972). A. O. Philips 'Fiscal Policy and Rural Development in Nigeria' NES, esp. p. 125. Third Plan, pp. 32, 68 declared an end to the use of marketing boards to tax producers. See Williams, 'The World Bank and the Peasant Problem'.

[27] See Corrigan, et al., *Socialist Construction*.

[28] See Bukharin and Preobrazhensky, *The ABC of Communism* ({1920} Harmondsworth, 1969), pp. 318-9.

[29] Engels, 'The Peasant Question in France and Germany,' ({*Neue Zeit*, 1894-1895} 1894), Selected Works, vol. 3, and in (CW 28); B. Russell and A. Russell, *German Social Democracy* (London, 1896), Lecture V.

[30] K. Kautsky, *The Agrarian Question* (1894), English Summary by J. Banaji, *Economy and Society*, 4 (1975); cf. Lenin, "Preface" to *The Development of Capitalism*.

ensure a proper allocation of resources, and must be superseded by the rational planning of inputs and outputs.'[31] The principles of enterprise management are thus applied to the organization of the national economy.

State socialist ideology identifies peasant production as pre-capitalist. The development of the productive forces requires the displacement of peasant production. Lenin did recognize the superiority of the American paths in which a capitalist class emerged out a peasant (family farm) production for the market, over the Prussian paths in which the 'feudal' landlords became capitalists. [32] Unlike Marx, [33] he never doubted the necessity for the elimination of peasant producers. Alternatively, the state reorganizes agricultural production along cooperative lines in order to realize the economies of scale necessary for the application of advanced technologies and systems of management, and to prevent the development of private farming and trading.[34]

State control of crucial means of production (e.g. tractors) and of the terms of exchange between agriculture and industry enables the state to exact from the peasants its tribute to what Preobrazhensky grimly called 'primitive socialist accumulation.'[35] State socialists assume the capacity of the state to organize agricultural production and allocate

[31] See O. Oni and Onimade, *Economic Development*, pp. 86-111. This appears to be the goal of Olayide *et al.*, *Quantitative Analysis*, pp. 95-103 and even the *Third Plan*, pp. 70-77.

[32] K. Marx, 'Preface' to the Russian Edition of the Manifesto of the Communist Party ({1882} (*CW* 29), (*MW* 45); V.I. Lenin, 'Preface' (1907) to *Development of Capitalism*, and *The Agrarian Programme of Social Democracy in the First Russian Evolution* vol. 14 (1907); O. Oni and Onimade, *Economic* Development, p. 198; cf. Bukharin and Preobrazhensky, *The ABC of Communism*, pp. 312-76.

[33] K. Marx, Letters to Mikhailovskii (*CW* 45), and to Vera Sassulich, and drafts (*CW* 46); Preface to the Russian edition of the *Manifesto* (1877-1881), *MW*, ch. 41, 43, 45.

[34] Lenin, "On Cooperation", in Lenin, *Collected Works*, vol. 33 ({1923} Moscow, 1960).

[35] Ye. Preobrazhensky. *The New Economics* ({1924, 1926} Oxford, 1965).

productive resources. The producer is to be subordinated to centralized direction – in his own ultimate interest![36]

Peasant Ideologies and Strategies

Both capitalist and state socialist ideologies assume that the development of commodity production must lead to the displacement of backward peasant producers by more efficient capitalist producers, at least once 'feudal' institutions have been abolished. Peasant communities are differentiated into capitalist farmers and proletarians, rural and urban, and the specialization of tasks among productive enterprises and classes of producers proceeds to its logical culmination in the farms of California.[37] However, peasant producers have never conceded gracefully to the forces of historical progress, and have had to be forcefully eliminated by the expropriation of their land. Alternatively pastoral and hunting people have been eliminated to create an open territory for capitalist farming. Elsewhere peasants have persistently survived into the twentieth century, to the embarrassment of capitalist and socialist planners in the E.E.C. and COMECON alike.

Prior to his own elimination by Stalin, A. V. Chayanov had argued that a peasant economy was based on principles distinct from capitalism.[38] Ideally, peasants use family labour and their own tools to work family land in order to meet the substantive needs of the family. Since the producer does not

---

[36] Belief in the virtues of state regulation of production and distribution is not peculiar to state socialists. It justified colonial policies, and particularly the marketing boards, and is blithely assumed in much contemporary literature on development. E.g. Olayide and Olatunbosun, 'New Dimensions in the Administration of Agriculture in Nigeria,' *QJA* 6, 1 (1971), NISER 76. p. 56; O. Oni and Onimade point out, socialism requires institutions of popular planning and control, *Economic Development of Nigeria*, pp. 103-118, 195-197.

[37] See W. O. Jones, 'Measuring the Effectiveness of Agricultural Marketing in Contributing to African Development,' *Food Research Institute Studies* (*FRIS*) 9, 3 (1970) pp. 178-80; compare to Lenin, *Development of Capitalism*, pp. 175-190.

[38] *The Theory of Peasant Economy* ({1923} London, 1991),

pay either himself or his family a wage, we cannot apply the capitalist category of net profit to the operation of the farm.[39] By contrast, capitalist farms employ hired labour for profit, and treat land as capital and commodity.[40]

Peasants can produce crops more cheaply than hired workers. Chayanov argued that as long as the subsistence needs of the family had not been met, family labour could continue to be employed up to the point at which each extra unit of labour time added virtually nothing to output. Understandably, peasants prefer the security and independence of controlling their own land and labour time to the 'slavery' of wage employment, even though public and private wage rates exceed the average and marginal returns to their own labour time. Wage labour is only a means of meeting immediate cash needs, or of financing savings to invest in independent farming or business. It is not a proper way of life.

Wage earners need to be coerced or induced into working hard and efficiently. Mechanized inputs are expensive to buy, and maintain, and require skilled workers to operate and repair them. Unskilled labour may have to be employed for stumping, ploughing and weeding before tractors and ploughs can be used. Top-soil may be lost, fertilisers are needed only to maintain soil fertility, and other crops cannot be intercropped.[41]

---

[39] Not that this stops economists and planners from doing so. e.g. J. C. Wells, *Agricultural Policy and Economic Growth in Nigeria, 1962-1968* (Ibadan, 1974).

[40] R. Redfield, *Peasant Society and Culture* (Chicago, 1956), pp. 18-19.

[41] L. Are, 'An Assessment of some Plantation Problems in Western Nigeria,' *Tropical Agriculture*, 41, 1 (1964), p. 3; Essang and Ogunfowora, 'Plantation Agriculture and Labour Use in Southern Nigeria', *NRDS*, 15 (1975); M. Kolawole, 'Mechanization of the Small Farm: Possibilities and Problem,' *WAJAE* 1, 1 (1972); W. T. Newlyn, 'A Study of Costs of Mechanized Agriculture in Nigeria,' *West African Institute of Social and Economic Development (WAISER)*, (n.d., c. 1954); M. J. Purvis, 'A Study of the Economics of Tractor Use in Oyo Division of the Western State,' *Consortium for the Study of Nigerian Rural Development, CSNRD*, Michigan

Whereas wage earners rely on their employers to pay for their subsistence, peasants must save out of their incomes and invest their savings in order to secure their own sources of livelihood. Thus several studies show high marginal and average rates of savings for a wide range of peasant incomes.[42] To the peasant, land is a source of livelihood, to be preserved if at all possible for the future. It is not a source of quick profit while land deteriorates. In periods of falling prices, peasants will maintain production, while capitalists abandon unprofitable farms.[43]

Peasants are knowledgeable about the availability and relative costs of local resources, and adapt them to the requirements of particular farms and localities. New crops have been introduced alongside tried methods for producing subsistence crops. Systems of credit, labour recruitment and land tenure have been adapted to take advantage of lucrative innovations. In general, peasant farming is characterized by the cautious management of available resources to good advantage.[44]

It is clear that wealthier peasants have better access to land, labour, credit, extension services and fertilisers and on better

State University and NISER, 17 (1968); Baldwin, The Niger Agricultural Project; and cf. Olatunbosun, 'Western Nigerian Farm Settlement: an Appraisal,' *Journal of Development Administration, JDA,* 5, 3, (1971) NISER, 75; or 'The Farm Settlement: A Case Study of an Agricultural Project in Nigeria', *BRES,* 6, 1, (1971); J. C. Wells, *Agricultural Policy and Economic Growth in Nigeria.*

[42] Galletti *et al., Nigerian Cocoa Farmers* (Oxford, 1956), pp. 471-475; M. Upton, *Agriculture in South-Western Nigeria* (University of Reading, 1967), p. 42; G. E. Okurume 'The Food Crop Economy in Nigerian Agricultural Policy', *CSNRD,* 31 (1969) pp. 91-92; M. Tiffen, *The Enterprising Peasant, Economic Development in Gombe Emirate North Eastern State, Nigeria 1900–1968* (London, 1976).

[43] Hancock, *Survey,* vol. 2, part 2, p. 193; J.K. Olayemi and S. Oni, 'Asymmetry in Price Response: A Case Study of Western Nigerian Cocoa Farmers,' *NJESS,* 14, 3 (1972), NISER no. 84.

[44] E. M. Abasiekong, SAN, 10, 6 (1968); R. O. Adegboye and J. A. Alao, 'Some Socio-Economic Factors Influencing Farmers, Participation in the Western Nigeria Cocoa Pilot Project,' *BRES,* 7, 2. (1972) pp. 235–6; Berry, *Cocoa, Custom and Socio-Economic Change.*

terms than poorer farmers. They apply these resources more effectively and market their products on more favourable terms. They may be better equipped to take advantage of yield-increasing innovations.[45] But these advantages operate within a limited range of farm sizes. Beyond that range the enterprise must bear the costs and shortcomings of capitalist or other forms of production.[46]

There are clearly advantages to be gained by cooperating in certain productive activities. Farmers may cooperate clearing land for settlement, protecting it from wild game and building camps and villages.[47] Cooperative labour can build roads and other public facilities. Cooperation may facilitate saving, and reduce the costs of storage, marketing and the use of inputs and services. Peasant communities have developed a variety of arrangements for organizing cooperative activities, when these are clearly to mutual advantage.

As Governor Clifford told the Nigerian Legislative Council in 1920:

> Agricultural interests that are mainly or exclusively, in the hands of the native peasantry (a) have a firmer foot than similar enterprises when owned and managed by Europeans,

---

[45] Essang, 'Institutional Arrangements',; Norman, 'Economic Analysis', AREP, 4, pp. 5, 16; Hill, *Rural Hausa*, p. 162. M. J. Purvis, 'Report on a Survey of Oil Palm Rehabilitation Scheme in Eastern Nigeria', *CSNRD*, 10 (1967); but cf. to this A. U. Patel and Antonio, 'An Analysis of Selected Factors that Influence the Adoption of Improved Practices among Tobacco Farmers in the Western State,' *NAJ*, 8, 2 (1971).

[46] D. E. Osifo and Q.B.O. Anthonio, 'Costs and Returns: A Study of Upland Paddy Production under Traditional Farming Conditions of the Wasimi and Ilaro Areas of the Western State of Nigeria,' *NJESS*, 12, 3 (1970); Olayemi and Oni, 'Costs and Returns in Peasant Cocoa Production: A Case Study of Western Nigeria', BRES, 6, 2 (1971) p. 147. On the extent of inequalities, cf. Galletti *et al.*, *Nigerian Cocoa Farmers*, pp. 145, 151-3; Olayemi, 'Some Economic Characteristics,' *BRES*, 7.2; Norman, 'An Economic Study of 3 villages in Zaria Province, Part 1, Land and Labour Relationships', *SMP*, 19, (1967); A. D. Goddard, Fine and, 'A Socio-economic Study of Three Villages in the Sokoto Close-settled Zone', *SMP*, 33 (1970); Hill, *Rural Hausa and Population, Prosperity and Poverty*.

[47] N. A. Fadipe, *The Sociology of the Yoruba*, ed. F. O. and O. O. Okediji, (Ibadan, 1970) p. 150.

because they are natural growths, not artificial creations, and are self-supporting, as regards labour, while European plantations can only be maintained by some system of organized immigration or by some form of compulsory labour; (b) are incomparably the cheapest instruments for the production of agricultural produce on a larger scale than has yet been devised and (c) are capable of a rapidity of expansion and a progressive increase in output that beggar every record of the past, and are altogether unparalleled in all the long history of European agricultural enterprises in the tropics.[48]

Theoretical analysis, common sense reasoning and a large body of empirical evidence all lend continued support to Clifford's judgements.

Peasants, Capitalists and State Relations

Do we therefore accept the ideology of the 'peasant economy,' and leave the business of farming to peasants, on the grounds that they know their own business best? Peasant ideology treats the 'peasant economy', as a self-sufficient mode of production. It isolates the organization of peasant production from its reaction to the wider political economy which determines the conditions of its own existence.

The survival of peasant production depends on the household's command of family labour. The expansion of opportunities to earn a living off the farm enables, sons, and may even enable wives and daughters to reject the authority of the head of the household and deprive him of his control over family labour. As labour-time itself acquires a cash value, customary arrangements for mobilizing labour are replaced by the hiring of wage labour. Although family labour remains the

---

[48] Cited Lord Hailey, *Africa Survey* (Oxford, 1940).

backbone of Nigerian farming, if agriculture cannot offer an attractive future, hired labour will increasingly have to replace family labour rather than supplement it.[49]

Peasant producers will only be able to increase production to take advantage of expanding markets if they have the incentives, and resources to do so. The costs of credit, transport, storage and marketing must be minimized to ensure peasants the full benefit of increased urban prices. State provision of credit, marketing facilities, inputs and cooperative institutions tends to be expensive, limited in their impact and ineffective. Credit programmes usually divert public money to private commerce or consumption. They reach few farmers and help to finance a privileged elite of capitalist, and often part-time farmers. Money is not available when the farmers need it. Few loans are ever fully repaid. But worst of all, the administrative costs may exceed the total sum loaned. Proposals for correcting abuses usually suggest stringent administrative and accounting procedures which increase the cost of loans, and limit them to capitalist farmers who can meet the procedural requirements of public or private banks. It would be cheaper to give money away. Where the initial costs and risks of innovations inhibit peasants from adopting them, inputs can be subsidized or given to peasants, rather than provided on credit.[50]

---

[49] Goddard, 'Changing Family Structures Among the Rural Hausa,' *Africa*, 73, 3, (1973), SRB, 196; B. J. Buntjer, 'Aspects of Change in rural Zaria', *SAN*, vol. 12, 2 (1970). Olayemi, 'Some Economic Characteristics,' *BRES*, 7, 2; Ogunfowora *et al.*, *NRDS*, 8, p. 27; Essang and A. F. Mawabonku, 'Determinants and Implications of Rural-Urban Migration: A Case Study of Selected Communities in Western Nigeria,' *NRDS*, 10 and AREP 10 (1974).

[50] H. Baumann, C. Connolly and J. Whitney, 'A Situation Report on Agricultural Credit in Nigeria,' *CSNRD* 3 (1966); Ogunfowora *et al.*, 'Capital and Credit', *NRDS*, 6. O. Teriba, also S. Oni, 'Credit in Rural Development: An Appraisal of the Supervised Credit Scheme for the Farm Settlers in Western Nigeria', all in *NES*; A. Ijose and J. N. Abaelu, 'Institutional Credit for Small Holder Farmers: A Case Study of the Western Nigerian Agricultural Credit

State marketing institutions, particularly of consumer goods, impose heavy administrative charges on both consumers and producers. This discourages production and accentuates the costs. State supplies are easily diverted to a few private traders who can thus corner the market. The Marketing Boards for export crops have been used to tax producers, ensure monopolistic profits to licensed agents, and slowed down the evacuation of crops, with all the attendant costs of storage, wastage, and delayed payment, thus inhibiting the flow of funds and credit to farmers.[51]

State programmes for supplying seeds, tractor services or fertilisers may concentrate scarce, subsidized inputs on to a few capitalist farmers. Supervised credit and extension schemes, the current panacea for the peasant problem,[52] employ expensive officials to direct compliance with the outputs dictated by the state, and the cultivation practices recommended by its experts, without regard for the farmer's own judgement of market conditions and the best way of increasing the return from his expenditure of cash and labour time.

Corporations'; S. Ugoh, 'Smallholder Agricultural Credit in Eastern Nigeria: An Analysis of the Fund for Agricultural and Industrial Development'; A. Osuntokun, 'Agricultural Credit Strategies for Nigerian Farmers', all in A. I. D. Spring Review of Small Farmer Credit, *AID*, 6, (1973); yet cf. Recommendations by T. L. Jones et. al., 'A Proposed Agricultural Credit Programme for Nigeria', *CSNRD* 4 (1966), blithely followed by I. J. Ebong; Anthonio; Teriba; all in *NES*, pp. 21, 34-5, 177; Olayide et al., *Quantitative Analysis*, p. 86. *Third Plan*, p. 82.; Olatunbosun, *Nigeria's Neglected Rural Majority* (Ibadan, 1975); and cf. A. E. Ekukinam, 'Comments', *NES*, p. 209; R. King, *Farmers Co-operatives in Northern Nigeria*, Institute for Agricultural Research, Zaria, 1976), and 'Cooperative Policy and Village Development'.

[51] For a critical review of the literature on foodstuffs marketing, see B. Harriss, *Cereal Surpluses in the Sudan-Sahelian States* (ICRISAT, Hyderabad and School of Development Studies, Norwich, 1978).

[52] See the National Accelerated Food Production Programme, *Third Plan*, pp. 69-73. A. U. Patel and A. A. Agboola, 'Strategy for Revolutionizing Maize Production in a Nigerian Village,' *BRES*, 8, 2 (1973). S. K. T. Williams et al., *Second Annual Report. Isoya Rural Development Project*, (University of Ife, 1974). For a sharp critique, see Alao, 'Increasing Food Productivity in West Africa through Improved Technology: The Human Factor', *WAJAE*, 1, 1 (1972).

State-sponsored cooperatives often exist only to meet the conditions on which public and private institutions will provide resources, rather than in response to peasant needs. They can easily become a means for wealthy members of rural communities to appropriate state and community resources for themselves. Official cooperative institutions and programmes are rarely adapted to the form and scale of farmers' activities. They fail as soon as no clear relation can be established between a man's return and the effort and efficiency of his work. The range over which economies of scale may be realized through cooperation varies from one activity to another, and cannot be catered for by state institutions whose form and scale is dictated by administrative convenience.[53]

State settlement schemes have spent large sums of money on acquiring land, building houses and facilities for officials and settlers, buying and maintaining tractors and fertilisers, hiring labour and advancing allowances to settlers. Settlements have been managed by authoritarian controls.

As Olatunbosun wrote of the Western Nigeria farm settlements echoing Baldwin's comments on the Niger project a decade previously:[54]

> the farmer's land is plowed for him; he plants seed given to him in prescribed rotations, he fertilizes and cultivates as recommended, and he hands over the crop for processing and marketing – for all of which operations he is, of course, financially responsible. In addition his house is built for him, and his farm labourers are hired and paid by the government –

---

[53] Beer, *Politics of Peasant Groups*; M. Koll, *Crafts and Cooperation*. R. King, *Farmers Cooperatives*.
[54] *Niger Project*, pp. 159-60.

which expenses the farmer must also repay. This extensive control has helped to reduce the farmer's status from that of an owner-operator to a labourer acting under orders.[55]

Most settlers were recruited unwillingly to the Mokwa scheme; the majority of Western Nigerian farm settlers defected, while Okediji found among the remainder 'anxiety, day-dreaming, displaced aggression, general hostility and, in some cases, violent tendencies toward the staff."[56]

Not surprisingly, returns were meagre and the only lessons demonstrated to settlers and farmers (but not it appears to planners) were the lack of future in farming, the incompetence of government and the futility of initiatives of this kind.[57] State agencies are simply not organized to assist peasant farmers, but rather require peasants to organize themselves to meet the state's convenience. By contrast with direct, and directive state policies, the building of farm roads cuts transport costs directly. Farmers can respond more quickly to urban prices, thus evening out the price fluctuations which are exploited by middlemen. Better roads bring more middlemen to rural markets and forces them to offer more competitive prices. Prospects of better returns, and not just higher yields, encouraged farmers to spend money on sprays, seedlings and fertilisers, and to invest time and money in careful cultivation.

---

[55] Olatunbosun, 'Western Nigerian Farm Settlements', JDA, 5, 3, 422; see also W. Roider, *Farm Settlements for Socio-economic Development: The Western Nigerian Case* (Munich, 1971).

[56] O. O. Okediji, 'Motivating Youths to Settle in Rural Area' (NISER, mimeo).

[57] Adegboye, A. C. Basu and Olatunbosun, 'Impact of Farm Settlements on Surrounding Farmers', NJESS 11, 2 (1969), NISER. 66; F. S. Idachaba, 'The "Demonstration Effect" of Farm Institutes and Settlements: Theory and Evidence,' *BRES*, 8, 2; J. C. Wells, Agricultural Policy; but cf. refusals to recognise failure: L. K. Opeke, 'Rapporteur', *WAJAE*, 1, 1, (1972); *Farmers Crusade Project*, A Midwestern Nigeria Publication (n.d., c. 1972); *Third Plan*, p. 82.

Farmers are more inclined and better able to seek out credit from middlemen and local moneylenders.[58]

The slogan of 'laissez-faire' provides a corrective to massive proposals, such as those embodied in the Third National Development Plan, for wasting public money and turning agriculture upside down. But it blithely evades the realities of market regulation, both by public agencies and private monopolies, in any capitalist society. A capitalist state does not correct the market power of the rich, so much as strengthen the ability of the rich to corner the market.[59]

The accumulation of capital by the exploitation of the peasantry does not increase the capacity of the economy to secure the livelihood of the people. The development of heavy industry as the leading sector of the economy can only be built on an agricultural foundation. The development of agriculture and light industry provides markets for heavy industry, and accumulates investment funds more rapidly than heavy industry itself. But more importantly, agriculture and light industry produce daily necessities, which are essential to mobilizing the creative and productive capacities of the people. Increases in farm incomes increase demand for food crops from other regions, and for the products and services of rural, as well as urban craft producers and traders. Improved farm incomes are a condition of the development of the national economy.[60] But this can only be achieved when peasants

---

[58] Anthonio, 'Costs and Returns: A Study of Upland Paddy Production under Traditional Farming Conditions of the Wasimi and Ilaro Areas of the Western State of Nigeria,' *WAJAE*, 1, 1 (1972); B. Ogundara, 'The Transport Constraint on Rural Development in Nigeria,' *NES*.
[59] See Weeks, 'Employment, Growth, and Foreign Domination'.
[60] Essang and Olayide, 'Economic Development'. D. Byerlee, 'Indirect Employment and Income Distribution Effects on Agricultural Development Strategies,' *AREP*, 6 (1973).

organize themselves in their own interests against the capitalists and bureaucrats who rule them.

Peasants usually accommodate themselves to the realities of capitalist and bureaucratic power. They compete for the favour of the influential and evade objectionable policies by a show of formal cooperation or plain dumb insolence. However, in Western Nigeria, over a period of fifty years, peasants have taken up arms against oppressive regulations, extortionate exactions, and unreasonable taxes imposed by the state, at a time when they found themselves getting less for their produce but having to pay more for their purchases. They have attacked government institutions, courts, offices, even schools and railways, officials, court and tax officers and the ubiquitous sanitary inspectors, and local rulers and their allies who supported their masters rather than their people.[61] Peasants then, can be mobilized, not by the state in the cause of development, but by themselves in opposition to the state, and such mobilization is a condition of a successful 'peasant strategy'.

Research and Policy Strategies in Nigeria

It is clear that rural development policy in Nigeria is in a crisis. There are obvious unanswered problems which cannot be resolved by *a priori* reasoning unassailed by practical experience. Significant bodies of data have been assembled, but we remain ignorant about the basic features of rural society in much of the country.[62] When careful studies have been

---

[61] Beer, *The Politics of Peasant Groups*; Beer and Williams, Politics of the Ibadan Peasantry; Adeniran, 'Dynamics'.

[62] Recent and current research [in 1975] is reviewed in Olayide, 'Stimulating Integrated Rural Development through Research', *NRDS*, 18 (1975). See also Norman, 'Interdisciplinary Research', *ACE*, 6. For a historical overview, see Forrest, 'Agricultural Policies'.

conducted, they have often brought into question many taken for granted assumptions. Professor Olayide has argued that the major constraint on rural development is the poor financing of research by government, and the government's failure to implement research results.[63] Researchers should orient their enquiries to the solution of specific problems.[64]

However, this is to put the cart before the horse. The facts are dumb, they don't speak for themselves. They can only be made to speak within an explanation, which itself is dependent on the standpoint from which the problem is defined. Consequently, any evaluation of research and investment programmes must begin by clarifying the assumptions in which they are grounded, and the objectives which they seek to realize.

Professor Olayide's arguments proceed from the assumption that rural development problems are to be discovered and devised by researchers, and implemented by government agencies.[65] The concern of the state to solve these problems and its capacity to do so are not questioned, though its current record is roundly criticised. Solutions cannot be devised by peasant farmers themselves. These assumptions have had important consequences for the form, style and conclusions of research.

---

[63] Olayide, S.O.,'Stimulating Integrated Rural Development'.

[64] Olayide *et. al., Quantitative Analysis*; Norman and E. B. Simmonds, 'Determination of Relevant Research Priorities for Farm Development in West Africa', *SRB* 204 (1973), ironically argue that research should be concentrated on government policies, which focused on small farmers!

[65] Olayide, 'Stimulating Integrated Rural Development', *NRDS*, 18 and 'Research on Rural Integrated Development, Employment and Food Production in the Guinea Savannah Zone of Nigeria', *NRDS*, 1 (1971), for which figures of $150,000 over 3 years, and $435,000 over 6 years are cited. The ILO Rural Employment Project asked for $3 million, thanks in part to staff costs of $1,344,000. One part of the project planned to train 140 'master farmers' over 5 years at a cost of almost $2,500 per farmer, I. L. O. Mission, 'Draft of a Preliminary Report', vol. 3.

Firstly, the collection of comprehensive and quantifiable data suitable for planning purposes is very expensive indeed. Figures run into hundreds of thousands, or even millions of dollars.[66] Although programmes involve extension work, in addition to research, such expensive extension programmes can only be justified by their research potential. Professor Olayide calls for a comprehensive survey of agriculture in Nigeria at a cost of several million naira, despite the experience of Nigerian censuses, and the limitations of Federal rural surveys.[67] Now it may be that good research cannot be done on the cheap. But we should ask at what point diminishing marginal returns set in, and whether the marginal product of research programmes, if not of farmers' labour, might not become negative.

It is significant that proposals are couched in dollars, since they are made to international agencies. Although they are addressed to specifically Nigerian problems, they do reflect the definitions of issues popular with capitalist foundations and international agencies, namely the promotion of employment and the implementation of the seed-fertiliser (Green) revolution.[68] They cannot explore the possibilities of, or need for, a 'Red Revolution'.

Secondly, farmers, their attitudes and their activities tend to be treated simply as data, to be recorded, processed, correlated and analysed. They are not treated as a source of

---

[66] Olayide *et al.*, *Quantitative Analysis*, p. 82.

[67] I.L.O. Mission, 'Draft of a Preliminary Request'; Essang, 'Agricultural Development and Employment Generation in Nigeria,' *NRDS*, 2. For a critique see Weeks, 'Employment: Does it Matter?' in R. Jolly *et al. Third World Employment*, (Harmondsworth, 1973).

[68] Patel and Agboola, 'Strategy for Revolutionizing Maize Production'; S. K. T. Williams *et al.*, *Second Annual Report, Isoya Rural Development Project*; Olayide *et al.*, *Quantitative Analysis*; and cf. too Essang, 'Agricultural Development,' *WAJAE*, 2, 1, (1973) pp. 66-7; Norman, 'Interdisciplinary Research,' *ACE*, 6. See also the promotion in Nigeria of the green revolution by the World Bank, in Williams, 'The World Bank'.

knowledge and wisdom to be learnt from, argued with and respected. Most fieldwork is carried out by field assistants who enumerate responses to pre-ordained questions. Farmers tend to reflect the context of the interview, and their assumptions about the likely consequences of research findings. In my view, the recurrent emphasis in surveys on the credit needs of farmers does not reflect a general rural 'capital shortages,' but the concerns of researchers with the introduction of expensive innovations and the farmers' assumption that surveys might lead governments to favour communities with credit programmes.[69] The reasons for farmers' actions are not explored and contested in dialogue but recorded as responses, or hypothesized post factum. Researchers even measure the rate at which different categories of farmers adopt recommended practices, without examining the costs and benefits of the practices themselves.[70]

Action programmes similarly are oriented to inducing farmers to adopt practices which the researchers wish to experiment with and take to be good for the farmers. They do not begin by keeping open their assumptions about the situation, views and requirements of the farmers, but with the anticipated benefits of developing production of high-yielding maize – even in the absence of effective demand for the

---

[69] Ogunfowora et al., 'Capital and Credit', NRDS 8, p. 41; Ogunfowora and Norman, 'Farm firm Normative Fertiliser Demand Response in the North-Central State of Nigeria,' Journal of Agricultural Economics, 24, 2 (1973); Norman, 'Interdisciplinary Research,' ACE, 6 (1971), pp. 34–8; Patel and Agboola, 'Strategy', BRES 8, 2 (1973).

[70] M. Upton, 'Socio-economic Survey of Some Farm Families in Nigeria, Part 3: Social and Psychological Factors', BRES 3, 2 (1968); B. van den Borne and N. Roling, 'Extension Workers and Farmer Characteristics', BRES, 8, 1 (1973); B. Falusi, 'Multivariate Probit Analysis of Selected Factors Influencing Fertilizer Adoption among Farmers in Western Nigeria', NJESS, 16, 1, (1974); but cf. B. Buntjer, 'Whom to Blame: The Farmer or the Extension Workers', SAN, 14, 1 (1972); Adegboye and Alao, 'Some Socio-Economic Factors' BRES, 7, 2.

product.[71] More generally, proposals reflect a concern to develop and apply technologies which increase production. In the real world of farmers, as in neo-classical economic theory, it is effective demand in the market which must come first.

The assumptions on which research is based generate their own conclusions. If we presume that rural development comes about when governments apply the findings of researchers, then our first priorities must be the financing of research, and the training of managers, extension officers and technicians. Next comes the application of packages of technology to agricultural production. This is done by financing capitalist farms and government plantations, along with government storage, processing and marketing companies. Peasants are to be organized into 'the appropriate institutional set-up' for planners to 'use' them to meet production targets.[72]

This line of reasoning has led the planners to propose a massive reorganization of agricultural production and distribution into complex, large-scale units. This itself will create the very problems identified as most important in the plan by requiring more managers, technicians, extension workers, and farm labourers than can possibly be found, and the financing and application of fertilisers and other inputs on a massive scale. No attention is paid to the most important productive power the creative and productive capacities and agricultural experience of millions of peasants. Instead, the *Third Plan* proceeds from an unthinking belief in the capacity

[71] Patel and 'Strategy for Revolutionizing Maize Production', *BRES*, 8, 2; S. K. T. Williams *et. al.*, 'Second Annual Report, Isoya Rural Development Project'; Cf. C. K. Laurent *et. al.* 'Agricultural Investment Strategy in Nigeria,' *CSNRD*, 26 (1969), p. 23.

[72] *Third Plan*, pp. 61-90, which relies heavily on the analysis of Olayide *et al.*, *Quantitative Analysis*; and cf. too Essang, 'Agricultural Development', *WAJAE*, 2, 1, pp. 66-7; critique by Anthonio, 'Costs and returns', *WAJAE*, 1, 1.

of government to succeed where peasants have not been able to, coupled with a naive faith that spending money will produce real resources to meet the needs of real people. The mistakes of the colonial groundnut projects - state production in Tanzania[73] and supervised settlement in Nigeria,[74] of the Nigerian National Supply Company,[75] state agricultural credit schemes, and tropical plantations will all be repeated, but on a scale where costs are counted in millions, rather than thousands, and billions rather than millions. To say the least, it will be an expensive and unnecessary programme of action-research.

Successive studies of programmes of the type proposed in the plan have revealed their failure to come near achieving their objectives. They have usually focused on problems of mismanagement and often implied fraudulent administration and recommended ameliorating measures, which involve more stringent administrative procedures that will increase costs and make programmes less flexible.[76]

The basic assumptions are not usually brought into question. It is striking how rarely it is suggested that such programmes and institutions as plantations, settlement schemes, credit corporations, marketing boards and other schemes for wasting money and exploiting farmers should be abolished, pending clear evidence that new projects along such

---

[73] See A. Wood, *The Groundnut Affair*. Compare the proposals by I. J. 'Nigerian Social Objectives and the Rural Sector', NES, p.21; Olayide *et al.*, *Quantitative Analysis*, p. 82; and for ten states, (excepting only Kwara and Kano) in the Third Plan, pp. 70-3.

[74] Kwara State proposals to spend N25 million on a project conceived on the same lines as the Niger Project, which was wound up after wasting only £124,000; *Third Plan*, pp. 71, 82; Baldwin, The *Niger Agricultural Project*.

[75] *West Africa*, 18, 25 February, 1975, cf. S. O. Olayide *et al.*, *Quantitative Analysis*, p. 86; *Third Plan*, p. 68.

[76] L. Are, 'Assessment', *Tropical Agriculture*, 41, 1; Olatunbosun, 'Western Nigerian Farm Settlements', *JDA*, 5, 3, pp. 427-428; Osuntokun, 'Agricultural Credit Strategies' *AID* 6, 3.

lines will improve lives of farmers and increase agricultural production at costs commensurate with the probable benefits.[77] It is unusual for anyone to suggest that rural development schemes imposed on farmers by their betters are likely to fail and that effective rural development requires that farmers organize themselves to protect their own interests.[78]

An Alternative Approach to Research

We should start by recognizing that 'economic relations' are relations among people. They are not relations between things, though they may appear so under capitalism when labour itself takes the form of a commodity which is bought and sold on the market.[79] Social relations cannot be adequately understood if we treat them as matters of voluntary choice. They are governed by the power of classes of people to require other classes of people to do their bidding as a condition of providing for their own sustenance and realizing their objectives. Economic relations are therefore social relations, and necessarily political. They involve conflicts of interest and questions of oppression and exploitation. In defining the values and objectives we wish to realize, we cannot avoid answering the question: whose side are we on? From whose point of view are we defining our problems?

Similarly, studying people involves us in relations with them. We must negotiate with them, talk with them, and judge their motives, ideals and actions. We should not use routinized research techniques, technical terms and statistical operations

---

[77] But see A. O. Philips, 'Fiscal Policy and Rural Development in Nigeria', *NES*, p. 130; Anthonio, 'Costs and Returns', *WAJAE*, 1,1.

[78] But cf. see Oni and Onimade, *Economic Development*, pp. 195, 197; Williams, 'Taking the Part of Peasants'. Part **V**.

[79] Marx, *Capital*, vol. 1, ch. 1; *MW*, ch. 32A, pp. 458-482.

to neutralize our personal involvement, though they may well serve to check precipitous judgements. 'Value-neutral' research usually aims to offend nobody in power and simply add to our list of publications so that we can acquire a greater share of the surplus value produced by workers and peasants. 'Policy-oriented' research usually takes the objectives of the powerful for granted, and seeks to ask how they can refine and realize their aims. Recognition of our value commitments and personal involvement does not preclude a continuing critique of the substantive, methodological and value assumptions which both govern and limit our research. My own assumptions are simple. As Polly Hill has argued:

> We must study the farmer, not patronize him: we must assume that he knows his business better than we do, unless there is evidence to the contrary.[80]

> We must discuss issues with farmers, and learn from them, not merely about them. Dialogue requires us to show farmers the respect of listening to their arguments, and presenting our own. In this way, research can be a process of mutual education.

Secondly, we should examine critically the historical record, with its abundant evidence of the modest capacity of researches and governments to solve the problems of rural development.[81] Failures are too easily attributed solely to bad policy implementation. When failures are repeated we should enquire more deeply into the assumptions underlying policies, and when successes are announced we should be cautious enough to ask for whom it was a success. It is irresponsible to propose solutions without clear evidence that they are likely to

---

[80] Hill, *Rural Capitalism*, p. 29.
[81] Forrest, 'Agricultural Policies'.

improve the lives of farmers, and unlikely to worsen them, nor to waste resources which can be put to clearly better uses.

Thirdly, we should recognize that state actions are not determined by the disinterested advice of academics, but by the requirements of the dominant classes. It is not enough to ask farmers what government should do for them, nor to devise appropriate policies for a mythical government of just men. We must face the question: under what conditions can farmers advance and protect their interests, and how can they, in alliance with others, establish and maintain those conditions?

At a more mundane level, dialogue with farmers and an understanding of the possible courses of action open to them does not require a comprehensive survey but a knowledge of the history and social and political relations of specific communities and their relation to the wider society. This requires time, patience, enjoyment of long-winded discussion and a willingness to be satisfied with partial answers, drawn from specific and thus unrepresentative communities. It does not require vast research grants, or a compromise of the researcher's commitments. If it does little for farmers, it may help to protect them from the errors of ambitious men, and it will educate the researcher, and education is surely a condition of a democratic polity. And is man not a political animal?

September 1975

Part VII

Politics and Society - State and Society in Nigeria Revisited[1]

I was asked by Professor Adigun Agbaje to revisit *State and Society in Nigeria*, which had been published thirty years previously. This essay revises and extends that lecture. It bridges over a long period and takes me from one intellectual environment to another. I may perhaps be excused for the autobiographical and self-referential aspects of this final essay, and for the repetition from the previous essays of some of the text.

Politics and political science

The academic world and intellectual fashions have changed since 1980. 'Politics', which I studied and taught at Oxford until 2010, used to be the study of politics. It is now, though not as yet in Oxford, 'political science'. Five approaches have come to dominate this discipline. The first is rational choice or rational actor theory. The second is quantitative analysis. Three more, related to one another, have taken leading positions in the study of African politics. These find a common place in 'development studies': how they fit, or don't into the imaginary of 'development'. The first of them is political culture. The next

---

[1] An Address to the Inter-disciplinary Research Discourse series at the University of Ibadan, 16 February 2010, extended and revised March 2010, and revised 31 December 2016 and October 2018

is 'neo-patrimonialism'. The third is democratization. They have all found a place in the study of Nigerian politics.

The first two borrow their logic and methods from the 'higher' disciplines of micro-economics and macro-economics and look for space for them in the field of political science. Their abstraction is both their virtue and their limitation. Rational choice provides a generally applicable method for analysing aspects of particular cases. At the University of Ibadan, Billy J. Dudley applied coalition theories and the analysis of political institutions to his study of *Instability and Political Order in Nigeria*, which he published in 1973,[2] well before they became internationally fashionable. He is recognized by the current generation of students of politics as the founder father of the discipline.[3]

Statistical methods makes it possible to test generalizations from large 'N' samples, to analyse the relations among variables or to interpret changes in enumerated series over time, Numbers are valuable, when they count what can be counted, such as vines, votes, or population. Then again, they may not be. *Afrobarometer* surveys, for example, give us some independent knowledge of the response of Nigerians in the aggregate to the principles of democracy and the practice of democratic politics.[4]

The remaining three can all be situated broadly within the study of 'political culture'. They tend to rely on sweeping generalizations, usually on a national or even continental scale. Peter Ekeh identified 'dual' publics in order to explain strong

---

[2] B.J. Dudley, *Instability and Political Order*, p. 75; 'Federalism and the Balance of Political Power'; *An Introduction to Nigerian Government and Politics* (Basingstoke, 1982)..
[3] This was the shared view among Masters students at a workshop that I took part in at the University of Ibadan on 8 February 2010.
[4] Afrobarometer (www.afrobarometer.org/results/results-by-country-n-z/nigeria).

loyalties to kin and ethnic group by contrast with an instrumental or indifferent attitude to wider moral and political commitments.[5] Ekeh paralleled the distinction that John Lonsdale made in his study of the Mau Mau rebellion and Kenyan politics between 'moral ethnicity' and 'political tribalism'.[6] Behind democratization theory are evolutionary assumptions that are embedded, as they are exposed in the title of Cowen and Shenton's critique as *Doctrines of Development*[7] and most clearly expressed in Brazil's national motto: *ordem et progresso*, Order and Progress.

Political scientists have constructed a neo-Weberian conception of 'neo-patrimonialism' to explain the failures of state institutions *or* their survival despite these failures. Their primary attributes are corruption and clientelism.[8] Christopher Clapham gives an institutional meaning to 'neo-patrimonialism' as a 'form of organisation in which relationships of a broadly patrimonial type which is formally constructed on rational-legal lines.'[9] In 1977, Richard Joseph adopted the more specific 'prebendalism', to provide a plainer descriptive term that fitted of how political processes work in Nigeria: 'state offices are regarded as prebends that can be appropriated by officeholders who use them to generate material benefits for themselves and their constituents and kin groups.'[10] From the publication of Joseph's influential article

---

[5] P. Ekeh, 'Colonialism and the Two Publics in Africa,' *Comparative Studies in Society and History*, 17 (1975).

[6] J. Lonsdale, vol. II of B. Berman, and J. Lonsdale, 'Moral ethnicity and political tribalism', *Unhappy Valley* (London 1972).

[7] M.P. Cowen, and R.W. Shenton, *Doctrines of Development* (London, 1975).

[8] D. Bach and M. Gazibo (eds), *Neo-patrimonialism in African States* (Cambridge 1982); see T. Mkandawire, *Thinking About Development States in Africa* United Nations University (1996).

[9] C. Clapham, *The Nature of the Third World State* (Madison, 1985).

[10] R. Joseph, 'Class, State, and Prebend Politics in Nigeria', *Journal of Comparative and Commonwealth Politics*, 21 (1983); *Democracy and Prebendal Politics in Nigeria: the Rise and*

1983 on 'Class, state and prebendalism', his concept took a central place in Nigerian political analysis.[11] Anne Pitcher and her co-authors show that 'neo-patrimonialism' found its own legitimacy as an analytic concept in a misreading of Weber, for whom 'patrimonialism' was 'a legitimate type of authority not a type of regime and which included elements of reciprocity and compliance [which] enabled subjects to check the actions of rulers'.[12] 'Neo-patrimonialism' is a lazy concept, labelling instances at the expense of explaining the interactions within and among institutions.

The literature on democratic transition represents democratization as a game of snakes and ladders in which the actors climb up the ladders only to slide down the snakes. The practice and analysis of 'democratization' has thus far (2010) proved problematic in Nigeria. It is neatly exemplified by the titles of two edited collections on the 1993 elections that was followed by Babangida's electoral coup: *Transition to Democracy*,[13] and *Transition without End*.[14]

These paradigms of political science abstract the study of politics from historical processes and displace them from class

Fall of the Second Republic (Cambridge, 1987), pp. 56-8, citing M. Weber, *The Religion of China: Confucianism and Taoism* ({1915} Glencoe, 1951)', p. 56. Prebends paid the 'official income from administering a district from which [his] private income was not really separated.

[11] W. Adebanwi and E. Obadare (eds), *Democracy and Prebendalism in Nigeria* (New York, 2012).

[12] A. Pitcher, M.H. Moran, and M. Johnston, 'Rethinking patrimonialism and neo-patrimonialism in Africa', *African Studies Review* 52 (2009); J.-F. Bayart, *The State in Africa*, (London, 1989, 1993, 2009). M. Weber, *Politik als Beruf* (1918) Phillips Reclam jun, (Stuttgart, 1992), pp. 8; 'Herrschaft' is translated as as 'rule' in D. Owen and Tracy B. Strong *The Vocation Lectures*, trans. R. Livingstone, p. 34 & li.; and as 'domination' in Weber, *Economy and* Society, II, ch 12, 13, pp. 1013-15, ff,; and in Gerth and C. Wright Mills, *From Max* Weber, p. 80;

[13] A. Jinadu, T. Olagunju, and S. Oyovbaire (eds), *Transition to Democracy in Nigeria* (Ibadan, 1997).

[14] L. Diamond, A.H.M. Kirk-Greene, O. Oyediran (eds), *Transition without End: Nigerian Politics and Civil Society under Babangida*, (Boulder, CO 1997); O. Oyediran and A. Agbaje (eds), *Nigeria: Politics of Transition and Governance* (Dakar, 1999).

analysis. They leave behind, firstly, the study of political institutions, how they work, and how they constitute their procedures; and secondly, political economy, which situates politics within economic institutions and class relations.

The Political Economy of Underdevelopment

In Parts II, III,[15] and IV,[16] the original essays on political economy and politics in Nigeria republished in this volume, I took a more encompassing view of politics. The essay which I wrote with Terisa Turner on 'Politics in Nigeria'[17] distinguished between 'politics as the allocation of scarce resources;[18] 'politics as the determination of public policy'; and 'politics as the relations and conflicts among classes'.[19] Economic relations and state relations are social relations. Hence the titles of the essays, *Nigeria: Economy and Society*, which was published in 1976 and of this collection, *State and Society in Nigeria*, originally published in 1980.

I was among a generation of expatriate 'radical' scholars researching and writing in the decade following the end of the Nigerian Civil War. We were mainly young and not from Nigeria itself. Few of us had very close links with our counterparts among radical Nigerian scholars.[20] Our most

---

[15] I wrote Part II with Terisa Turner.
[16] Part IV is taken from the 'Postface' to the first edition.
[17] Part III.
[18] Part III.
[19] Shehu Othman and I returned to these themes in S. Othman and G, Williams, 'Politics, Power and Democracy in Nigeria' in J. Hyslop (ed.) *African Democracy in an Era of Globalization* (Johannesburg, 1999).
[20] Nigerian radical nationalists and Marxist academics at that time of our own or of an older generation included the economists, Eskor Toyo (1929-2015), Bade Onimode (1944-2001), and the irrepressible Comrade Ola Oni (1933-1999); Claude Ake, a political scientist (1939-1996); the historians, Segun Osoba (b. 1935), and Yusufu Bala Usman (1945-2005); and Edwin Madunagu (b. 1946) a mathematician. Osoba and Usman wrote the subversive 'Minority Report' of the Constitutional Drafting Committee in 1977. Madunagu, in a similar way, produced a minority report and resigned from the constitutional Political Bureau in 1986.

common academic affiliations were with sociology. What we were trying to do in the 1970s was to make sense of the international economic context, the formation of a capitalist society, the social relations of classes and class politics at local, regional, and national levels, and the nature of 'the state' in Nigeria. If we had anything to bring to the analysis of Nigerian societies, it was firstly the radical tradition in political economy; [21] secondly, radical interpretations of Nigerian history;[22] thirdly, the study of workers and not just trade unions;[23] fourthly, to participate in the analysis of inequalities and local economies and of politics in farming areas and towns;[24] and fifthly, to contribute to the literature on the

---

[21] Parts II, III. G. Williams (ed.), *Nigeria: Economy and Society* (London, 1975). See P. Waterman, 'On Radicalism in African Studies'; O. Onoge, 'The Concept of Pluralism: a Critique', C. Allen, 'Incomes Policy and Union power', O. Nduka, 'The Rationality of the Rich in Nigeria', S. Osoba, 'The Nigerian Power Elite: 1952-1965'; G. Williams 'Class Relations in a Neo-colony Political Economy: the case of Nigeria' in P. Gutkind and P. Waterman (eds), *African Social Studies; a radical reader*, New York 1977; P. Gutkind and I. Wallerstein eds), *The Political Economy of Contemporary Africa*; C. Allen and G. Williams (eds.), *The Sociology of Developing Societies: Sub-Saharan Africa* (New York 1982); G. Williams (ed), *Special Issue on Nigeria, ROAPE* 13 (1978); E. Toyo, 'An Open Letter to the Nigerian Left' *ROAPE*, 32 (1985); T. Abdulraheem *et al.* (eds), Oil, Debts and Democracy in Nigeria, *ROAPE*, 37 (1987); S, Osoba, 'Corruption in Nigeria: historical perspectives,' *ROAPE*, 69 (1996).

[22] R.W. Shenton and W. Freund, 'The Incorporation of Northern Nigeria'; R.W.Shenton, *The Development of an African Capitalism* (Oxford, 1986); W. Freund, *The Making of Contemporary Africa: The Development of African Society since 1800* (Cambridge, 2nd. ed. 1998) add 3rd ed.

[23] R. Cohen and R. Sandbrook (eds), *African Working Class*; R. Cohen, *Labour and Politics*; A, Peace, *Choice, Class and Conflict*; C. Jackson, 'Hausa women on strike', *ROAPE* 13 (1978); W, Freund, *Capital and Labour in the Nigerian Tin Mines* (London 1981), and *The African Worker* (Cambridge 1988); P. Lubeck, *Islam and Urban Labour in Northern Nigeria* (Cambridge 1986); G. Andrae and B. Beckman, *Union Power in the Nigerian Textile Industry: Labour Regime and Adjustment* (Uppsala; Kano 1998).

[24] Part IV. C. Beer, *Politics of Peasant Groups*; C. Beer and G. Williams, '*Politics of the Ibadan Peasantry*'; T. Forrest, 'Agricultural Policies'; T. Wallace, 'Kano River Project' in J. Heyer, *Rural Development;* G, Williams, 'Taking the Part of Peasants', 'and Why is there no agrarian capitalism?'. P. Clough, *Morality and Economic Growth in Rural West Africa: Indigenous Accumulation in Hausaland* (New York/Oxford) ; T. Adeniran, 'Dynamics';. T. Turner, 'The Transfer of Oil Technology. and 'Two Refineries'

formation of and politics of ethnic identities, and the politics of the oil industry.[25]

Our research did not mark as radical a break as we might have thought we had done from previous writing on the politics of nationalism, of tradition, constitutional crises, political parties, elections, violence and corruption, and of the origins of the Civil War. The previous generation of authors on Nigerian politics combined detailed political narratives of accounts of political contestation with institutional analysis that have not yet been surpassed.[26]

My own interpretation of Nigerian politics began from my critical encounter with Sklar's analysis of the politics of Ibadan. In his study of *Nigerian Political Parties*, Richard Sklar counterposed 'class' and 'community'. He wrote in 1967 that 'class formation would appear to be more significant than class action as a form of class action in contemporary Africa.'[27] Ken Post and George Jenkins wrote the biography of Adegoke Adelabu, a man with no discernable principle other than to win votes, who exemplified the style and purposes of populist politics and who would set the precedent for civic politics in Ibadan. [28]

---

[25] Peel, *Ijeshas and Nigerians*; *Religious Encounter*; A. R. Mustapha, 'Ethnicity and the Politics of Democratization in Nigeria', in B. Berman, D. Eyoh, and W. Kymlicka, (eds.), *Ethnicity and Democracy in Africa* (Oxford 2004).

[26] Part III. J.S. Coleman, *Nigeria*; R. Sklar, *Nigerian Political Parties*; R. Sklar and C.S. Whitaker, 'Nigeria', in J. Coleman and C.G. Rosberg, eds. *Political Parties and National Integration in Tropical Africa* (Berkeley, 1964); K. Post, *The Nigerian Federal Election of 1959*, and *The New States of West Africa* (London, 1964); Post and Vickers, *Structure and Conflict in Nigeria*,; Mackintosh, et al., *Nigerian Government and Politics*; B.J. Dudley, *Parties and Politics in Northern Nigeria* (London, 1968), and *Instability and Political Order*; C.S. Whitaker, *The Politics of Tradition* (Princeton, 1970); First, *Barrel of a Gun*; Luckham, *Nigerian Military*; Melson and Wolpe (eds) *Nigeria*.

[27] Sklar, 'Political Science and National Integration' *Journal of Modern African Studies*, 5 (1967).

[28] Post and Jenkins, *The Price of Liberty*; A. Adelabu, *Africa in Ebullition*.

Nigeria was changing. The period we were writing about, 1966-1979, included three military coups, the pogroms of May 1966 which continued to the beginning of October 1966, a civil war and its aftermaths, the first oil boom, the emergence, consolidation, and reduction of the authority of a small cadre of federal civil servants,[29] the division of regions to create 12 and later 19 (and then 21, now 36) states, the differential reincorporation of Igbo elites into the federal political economy after the War ended, the indigenization decrees, a third military coup, a radical constitutional change, and a federal election. Politics was not all from the top down, as evidenced by a wartime farmers' rebellion in rural Ibadan, and by strikes in Agege and Kano.

How were we to make sense of all this? A reduction of the 'legal, political and ideological superstructures' to their 'economic structure'[30]. simply could not work. These are all parts of complex processes in which each element links with the others. Therefore they cannot be read off any general theory.[31] Our explanations depended on empirical fieldwork and on an analysis of how institutions work, formally and informally, as the consequences, foreseen and unforeseen, of decisions and not of impersonal processes. They required us to put the politics back into the study of politics.

Theories of underdevelopment provided a starting point for macro-political economy: were Nigerian business dependent on their relations with foreign capital or was an

---

[29] See Parts I, III. A. Ayida and H. Onitiri, 'Reconstruction and Development,' A. Ayida, 'The Nigerian Revolution'.

[30] K. Marx, 'Preface' to *A Contribution to the Critique of Political Economy* ({1859}*CW*, 29) pp. 263-4), D. McLellan, *Karl Marx: Selected Writing*, 2nd ed. (Oxford, 2000) (*KM*), ch. 30, p. 425. D. Sayer, *Marx's Method: Ideology, Science and Critique in Capital* (Hassocks, 1979); Williams, 'In Defence of History', *History Workshop Journal*, 7 (1979).

[31] Part II, Peel, *Ijeshas and Nigerians*, pp. 4-7.

indigenous capitalist class developing in Nigeria? Colin Leys made the cases convincingly for both sides in successive publications on capitalism in Kenya.[32] The Igbo business families, exemplified by Sir L. P. Ojukwu; Muslim Yoruba traders, such as Chiefs Salami Agbaje, Adebisi Giwa, and Folarin Solaja in Ibadan; and Alhassan Dantata, the richest among the Kano merchants, all had ties with the colonial trading houses who controlled the trade in imports and exports and were favoured by colonial administrators. But Tom Forrest's historical research showed that they weren't pawns of colonial interests either.[33]

Underdevelopment theory was ahistorical and its questions were wrongly posed. It presumed that Nigerian businessmen could only depend on government and on European firms for their economic advancement.[34] In his critique of Part II in this volume, Bjorn Beckman rightly observed that 'conflict is hardly a more striking feature of this relation between the Nigerian bourgeoisie and imperial capital than is co-operation or mutually lucrative interaction.'[35] The question should have been more open: in what ways, and why, did which Nigerian businessmen relate to one another, to governments, and to foreign companies? This is obviously central to the

---

[32] C. Leys, *Underdevelopment in Kenya* (London 1975). and 'Capital Accumulation, Class Formation and Dependency. The Significance of the Kenyan Case', *Socialist Register* (1978); both excerpted in Allen and Williams (eds), *Sub-Saharan Africa*.

[33] Forrest, *The Advance of African Capital: the Growth of Nigerian Private Enterprise*, (Edinburgh 1986).

[34] Williams, 'The Social Stratification of a Neo-colonial Political Economy: Western Nigeria', In C.H. Allen and R.W. Johnson (eds), *African Perspectives: Papers in the History, Politics and Economics of Africa: Presented to Thomas Hodgkin* (Cambridge 1970). It is now my view that, as in this case, concepts prefaced by 'neo-', as in 'neo-colonial', 'neo-patrimonial', 'neo-liberal' should be abandoned. They lack definition and tell us what they do not mean rather then specifying what they do mean.

[35] B. Beckman, Review of Williams (ed.), *Nigeria. Review of African Political Economy* 10 (1978); see Beckman, 'Imperialism and the National Bourgeoisie; Whose state? State and Capitalist Development in Nigeria'. See also *ROAPE* 22, 23.

contemporary political economy of Nigeria and to its international relations.

Ironically, dependency theories have lost their influence when African governments have become ever more dependent on foreign governments, 'international donors' and 'the international agencies' for foreign aid transfers. Mosley, Harragin, and Toye use a neat game theory to illustrate one aspect of their case studies: governments that could claim to have met the conditions imposed on them could expect rewards for their fiscal virtue; those who had not could plead continuing need.[36] Whitfield and others have shown more recently that the continuing dependence of African governments for capital and even for current budgets does not remove their bargaining power in relations with foreign governments and international agencies. [37]

International economic relations in Nigeria did not fit it with the theory.[38] A massive oil producer depends on the fluctuations of international oil prices for its public revenues and demand in the economy. Rising prices and expanding revenues enabled Nigerian governments and government agencies to borrow money from international banks and commit themselves to increasing spending. The inevitable fall in prices and revenues left the federal government and its dependent state governments with extraordinary debts in relation to their revenue commitments. Successive governments fixed the exchange rates, controlled imports and kept food imports and petroleum below international prices. Notoriously, one of the world's major oil exporters has to

---

[36] P. Mosley, J. Harragin, and J. Toye, *The Politics of Aid: the World Bank and Policy-based Lending*, vol. 1. (Oxford 2009).
[37] L. Whitfield, *The Politics of Aid: African Strategies for Dealing with Donors* (Oxford, 2009).
[38] Ricardo de Oliveira, *Oil and Politics in the Gulf of Guinea* (London, 2007), pp. 207-214.

import petroleum. Access to foreign currency, imports of rice and wheat, and other commodities was determined by proximity to political office and political power. [39]

To represent the Nigerian 'state' as a petro-state misses out crucial parts of the political economy. They could be summed up in the *state-system* of forms of rule, institutions of governments, armed forces, and petroleum companies; the *power relations* among the 'political class', local activists, business interests, and international corporations; and the 'official' and 'unofficial' *channels of distribution*.[40]

These days underdevelopment is called 'globalization', in the abstract and the singular, with no subject, which makes it a banal and even less an historical concept. At least our concepts had some bite.

'Political Class', 'Power Elite', 'Ruling Class'?
Max Weber distinguished between class, as referring to economic relations 'ultimately market situation' and 'status group' (*Stand*), claiming recognition of 'status honour',[41] as exemplified by 'style of life' and in Nigeria, as in Britain, by the conferment of titles. Weber described the state as 'a relation of rule' (*Herrschaftsverhältnis*) of people over people, supported by means of legitimate (i.e. assumed to be legitimate) use of violence.'[42] 'Class' and 'status' are analytically separate. How they relate to one another is an empirical question. I am now, if anything, inclined to think that 'everything' is ultimately about status honour. It often appears to be so in Nigerian public life.

---

[39] Tajudeen Abdulraheem and others, 'Editorial', Bright Okogu, 'The Outlook or Nigerian Oil, 1985-2000'; Yusuf Bangura, 'Structural Adjustment and the Political Question,' in *ROAPE* 37.
[40] Part III. Turner, 'Multinational corporations' /'Commercial capitalists'.
[41] M Weber, 'Class, status, party.'
[42] Weber, *Politik als Beruf*, p. 8.

In *The Manifesto of the Communist Party*, Marx and Engels situated the 'bourgeoisie' in their relations to society and state.[43] Reference to the 'bourgeoisie', when it is taken to mean capitalists, obscures their social character. We can refer to a Nigerian bourgeoisie as a 'status group (*Stand*).[44] Indeed we must do so, if we are to be able to bring capitalists/business-owners, professionals, bureaucrats, military officers, politicians, and patrons of their communities, into an overarching category. In the period before and since Independence these élites were recruited into their situations up a variety of routes, and their opportunities differed in kind and according to ethnic identity' and their 'state of origin and the capacity to translate advancement in one arena into another."[45] Material interests and social standing are not independent of their political connections, As Peter Waterman once pointed out to me, prominent Nigerians have been several of these at any one time or over their lifetimes. Encompassing all of these into a 'bourgeoisie', as I originally did, does not allow for a layering of positions within and among each of these categories.

In 1966 and 1967 respectively, James O'Connell, and Richard Sklar referred to politicians and their close associates as a 'political class'.[46] I started out in my B. Phil. thesis using the concept 'political class' 'not only [to] include incumbents of political offices, but everyone whose offices, employment and income - and his prospects thereof – depend on their gaining

---

[43] K. Marx and F. Engels, *Manifesto* (*CW* 6), p. 486; (*KM* 18), p. 247.
[44] Williams, 'Class, status, elite in a neo=colonial' political economy'.
[45] First, *Barrel of a Gun*, p. 113, citing a 1968 seminar paper by Ken Post.
[46] J. O'Connell, 'The Political Class and Nigeria's Economic Growth', *Nigerian Journal of Economic and Social Studies* 8 (1966); R. Sklar, 'Political Science and National Integration – A Radical Approach' *Journal of Modern African Studies* 5, 1 (1967); Akeredolu-Ale, 'Private Foreign Investment'.

the favour of the government in power.'[47] I then backed away from the term because as Christine Whitehead told me, 'any given economic order will be affected by specifically political activities and decisions. Thus all classes are, in a sense, '"political classes" in that their market situation is partly dependent on the political resources at their disposal.'[48] Perhaps, now that 'politics' and 'politicians' claim their own institutional space, it may be time to bring it back into our analytic vocabulary.

Ruth First perceptively complemented the idea of a 'political class' by referring to competition which would develop within the 'power élite' between politician-businessman and 'power bureaucrats, the army men and the civil servants'.[49] The 'power élite' 'used the state to manipulate contracts and jobs for themselves and ultimately to facilitate their emergence as a class. And the conflict of classes in formation can be as intensive, if more elusive of analysis than that of classes long and established'.[50]

Allison Ayida used the term 'political class' in 1971 from within the heart of the military government.[51] The term has now become conventional in Nigerian political discussions'. It is used in Britain to describe the extending number of people who engage in politics, no longer as elected representatives but as policy advisers and as titled City businessmen. Retired

[47] Williams, 'The Political Sociology of Western Nigeria', B. Phil. thesis (University of Oxford 1967), p. 104, cited First, *Barrel of a Gun*, pp. 104, 459, and in 'Social stratification', p. 226.
[48] C.E. Whitehead, The Political Implications of Social Change in Ghana, 1947-1957', (B.A. dissertation, Department of Social Theory and Institutions, University of Durham, unpublished, 1968), p. 42-4, cited in Williams, 'Social stratification', p. 226. Shehu and Othman and I used the term descriptively in 'Power, Politics and People'.
[49] First, *Barrel of a Gun*, pp. 462, and pp. 112-3, citing a 1968 seminar paper by Ken Post.
[50] First, *Barrel of a Gun*, p. 411.
[51] A. Ayida, '*The Nigerian Revolution, 1966-76*', and in *Reflections on Nigerian Development* (Malthouse, Lagos, 1987). Part II.

politicians, civil servants, and military officers move with indecent haste to join the directors of companies interested in acquiring government contracts or protecting themselves from legislative interference. Does that sound familiar to Nigerians?

C. Wright Mills built his sociology of 'the 'power élite' in the U.S.A. on an analysis of institutions. Military, corporate, and executive élites colluded in the exercise of power and advancing their interests and enjoyed and displayed their wealth and celebrity. Power is exercised both overtly and implicitly. It is a feature of formal institutions and masked by informal negotiations and hidden processes of decision-making.[52] Wright Mills's account depended on the assumption that, whatever their institutional and political differences, the elite triumvirate were able to exercise a common system of political domination. But if, as I had originally argued,[53] the Nigerian 'bourgeoisie' were a 'class', conscious of their collective interests, why did they persistently come into conflict with one another. This was never just an inter-regional practice. It is often more bitter among rather than between state and regional elites.

Segun Osoba adopted the concept of a 'power élite' in his account of the growth of interlocking bureaucratic, business and military élites and their dependence on oil revenues and foreign firms. It was tied together by collusion and convergence among institutions but delineated the career paths of individuals and their cohorts. Military careers open the way to business opportunities. Politics is business by another name:

---

[52] C. Wright Mills, *The Power Elite* (Oxford, 1956).
[53] Williams, 'Social Stratification'.

The essentially business attitude which most of the elite developed to the affairs of the nation meant that most of them devoted all their thinking and scheming to how well they could do for themselves from the material resources available to the whole populace...there was no room for creative intellectualism or idealism in Nigerian politics.[54]

Osoba's comments may still stand.[55]

In the 1970s, Marxists differed as to whether Nigerian capitalists were an 'intermediary class'[56] or constituted an indigenous capitalist class. Edwin Madunagu now places Marx and Engels conception of the 'ruling class' (*herrschende Klass*) at the core of his analysis. It is united and divided. It is 'united by capitalism' 'and capitalist rules and logic, which enable it to enforce, protect and defend its collective interests against the interests of other classes and strata, and be able to close ranks at critical times when its rule, as class rule, is challenged. It is divided among by histories, economies, ethnicities, regions, political parties and factions, fraternities, insurgents, sectional interests and organisations.[57]

The State, Engels writes:

is the form in which the individuals of a ruling class assert their common interests and in which the whole civil society of an epoch is epitomised , i.e. follow that the State mediates in the

---

[54] Osoba, 'The Nigerian power elite', ({1970} New York), p. 377.

[55] They are echoed by Attahiru Jega, *Democracy, Good Governance and Democracy In Nigeria* (Ibadan, 2007), pp. 27-8.

[56] F. Fanon, *The Wretched of the Earth* ({1961} London, 1966), p. 122 .

[57] E. Madunagu, Forces in the current power struggle in Nigeria, *Pambazuka News* 29 June 2018, See C. Obi 'The Impact of Oil' at n. 71,

formation of all common institutions and that the institutions receive a political form.[58]

It is an '*illusory* communal interest'.[59]

From 1966 to 1975, a Nigerian 'power élite' brought military and business interests into contests with regional interests, presided over by and, the 'Super Permsecs' of the federal administration, over the allocation of oil revenues, government spending, and political rule.[60] General Murtala Muhammed and after he was assassinated General Olusegun Obasanjo took power from the government of General Yakubu Gowon, and reduced the influence of the federal bureaucrats. It was an institutional coup, which reconfigured the 'power elite', with the military taking over direction from the bureaucracy. It also demonstrated the tendency of the powers-that-be to fragmentation along intersecting axes of differentiation. It brought into question in the Nigerian case the coherence of purpose and institutions that was central to Mills' analysis of power elites.

The 'political elites' did not share a common view of their own social standing and place in the political world. The military, with a few exceptions, were looked down upon, all the more so perhaps when they monopolised political power and enriched themselves. They felt that they had been usurped from their rightful claim to political office. Politics provides one route for people to be recognised by the conferment of

---

[58] F. Engels, Feuerbach, Opposition of the Materialistic and Idealistic Ideology, *German Ideology* I, ch. 1, (*illusorischen gemeinschaftlichen Interessen*, translated as 'general interest').

[59] Engels, Feurbach, p. 35 marginal note. See P. Abrams, Notes on the Difficulties of Studying the State (1977), *Journal of Historical Sociolgy* 1, 1, 1988. See Marx and Engels, *The Manifesto of the Communist Party, and the Prefaces.*

[60] Citing Part III, 'Commercial Capitalists'; 'Transfer of Oil Technology; Othman and G, Williams, 'Power, Politics and People.'

chieftaincy titles; to bring back a share of the cake for their home communities; to be promoted in bureaucracies, and in universities. Class interests may matter but the status of 'political elites' takes precedence.

The Civil War and the 'institutional revolution'

Exceptional studies were written during and soon after the end of the war on the military in politics, the sociology of the Nigerian military, the origins of the war, the politics of communalism, and the international politics of the war, and sources were copiously documented.[61] Participants' narratives from either side were naturally partisan in the extreme but they us much about their experiences and understandings of past events and recent memoirs still have more to tell us than most accounts by academics. Subsequent writing on the civil war has often been more significant for what it doesn't tell us as for what it does.

After 1975, the war itself was no longer a polite subject for serious academic inquiry and debate. Few researchers have been very keen to go back to those events seriously, not least for fear of what they what they may uncover. The war itself has had continuing consequences for Nigerian politics: accentuating the rivalries regarding rank and promotion among serving and retired military officers, the rise of new and ambitious generations of junior and middle-ranking officers, the grievance of Igbo businessmen that they were excluded from the opportunities created by the indigenization decrees,

---

[61] For examples, First, *Barrel of a Gun;* Melson and Wolpe (eds), *Nigeria,* Panter-Brick (ed.), *Nigerian Politics and Military Rule: Prelude to Civil War* (London, 1970); A. H. M. Kirk-Greene (ed.), *Crisis and Conflict in Nigeria: A Documentary Sourcebook, 1966-69,* 2 vols (Oxford, 1971). R. Luckham, *The Nigerian Military;* J. de St Jorre, *The Nigerian Civil War* (London, 1972). Dudley, *Instability and Political* Order. J. J. Stremlau, *The International Politics of the Nigerian Civil War, 1967-1970* (Princeton University Press, 1977).

divisions among communities in the Niger Delta over their alignments within the federal political system. The volume edited by Eghosa Osaghae, Ebere Onwudiwu and Rotimi Suberu in 2002 on *The Nigerian Civil War and its Aftermath*[62] showed the way to reconsidering the histories of the war, while illustrating the difficulties of open engagement among scholars. Forty years after the end of the war, there is still a need for further studies of archival, documentary and also of oral sources – before even more of those engaged in the events die.

I will confess to passing over the events of the war in two pages in the essay on politics in *State and Society in Nigeria*.[63] Forgive me for spelling out my own simple attempt to make sense of these complicated and tragic histories:

> The events of 1966 to 1970 were most easily explained by grand theories: the Igbo plot, or the northern conspiracy. Evidence can be adduced for either account by incorporating them into two grand narratives. The coup-makers of January 1966 blamed the failures of Nigeria on tribalism, regionalism and politics, arguments, which resonate in subsequent and contemporary Nigerian politics. Their solution was abolish tribalism, abolish regions and exclude politicians. 'Tribalism' cannot deal with the ambiguities of Nigerian politics. 'Regionalism' emphasises the institutional bases of political power but does not explain why they could not be accommodated with one another or why Nigeria did not break up into its constituent regions. To explain political conflicts we

[62] E. Osaghae, E. Onwudiwu and R. Suberu (eds), *The Nigerian Civil War and its Aftermath* (Ibadan, 2002).
[63] I was subsequently asked to write a study of the war and its origins for the Open University. G. Williams, *The Nigerian Civil War* at www.gavinwilliams.org (website in progress), and *The Origins of the Nigerian Civil War* (Milton Keynes, 1982). There is a brief account in Othman and Williams, 'Power, Politics, and Democracy.'

must ask why politicians acted and why politics took the forms they did.

Sequences of events appear with hindsight to have been inevitable. We ask what made them happen rather than what made them possible. But history does not go backwards. In this case, we can conceive how different sequences of events might have followed from the elections in the Western Region in October 1965, or the Conference in Aburi, Ghana on 4-5 January, 1967, up to the declaration of secession on 30 May 1967 and beyond.

I identified the September 1966 Constitutional Conference, which placed the fate of Nigeria in the hands of the Regions. My own interpretation of this fateful moment was that

> (After) the Constitutional Conference adjourned on 3 October the Government of Eastern Nigeria and the Federal Government followed comparable strategies. Each was willing to find agreement but on their own terms; otherwise they would assert their own sovereignty. Lagos and the West were important in the calculations of the North and the East. So too was the creation, or not, of new states. Apparent agreement among soldiers broke down when its ambiguities were revealed. The key negotiators on both sides were civil servants, intent on securing their own governments' sovereignty.

Nigeria entered the Civil War, and left it under the direction of the 'Super Permsecs', or, to borrow from Gerald Aylmer, 'the state's servants'[64] who proved unable to carry through the

---

[64] G. Aylmer, *The State's Servants: The Civil Service of the English Republic, 1649-1660* (Oxford, 1973). The term and the idea are borrowed by P.R.D. Corrigan, 'Moral Regulation', pp. 109-179, and Appendices.

'national' revolution' that they had envisaged. [65] It was premised on the continuing expansion of federal oil revenues. The public sector would be extended, strategic industries reserved to the state and its executive capacity would be strengthened. The private sector did not much like this, but got the 'indigenization' decrees instead. When Murtala Muhammed overthrew the Gowon government in 1975, he reorganized it along the hierarchical lines of the military. The 'political class' got constitutional reform.

Where did these changes take us? The 'contractocracy' was already well ensconced during the civil war in the imports of cement and defence equipment at inflated prices.[66] The Central Bank retained something of its financial capacity but was hamstrung by trade and exchange rate policies, which increased import dependence, enriched the rich and encouraged smuggling and hoarding. Public funds were stolen and scarce rice imports were openly used to buy the support of politicians.

Indigenization did work. [67] At least some Nigerians benefited and got control of a larger share of the economy via government decrees and the stimulus to the stock exchange. These were intended to ensure protected areas for Nigerians

---

[65] Ayida, *The Nigerian Revolution, 1966-76* and in *Reflections on Nigerian Development* B. J. Dudley, *An Introduction to Nigerian Government and Politics* (Macmillan, London, 1982); A. D. Yahaya, `Nigerian Public Administration under Military Rule: The Experience of the Northern States' in O. O. Adamolekun (ed.), *Nigerian Public Administration, 1960-1980* (Heinemann, Ibadan, 1985) Kayode and Otobo, *Allison Akene Ayida.*

[66] Part III. Turner, 'The Nigerian Cement Racket'

[67] P. Collins, 'Public Policy and the Development of Indigenous Capitalism'. *Journal of Comparative and Commonwealth Political Studies* 19, 1997; C. Ake, `Indigenization: Problems of Transformation in a Neo-colonial Political Economy' in Ake (ed.), *Political Economy of Nigeria* (Longman, London, 1985); T. Biersteker, *Multinationals, The State, and Control of the Nigerian Economy* (Princeton University Press, 1987); A. Olukoshi, 'Economic Crisis, Structural Adjustment and the Coping Strategies of Manufacturers in Kano, Nigeria,' United Nations Institute for Social Development, DP 77, 1996.

and partnerships with foreign companies. Foreigners were to vacate space for Nigerians, and move into higher value and technically more advanced sectors in association with Nigerian investors. There was naturally collusion between Nigerians and foreigners, especially the Lebanese against whom the policies were directed in the first instance. Igbo businessmen complained that they had been kept on the edges of the game just when the prizes were being handed out. The policy probably increased Nigerian business capacities. It was a bonanza for politicians, civil servants, and military officers able to get foreign exchange and scarce imports; secondly, bankers with unsecured loans; thirdly, those who owned petrol tankers, presumably with political protection. The shift to national ownership would probably have happened anyway. The decrees affected its timing and who benefited.

I argued in 1994 that 'structural adjustment is necessary [but that] it doesn't work'[68] People revolt against economically rational reductions of the state subsidies of petrol prices which generates enormous profits for those in a position to exploit them but the costs of whose withdrawal fall on the ordinary people and not the profiteers. Macro-economic reforms have brought some of these enormous scams to an end and allowed modest benefits for the middle classes and some public institutions. There is little to show for the enormous increases in public expenditure. We must still ask: who got the contracts and who stole the money? Perhaps Nigerians know the answers.

---

[68] Williams, 'Why Structural Adjustment is Necessary and Why it Doesn't Work', Debates, *ROAPE* 60, 1994.

Fiscal Federalism

The U.S.A. provided the obvious model for the federal constitution, which was installed with modifications in Nigeria in the 1978 Constitution and which has remained in place in its institutional outlines during periods of civil rule. There were several things wrong with this institutional transfer. The U.S. Constitution starts with an assumption that state and city governments set taxes, raise revenues and – usually – pay the interest on their bonds. The central flaw in Nigerian federalism is that they don't. At its simplest, oil companies pay shares of taxes and profits to the federal government which takes its own share and distribute their allotted shares to the states and to local government. Neither the federal or the states or local government need to tax people to get money to spend.[69] Their revenues depend on the unpredictability of oil incomes.

Oil revenues have opened space for 'types of capitalistic orientation of profit-making' that encompass 'opportunities for predatory profit from political organizations or persons connected with politics' and, as Max Weber delicately adds, 'profit opportunities in unusual transactions in political bodies.'[70] 'The pursuit of 'Power for Profit', in the title of Othman's article[71] has promoted factionalism among political and military elites. Cyril Obi put it nicely: 'The issue of revenue allocation strikes at the very basis of existence of the Nigerian federation and the rules of entry and exit from the ruling class.'[72] Revenues were reallocated and the formulas for

---

[69] J. Guyer, *Representation without Taxation: An Essay on Democracy in Rural Nigeria*, 1952-1990, *African Studies Review* 35,1(1992).

[70] Weber, *Economy and Society*, ch. 2.13, p. 164-5. See Part II

[71] Othman, 'Nigeria: 'Power for Profit'".

[72] C. Obi, The Impact of Oil and Nigeria's Revenue Allocation System: Problems and Prospects for National Reconstruction, in Amuwo, K. et al., (eds) *Federalism and Political Restructuring in Nigeria* (Ibadan, 1998).

distribution between the three tiers of government and among the (rising number of) states were changed on successive occasions. Victor Lukpata lists fourteen principles that Commissions/Committees have hitherto recommended 'for the sharing of the national cake.'[73] The federal administrators took advantage of the Civil War and its aftermath to take control of the lion's share of revenues from oil production. However, Philip Asiodu's vision of the 'national' management or distribution of oil wealth could not be realised.[74] It had to give way to the allocation of revenues between the federation and the states and among state governments.

The Technical Committee for the Constituent Assembly (1977) and the Okigbo Presidential Commission (1980), headed by Nigeria's two most distinguished if rival economists, were unable to come up with proposals that could secure the agreement of the federal and state governments. The Shagari government, in effect, split the difference between the shares of 53 and 57 per cent proposed to go to the Federal Government.[75] Military governments held on to their control of the allocation of oil revenues, ignoring recommendations by the Revenue Mobilisation and Fiscal Commissions.

State governments wanted the Federal government to devolve more revenues to them but could not agree among themselves to the formulas for allocating revenues among themselves. The Federal government increased the share going

---

[73] V.I. Lukpata, 'Revenue Allocation Formulae in Nigeria: a Continuous Search', *International Journal of Public Administration and Management Research*, 2, 2 (2013), p. 35.

[74] Philip Asiodu, *Daily Times*, 19, 20 March 1973, cited Part IV.

[75] A. Aboyade, *Revenue Allocation Formula in Nigeria*, 1978. P. Okigbo, *Presidential Commission on Revenue Allocation*, 1980, p. 35; and 'Economic Implications of the 1979 Constitution of the Federal Republic of Nigeria' in Nigerian Economic Society, *The Nigerian Economy: A Political Economy Approach* (Longman, London, 1986). Jega, *Democracy*, pp. 217-9; Lukpata, 'Revenue Allocation Formulae.

to local government from 10% in 1988 to 20% in 2010, but did so at the expense of state governments and not their own. In the absence of a willingness to comprise, any change has to be laid down by a military ruler or a 'Presidential Executive Order'. Eventually in 2010, the government of President Goodluck Jonathan raised the 'special funds' to 13%, which it allocated to the states where oil is produced.[76]

Allocation of Revenues among Federal, State, and Local Governments[77]

	Federal	State	Local	Special
1975	59. 4 %	20.0%	20.6%	
1981	55.0 %	30.5 %	20.0 %	4.5 %
..	..	..	...	...
2010	52.68 %	26.72 %	20.6 %	
2013	39.68 %	26.72 %	20.6 %	13 %

shared among the oil-producing states of Akwa Ibom, Bayelsa, Delta, Edo, Imo, Ondo, Rivers.

Figures for the shares of tiers of government tell us a lot but also obscure much about the contentious rules regarding distribution and the political, often violent, conflicts among and within states and over the boundaries of local government areas. The rapid increase in oil exports put access to oil supplies and lucrative contracts into the hands of the federal state who are in a position to take over the allocation of oil taxes and profits. The creation of new states introduced new claimants for their rightful shares of federal revenues and destabilised alliances among them. Another increase by a half from 36 to 54 states was even proposed. It would squander

[76] Oyovbaire, 'The Politics of Revenue Allocation' in Panter-Brick, (ed.) *Soldiers and Oil*; and *Federalism in Nigeria: A Study in the Development of the Nigerian State* (London, 1985), pp. 162-200.
[77] Ikeji, 'Politics of Revenue Allocation', *Premium Times*, 28 April 2014.

even more public money, spread benefits further across the political class and turn minorities into majorities and create new 'minorities'. State governments are the fulcrum of access to personal and public resources. They are able to dispose over their own shares of federal resources and the ability to distribute them to LGAs and among their own clients at local and state levels. For most participants in politics, Abuja is a long way away. Consequently, since 1964, political violence has taken place and been most intense at the level of regions or states and over the multiplication and boundaries of local government areas (LGAs).[78]

It was inevitable that the governments of the oil-producing states would want to recover the share of oil royalties from which they had been deprived by the fiscal coups of 1970-1974. In 1998 the All Ijaw Youth Congress demanded 'resource control', whatever that might be, in its Kaiama Declaration, a claim that the governors of the littoral states subsequently took up. Revenues would still go through the accounts of the federal government before being transferred to the state governments. If state governments do not raise their own revenues, 'fiscal federalism', 'true' or otherwise, does not exist. This is no reason in principle for reallocating revenues among the tiers of governments in line with agreed formulas and scope for alteration. The competition for resources in a 'federal' *state* would require some state governments to forego advantages so that others may benefit.

Oil companies have spread extraordinary environmental damage in the oil-producing areas. The people living in the oil-producing areas of the Niger Delta have paid the appalling

---

[78] Post and Jenkins, *Structure and Conflicts in Nigeria*; Parts III and IV.

costs while their political 'representatives' claim on their behalf and appropriate their own shares of the profits for themselves and 'financially sponsor youth activists'. Kathryn Nwajaku-Dahou explains 'oil bunkering...the 'illicit theft and sale of oil that expanded against the backdrop of "insurgency" (in the Niger Delta states)...as an extension of the "parallel economies" that developed around the production, sale and marketing of oil since the oil boom of the 1970s.' 'Oil companies have lifted oil 'legally' by under-invoicing. More visible, if protected' has been the sabotage of well-heads.'[79] Self-proclaimed insurgents have used violence to collude and reach compromises with the oil companies, security companies, the Joint (military) Task Force, and their personnel, as well as state Governors, retired generals, and politicians.

Sects and Markets

Left-wing radicals, and political scientists for that matter, have not usually been well attuned to the meaning and significance of religious belief and observance, though it is obviously central to people's lives. Our tendency, with significant exceptions,[80] has been to marginalise its significance and to give more attention to economic interests and political alignments. I had myself nothing to say in my own essays about the political significance of religion![81]

Since the Civil War, religion has acquired a greater and more evident social and political salience than ever, forcing us to ask, what is it all about? The first answer is that religious

---

[79] A. Jega, *Democracy*, pp. 203-44; K. Nwajiaku-Dahou, 'The Political Economy of Oil and "Rebellion", in Nigeria's Niger Delta', *ROAPE* 132, pp. 299-300.

[80] P. Lubeck, *Islam and Urban Labour in Northern Nigeria: the Making of an Islamic Working Class* (Cambridge, 1986). See also I. Clarke and P. Linden, *Islam in Modern Nigeria: A Study of a Moslem Community in a Post-Independent State*, (Mainz, 1984).

[81] I made only two passing references to religion!

doctrines, beliefs and practices are not all the same thing. The second is that it is easy to say that religion is really about something else. This is particularly tempting to the irreligious. But religion is not *only* about religion.

There is nowhere more than in the study of religious ideas and practices that the multiple intersections of complicated social phenomena are to be found. To interpret them, we have to study them empirically and to situate them historically in their relations to religious doctrines and ritual practice; to mystical experience and millennial expectations; to sectarian and denominational divisions; to ethnic and pan-ethnic identities; to urban and rural place; to gender and generation; to family membership; to poverty and inequalities; to systems and boundaries of administration; to forms of livelihood; to class relations and status differences; to domination and subordination; to (mis)representations of 'others'; to material interests; to political alignments; to the dogmatisms of evangelizers and 'fundamentalists'; to complementary transactions and shared interests; to conflicts of different kinds at local, state, and federal levels between Christians and Muslims and among Christian and Muslim sects and denominations; and to competition for followers in the 'religious market place' among Muslims and among Christians. These elements each acquire their meaning and significance from their relations to one another; how they do so is not consistent across time and space. [82] Hitherto, the vast majority of northern Muslims have identified with the 'inner-worldly' *Sufi* brotherhoods (*tariqa*) within *Sunni* Islam. The *Qadiriyya*

---

[82] A.R. Mustapha and M.U. Bunza, 'Contemporary Islamic Sects & Groups in Northern Nigeria', in A.R. Mustapha (ed.), *Sects and Social Disorder: Muslim Identities and Conflicts in Northern Nigeria* (Woodbridge, 2014), pp. 56-63.

were associated politically with the Fulani aristocracy and the Native Administrations and Northern People's Congress (NPC); the 'social conservative and politically radical' *Tijaniyya* with the mercantile classes and farmer-traders in Kano, Zaria, and southern Katsina.[83] Party politics brought doctrinal disputes and economic differences into state, federal, and regional arenas.

In 1962, the *Sardauna* of Sokoto, the Prime Minister of the Northern Region, initiated the *Jama'atu Nasril Islam* for political as much as for religious reasons.[84] The *Sufi* brotherhoods were confronted by '*Yan Izala*,'[85] ('*Salafists*'), and by the emergence of a *Shi'a* rival.[86] *Izala*'s modernism provides a more rational religion to Western-educated Muslims, justification for avoiding costly religious rituals to the middle classes, to women by promoting women's education, and to Muslim migrants who were not integrated into the networks of the brotherhood.[87]

Jibrim Ibrahim divides Christian churches into four categories: Protestant and Catholic (originally mission); Ethiopian (nationalist); *Aladura*; and Pentecostal. In 1976, they found themselves creating the Christian Association of Nigeria, with an effective responsibility to protect the position of the churches in Nigerian society and the constitution.

---

[83] Mustapha and Bunza, 'Contemporary Islamic Sects', p.61; M. Last 'The genesis & development of reformist Islamic groups in northern Nigeria,' in Mustapha, *Sects and Social Disorder*.

[84] Lubeck, *Islam and Urban Labour*, pp. 76-84.

[85] *Jama'atu Izalatil Bid'a wa Iqamat al-Sunna* (*Izala*). See Mustapha and Bunza, 'Contemporary Islamic Sects', pp. 63-70; R. Loimeier, *Islamic Reform and Political change in Northern Nigeria*, (Evanston, IL, 1997); and O. Kane, *Muslim Modernity Postcolonial Nigeria: A Study of the Society for the Removal of Innovation and Reinstatement of Tradition* (Leiden, 2003).

[86] Muslim Brothers', (Movement for the Jihad and the Restoration of the Caliphate), Mustapha and Bunza, 'Contemporary Islamic Sects', pp. 70-74.

[87] Mustapha, *Sects and Social Disorder*, pp. 66-67, citing Loimeier, *Islamic Reform* p. 258; and O. Kane, *Muslim Modernity in Postcolonial Nigeria Leiden, 2003*).

The number of Pentecostal churches and their adherents exploded dramatically from the formation of the Deeper Life Church in 1973. Ruth Marshall interprets the 'born-again' movement as a *'religious* form in response to what is seen as a *spiritual* crisis.'[88] Pastor M. O. Olewole described it as 'spiritual warfare', 'in the battle of translating the victory of Jesus over the devil onto the everyday, natural realities of own personal lives and also of our political, religious, economic and social systems.' He rightly predicted 'a revival of an unprecedented dimension'[89]

Holiness churches have drawn their congregants from the established denominations, and also from the 'praying' (*Aladura*)[90] and apostolic churches that had come into existence between the two World Wars. The success of churches depends on their following. By 2001, the Deeper Life Church claimed a thousand churches, a membership of 200,000 and an enormous church complex alongside the Ibadan-Lagos expressway. It was even exceeded by the Redeemed Christian Church of God (RCCG) in attendance and in the number of its parishes, by its worshippers across Europe, Asia, and the Americas, and by its success in attracting membership from among social elites and its private university.

The 'wave' of the 1970s 'placed the accent on becoming born-again' and 'a new life in Christ'. The Holy Spirit was revealed in the "charismatic gifts" of speaking in tongues, faith healing, deliverance from evil spirits and prophesying'. Converts observed strict personal discipline, gave testimony of past sins, and of miracle deliverance. They 'were exhorted to

---

[88] R. Marshall, *Political Spiritualities: the Pentecostal Revolution in Nigeria* (Chicago, 2009), pp.1-2, citing M.O. Ojewale (1990), from B. Okri, *Infinite Riches* (Orion, 1999).
[89] Marshall, *Political Spiritualities*, p. 1.
[90] J.D.Y. Peel, *Aladura: a Religious Movement among the Yoruba* (London, 1968).

prepare themselves and live in constant expectation of "the rapture" '. A second 'new wave' of Pentecostalism emerged in the mid-1980s, which placed more emphasis 'on experiential faith, the centrality of the Holy Spirit, and the spiritual gifts of speaking in tongues and miracles.' They were distinguished by the 'doctrine of prosperity', that believers are 'rewarded depending on how much 'spiritually but especially materially,' they give to God (or his representatives), who reward him by 'prospering' him. [91]

Can the rise of the *Sunni Yan Izala* and the *Shi'ites* in the northern states be placed in line with the 'waves' of Pentecostalism, and any similarities be attributed to 'neo-liberalism'? There are similarities but *Izala's* doctrines and style of life seem more akin to Puritanism, than to being 'born again' and 'making anew'. *Yan Izala* and the Pentecostal churches both increased their followers rapidly in the early days of the oil boom in the 1970s,[92] preceding the economic crisis and the 'neo-liberal' policies of the 1980s. Their followers are both subject to the experiences and uncertainties of the lives of Nigerians, to which they find answers that differ among Muslims as among Christians. The important questions are why people and communities act in particular ways and places, and with what consequences, intended and unintended.

Religious Encounters

Mustapha observes '*how* we study religious encounters and conflicts matter.'[93] He cites Horowitz, 'Narratives matter in

---

[91] This paragraph cites or compresses, Marshall, *Political Spiritualities*, p. 79.

[92] Nigeria's oil production (26.3mn. barrels p.d.) and it current account balance (US$4.4mn) were at a peak in 1980. Okugu, 'The outlook for Nigerian oil: 1985-2000: Four scenarios ' *ROAPE*, 17 (1986), Tables 1 and 2, pp. 14-15.

[93] A.R. Mustapha, Religious Encounters in Northern Nigeria, in A.R. Mustapha and D. Ehrhardt,eds, *Creed and Grievance Muslim-Christian Relations & Conflict Resolution in Nigeria*. 2018, p.3.

situations of conflict. They are used to construct diagnostic (what happened) and prescriptive (what should happen) frames of reference...narratives frame both the understanding and the responses of the actors in the conflicts.'[94] Narratives also frame the ways in which conflicts are framed in the interpretations from outside the events.

As Mustapha and Bunza show in their study of Muslim identities in northern Nigeria, 'conflicts have been as much a defining feature of intra-Muslim relations over the centuries as in the recent history of Muslim/Christian relations.' They go on to say that among Muslims in the northern states 'traditionalists, modernists and radicals, organised in different sectors and groups, compete for followership and influence.' In the process, they have converted the sacred sphere into something akin to a market.'[95] Exclusive 'doctrinal claims often created the basis for violent conflicts between the sects [...] directed at the state or at segments of the wider society such as Christians or [Muslim] members of non-northern ethnicities'.[96]

Electoral contests cannot be reduced to ethnic or religious identities, land or material interests. J.D.Y. Peel identifies the contemporary accommodation of Islam and Christianity in Yoruba communities, who share a common loyalty to the *ilu* (*town*), and the institution of the *oba* (divine ruler, *ekeji orisa* second to the gods)' and *'orisa'*, such as *Sango* (Oyo), *Ogun* (Ilesa) or *Agemo* (Ondo), that were felt to embody the identity

[94] D.I. Horowitz, A Democratic South Africa: constitutional engineering in a divided society. Berkeley, 1971, in Mustapha, Religious Encounters, p, 7,
[95] Mustapha and Bunza, 'Contemporary Islamic Sects' p. 92, and Anon. at p. 91, and p. 55; Mustapha.
[96] Mustapha, 'Conclusion: Religious Sectarianism, Poor Governance and Conflict,' in *Sects and Social Disorder*, p. 200. See Mustapha and Ehrhardt, *Creed and Grievance*, Part 1,

of the whole town.'[97] Though their modes of greeting will differ, Nigerians expect one another to show respect for the adherents and faiths of different religious identities at formal and at informal occasions.

Kate Meagher's empirical research on informal enterprises between and within religious and ethnic relations between Hausa Muslims and mainly Igbo Christians found a 'remarkable capacity of informal institutions resources to maintain inter-religious cooperation', whether their activities were complementary or cooperative and organised in separate network as in Kano or mixed as in Kaduna, though the risks of violence has created tensions between them. [98]

Violence within and between communities should not be taken as microcosms of greater macrocosms. Ethno-religious tensions have been the consequences and not the causes of ethnic and religious conflicts in particular contexts. As always, the relations between them must be empirically interrogated. Conflicts may emerge out of local conditions. They will often take place where changes at a larger scale appear to place the interests and security of people at a smaller scale.[99] The most extreme cases, the pogroms against Igbos and others from the former Eastern Region in 1953 and on a massive scale in May and September 1966 originated in apparent threats to the interests of 'the North', and from the counter-coup against the Ironsi governments in July 1966 of northern troops, among whom Tiv Christians were the largest component.[100]

---

[97] J.D.Y. Peel, *Christianity, Islam, and Orisha Religion: Three Traditions in Comparison and Interaction*, University Press, 2016, cited Mustapha, pp. 6-7.

[98] K. Meagher, Complementarity, Competition, and Conflict, in Mustapha and Ehrhardt, *Creed and Grievance.*

[99] See Jibrin Ibrahim, 'The Politics of Religion in Nigeria: the Parameters of the 1987 Crisis in Kaduna State,' *ROAPE*, 45, 46 (1989), p. 65, and pp. 65-82.

[100] Part III. Othman and Williams, 'Power, Politics, and Democracy', references at n. 20.

Oil revenues, the creation of new states, revenue allocation, and constitutional disputes taken together brought religious affiliations to the fore in the politics of resource allocation. The creation of a Federal (civil) Shari'a Court of Appeal was made a divisive political issue in the 1977 Constituent Assembly by a northern establishment alliance consolidate and extend political allegiances at a time when control of Native Authorities and the erstwhile Northern Region would no longer suffice to ensure their political domination; the Muslim Students Society wanted the 'total application of the sharia both as a legal system and a way of life.'[101] The extension of the scope of sharia law in 2000 to twelve states[102] and Nigeria's membership of the Organisation of Islamic Countries (now) Conference (OIC) in 1986 appeared to Christians to put the Nigeria's secular constitutional status at risk.

Students have often provoked religious conflicts, which took on ethnic dimensions. In 1986, a dispute between at the Kafanchan College of Education on the alleged denigration of the Quran and the Prophet eventuated in extensive destruction of churches, mosques, houses and 'hotels' across southern Kaduna State. Grievances spread across numerous issues. A summary of fifteen of the issues submitted to the Donli Committee on the disturbances included religion, politics, the police and army, and structural adjustment and economic policies. For their own safety, Hausa-Fulani, and non-Muslim 'settlers' returned to the 'homes' where many had never resided. The main victims of looting were Igbos. The state was

---

[101] Ibrahim 'The Politics of Religion', p. 77.
[102] A.R. Mustapha and A.R. Gamawa, Challenges of Legal Pluralism: Sharia law and its aftermath, in Mustapha and Ehrhardt, *Creed and Grievance*.

no longer able or even committed to protect the security of residents. [103]

Confrontations between Christians and Muslims have often originated and spread within in and from and urban and rural areas as in Kano in 1982. The bloody conflicts in southern Kaduna state, between the Christian Kataf, locally a majority, and the Hausa-Fulani, locally in the minority. They brought out questions of the siting on the town market, land, religious opposition, ethnic difference, political power, virulent representations of the 'other', the partisan regionally-based national press, and turned on differential claims to histories of residence and of 'indigeneity' and death sentences on fourteen Kataf men, including retired General Lekwot, who were subsequently released.[104]

In Jos, the capital of Plateau State, repeated violent conflicts and even planned massacres began in 2001, and cost thousands of lives and extensive destruction. These have been even more complex in their origins, alignments and consequences than elsewhere in Nigeria. Jos includes the town, linked rural areas and mining settlements. It has been a centre for Christian missions and open to 'born again' revivals, and to reformist Islam. *Izala* was founded there in 1958. It is differentiated among local and migrant, ethnic and language groups, Fulani herdsmen, Yorubas and Igbos, each by generation and gender. Political cannot be reduced to land. Higazi writes that in Jos, in the rural areas, and in the

---

[103] Ibrahim, The Politics of Religion'.
[104] Mustapha, 'Ethnicity and Democratization in Nigeria; Case Study of Zangon Kataf,' in J. Ibrahim (ed.), *Expanding Democratic Space in Nigeria* (Dakar, 1994). J. Ibrahim, 'Ethno-religious mobilisation and the sapping of democracy' in Hyslop (ed.) *African Democracy*. W. Adebanwi, *Nation as Grand Narrative: the Nigerian Press and the Politics of Meaning* (Rochester, 2016), pp. 277-90.

abandoned mine settlements, each with their own demographic, cultural, and economic characters, 'the dominant discourses in the conflicts refer to political exclusion on the basis of religion on the Muslim side, and fears of religious and cultural domination, among Plateau Christians.' [105]

The fiscal allocation of economic advantages within as well as between states places an emphasis on certificated 'indigene' status', as decided by local government authorities but signed by ward and district heads. Even then certification did not in practice assure Muslims in Jos of their 'indigene' rights. The demographic ratio between Christians and Muslims was therefore important to the balance between political parties. So were the electoral advantages of incumbency. The political culture in 2011 was 'oriented to ethnic populism and patron-client relationships.'[106]

Kano, Bornu, and elsewhere in Northern Nigeria have been subject to sectarian violence on a large scale. The *Maitatsine* crisis caused over 9,000 deaths across northern Nigeria after 1979. Yahaya Hashim and Judith-Anne Walker describe it as 'mainly a violent attack on security forces and the dominant Muslim population'. [107] Murray Last observes that radical Islamic sects, *Maitatsine* from 1979 and *Boko Haram* from

---

[105] A. Higazi, 'The Jos Crisis: a Current Nigerian Tragedy', (Friedrich Ebert-Stiftung, Abuja, 2/2011), p. 3. See Higazi, 'Rural insecurity on the Jos Plateau: livelihoods, land & cattle amid religious reform & violent conflict' in Mustapha and Ehrhardt, *Creed and Grievance*, Part Three: Jos: Conflict and Peace Building.

[106] Higazi, 'The Jos Crisis'. p. 7.

[107] Murray Last observes that radically Islamic sects, Maitatsine from 1979 and Boko Haram from 1998 attracted and settled 'the disengaged, excluded young' in poor wards of Kano and Maiduguri respectively. M. Last 'The genesis & development of reformist Islamic groups in northern Nigeria' p. 49; also Y. Hashim and J-A Walker, 'Marginal Muslims': Ethnic Identity & the *Umma* in *Kano*', in Mustapha, 'Understanding Boko Haram', *Sects and Social Disorder*, p. 130; Marc-Antoine Peroud de Montclos, 'Boko Haram. Youth mobilization and jihadism' in Mustapha and Ehrhardt, *Creed and Grievance*; P. Lubeck 'Protests under Semi-industrial Capitalism', The Maitatsine Riots in Kano: An Assessment', in J.D.Y. Peel and C. Stewart (eds), *Popular Islam South of the Sahara'* (Manchester, 1985), pp. 76-77.

1998 attracted and settled 'the disengaged, excluded young' in poor wards of Kano and Maiduguri respectively.[108] What are the forms and extent of social exclusion that can recruit followers to sectarian violence? How do the *almajirai* that attend the Quranic schools live and experience their daily lives? Hannah Hoechner tells us of rural and urban poverty, religious outlooks, education and aspirations, and small opportunities in informal enterprises of the *almajirai* in Kano, who are not recruited to religious violence[109] – and the 'moral panic and stark prejudices to which they can give rise. Wole Soyinka writes of the *almajirai* that 'terrorists are deliberately bred, nurtured, sheltered, rendered pliant, obedient to one line of command, ready to be unleashed at the rest of society.' I heard a long and uninterrupted account from a Nigerian academic of 'what the *almajirai* are' – ending with drug smuggling ad providing recruits for *Boko Haram*.

Attributing sectarian violence can turn the answer unto a question. Neither conspiratorial nor single-stranded narratives will be able to make sense of the origins, transformations, and cycles of the violence of the notorious *Boko Haram*. Mustapha outlines its strategies since its first leader, Muhammed Yusuf, was summarily executed in 2009 after 800 people had been killed in violence in Bauchi state. He spells out its means and objectives:

> It has used targeted assassinations, drive-by shootings, suicide bombings, improvised explosive devices (IEDs), and vehicle-born IEDs to spread death and destruction across northern

---

[108] M. Last 'The genesis & development of reformist Islamic groups in northern Nigeria', in Mustapha, *Sects and Social Disorder* p. 49.

[109] H. Höffner, Quranic Schools in Northern Nigeria: everday experiences of youth, faith, and poverty (Cambridge, 2018), 137, Wole Soyinka blamed the *ajmajirai* attending Quranic schools:

Nigeria…The targets have been individuals with whom they disagree on doctrinal or political grounds, schools, churches, mosques belonging to their political opponents, the police, the military, traditional rulers, political leaders (and) symbolic targets.

Military and police have, as elsewhere in Nigeria, combined incompetence with brutality. Youth vigilantes who, together with retired servicemen and local hunters 'cleared Maiduguri of *Boko Haram*, deployed dane guns, talismans, and charms' together with 'cutlasses, swords, knives and bows and arrows' against AK-70s and other weaponry.[110] Mustapha emphasises religious doctrines, poverty and inequality, post-1999 electoral competition, the agency of the youth involved in *Boko Haram*, and the international context.[111]

Institutionalising Ethnic Politics

Nigeria is commonly described in the international press without attention to geography or demography, as divided between 'a mainly Muslim North' and a 'mainly Christian South'. The implication is that regional rivalries or religious antagonisms will explain the all too widespread communal and political violence in Nigeria.

In politics, in the national press, in public life, and within academia, Nigerians are too inclined to represent political and bureaucratic and military elites from other parts of the country as united political blocs subject to the hegemony of the ('northern') Hausa-Fulani oligarchy or as pursuing a 'Yoruba agenda' despite, for example, the historic divisions between Sokoto and Kano, and between political aristocracies and a

---

[110] In Ibadan in 1968-69, farmers and hunters were armed with 'dane guns, *ju-ju* charms and cutlasses.' Beer and Williams. 'Politics of the Ibadan Peasantry', p. 152, and V.

[111] Mustapha, 'Understanding Boko Haram', *Sects and Social Disorder* p. 166, and pp. 147-198.

looser network of power elites centred in Kaduna,[112] or violent conflicts in the former Western Region and political divisions within and between predominantly Yoruba states and political parties. The press and politicians have always been good at counting how many people from other different political or pan-ethnic ethnic groups are represented in official appointments.

The formation and reformation of local, religious, linguistic, ethnic, sub-ethnic, pan-ethnic identities and claims to 'nationhood' have real consequences. They have been constructed, often along the boundaries and institutions laid out by the colonial administrations and the Royal Niger Company. Narratives vary according to who is talking about whom, in what context and to what end? They may be combined into ethno-religious identities, or retain identities within wider formations: in rural Kano, for example, *wangarawa, talakawa, tijaniyya*, Hausa, (*Sunni*) Muslim. Only 'Muslim' can be classified in an order of precedence nor do they contradict one another. Their meaning and significance depends on context. Language is the most common synonym for 'ethnicity'. As the past and recent histories of the Niger Delta show, the borders of languages are not clear to draw and are liable to adapt to changes in economic and political circumstances.[113] Since Samuel Johnson wrote in 1916 his '*History of the Yorubas* from a patriotic motive that the history

---

[112] Shehu Othman, 'Classes, Crises and Coup': the Demise of Shagari's Regime', *African Affairs*, 83 (1984); 'Nigeria: "Power for Profit": Class, Corporatism and Nationalism in the Military' in D.C. O'Brien, J. Dunn, and R. Rathbone (eds), *Contemporary West African States* (Cambridge, 1989).

[113] K. Nwajiaku, Heroes and Villains: Ijaw Narratives of the Nigerian Civil War,' *African Development*, XXXIV, 1, (1) 2009.

of our fatherland might not be lost,'[114] histories have been recovered, and also reinvented to give meaning to the past and legitimacy to the present.

Ike Okonta, informs his research into the tragic 'struggle for self-determination' of the Ogoni with 'a concern to explores the viability of a new "grammar of politics" and development wherein imagined communities like the Ogoni, allowed to run their own affairs while still remaining a part of Nigeria, could bridge the fatal gap between state and society.'[115] Are the grammatical rules too deeply inscribed in the illusory but real system of the state in which the demand for communal representation is primarily a means for élites to claim a share of state resources?

Democracy is an Essentially Contested Concept[116]

In 1997, Jibrin Ibrahim and his colleagues published *Expanding Democratic Space in Nigeria*.[117] It argued that there should be opportunities to open and to defend democratic space in different places and in aspects of the life of Nigerian society, and democratic participation and commitment in public institutions, including universities. Accountability is not then just upwards. It is also downwards.[118] With accountability goes responsibility for consequences. We cannot hold others to account if we do not fulfil our own. Democratic politics is a site of continued contention. It is never accomplished but it can be

---

[114] Rev. S. Johnson, *The History of the Yoruba* ({1916] 11th reprint 2001, CSS Press) Author's Preface.

[115] S.C. Nolutshungu, Fragments of a Democracy: Reflections on Class and Politics in Nigeria," *Third World Quarterly* 30 (1) (1992), p. 101. G. Williams, Democracy as idea and Democracy as Process in Africa, *Journal of African-American History*, 86, 4, 2003.

[116] Williams, Democracy as Idea and Democracy as Process.

[117] J. Ibrahim (ed.) *Expanding Democratic Space in Nigeria* (Dakar, 1997).

[118] B. Beckman, 'Interest Groups and the Construction of Democratic Space, in Ibrahim (ed.) *Expanding Democratic Space*.

striven for. As Max Weber said, in Munich on 28 January 1919, 'Politics is a slow boring of hard boards.'[119]

---

[119] Weber, 'Politics as a Vocation', {1918, published 1999, London, 1948), p. 128.

Bibliography

A Midwestern Nigeria Publication, *Farmers Crusade Project* (n.d., c. 1972)

Abasiekong, E.M., 'Peasants and the Economic Man Model: Are Nigerian Peasants Economic Men?' *SAN* 17, (1975);

Abdulraheem, T. *et al.* (eds), Oil, Debts and Democracy in Nigeria, *ROAPE*, 37 (1987);

Aboyade, O. A. *Revenue Allocation Formula in Nigeria*, 1978.

Abrams, P., 'Notes on the Difficulty of Studying the State' (1977) *Journal of Historical Sociology*, 1, 1 1988.

Action Group, Democratic Socialism. Being the Manifesto of the Action Group of Nigeria (Lagos 1960).

Adamolekun, O. O. (ed.), *Nigerian Public Administration, 1960-1980* (Heinemann, Ibadan, 1985)

Adebanwi, W. and Obadare, E. (eds), *Democracy and Prebendalism in Nigeria* (New York, 2012).

Adebanwi, W., *Nation as Grand Narrative: the Nigerian Press and the Politics of Meaning* (Rochester, 2016).

Adegboye and Alao, 'Some Socio-Economic Factors,' *BRES*, 7, 2.

Adegboye, A. C. Basu and Olatunbosun, 'Impact of Farm Settlements on Surrounding Farmers,' NJESS 11, 2 (1969).

Adegboye, R.O. and J. A. Alao, 'Some Socio-Economic Factors Influencing Farmers, Participation in the Western Nigeria Cocoa Pilot Project,' *BRES*, 7, 2. (1972) pp. 235–6

Adegboye, R.O., 'Redemption of Pledged Property through Rural Credit,' *NES*, pp. 181-182.

Adeniran, T., 'The Dynamics of Peasant Revolt in the Western State of Nigeria: a Conceptual Analysis,' *Journal of Black Studies* (1974).

Adesimi, A. 'An Econometric Study of Air-cured Tobacco Supply in Western Nigeria, 1945-64' *Nigerian Journal of Economic and Social Studies*, (NJESS) 12, 3 (1970) p. 315

Afigbo, A. *The Warrant Chiefs* (London, 1972);

Aguolu, C. C., *Nigerian Civil War, 1967-70*, An Annotated Bibliography (Boston, 1973).

Bello, Ahmadu, *My Life* (London, 1960)

Ajayi, J.F.A., *Christian Missionaries in Nigeria, 1841-91* (London, 1965)

Ake, C. (ed.), *Political Economy of Nigeria* (Longman, London, 1985);

Ake, C., `Indigenization: Problems of Transformation in a Neo-colonial Political Economy' in Ake (ed.), *Political Economy of Nigeria* (Longman, London, 1985);

Akeredolu-Ale, O. *The Underdevelopment of Indigenous Entrepreneurship in Nigeria* (Ibadan, 1975)

Akeredolu-Ale, O. 'Private Foreign Investment and the Underdevelopment of Indigenous Entrepreneurship in Nigeria,' in Williams, (ed.), *Nigeria: Economy and Society* (London, 1975).

Akeredolu-Ale, O. 'The Competitive Threshold Hypothesis and Nigeria's Industrialisation Process,' (review of Kilby, Industrialisation), *Nigerian Journal of Economic and Social Studies*, (*NJESS*) 14 (1972).

Akinjogbin, I. A., 'The Oyo Empire in the Eighteenth Century,' *Journal of the Historical Society of Nigeria,* (JHSN), 3 (1966), pp. 458-9.

Aladejana, A., *The Marketing Board System: A Bibliography* (Ibadan, 1971)

Alao, 'Increasing Food Productivity in West Africa through Improved Technology: The Human Factor,' *WAJAE*, 1, 1 (1972).

Alavi, H., 'Peasants and Revolution,' *Socialist Register* (1965).

Alavi, H., 'The Post-Colonial State,' *NLR*, 74 (1972).

Albert, I., 'Ife-Modakeke Crisis,' in O. Otite and I. Albert (eds) *Community Conflict in Nigeria: Management, Resolution, and Transformation* (Ibadan, 1999)

Allen, C.H. and Johnson, R.W. (eds), *African Perspectives: Papers in the History, Politics and Economics of Africa: Presented to Thomas Hodgkin* (Cambridge 1970).

Allen, C. and Williams, G. (eds.), *The Sociology of Developing Societies: Sub-Saharan Africa* (New York 1982);

Allen, C. H., 'Unions, Incomes and Development,' *Developmental Trends in Kenya* (Centre for African Studies, Edinburgh, 1972)

Amsden, Alice H., *Asia's Next Giant. South Korea and late industrialization* (Oxford, 1992).

Amuwo, K. *et al.,* (eds) *Federalism and Political Restructuring in Nigeria* (Ibadan, 1998).

Andrae, G. and Beckman, B., *Union Power in the Nigerian Textile Industry: Labour Regime and Adjustment* (Uppsala; Kano 1998).

Anthonio, 'Costs and Returns: A Study of Upland Paddy Production under Traditional Farming Conditions of the Wasimi and Ilaro Areas of the Western State of Nigeria,' *WAJAE*, 1, 1 (1972)

Are, L., 'An Assessment of some Plantation Problems in Western Nigeria,' *Tropical Agriculture*, 41, 1 (1964), p. 3;

Arrighi, G. and Saul, J., 'Socialism and Economic Development in Tropical Africa,' *JMAS*, 6 (1968)

Arrighi, G. 'International Corporations, Labour Aristocracies and Economic Development in Tropical Africa,' in Rhodes, R. (ed.) *Imperialism and Underdevelopment* (New York, 1970)

Arrighi, G. and Saul, A., *The Political Economy of Tropical Africa* (New York, 1972)

Asiodu, P.C., 'Industrial Policy and Incentives in Nigeria,' (NJESS) 9 (1967),

Asiyanbola, R.A., 'Ethnic Conflict in Nigeria: a Case of Ife-Modakeke in Historical Perspective,' *ASSET:* An International Journal of Agricultural Sciences, Sciences, Environment and Technology, 4 1 (2010).

Atanda, J. A. 'The Iseyin-Okeiho Rising of 1916,' *JHSN*, 4 (1969).

Atanda, J. A., *The New Oyo Empire: Indirect Rule and Change in Western Nigeria, 1896-1934.* (London, 1975)

Atanda, *The New Oyo Empire*, Longman, 1973

Atta, A. 'The Development of Nigeria's Political Personality,' *Quarterly Journal of Administration* (*QJA*) 6 (1971).

Awolowo, O., *Awo* (Cambridge, 1960)

Ayandele, E. A., *Holy Johnson* (London, 1970).

Ayandele, E.A., *The Missionary Impact on Modern Nigeria, 1842-1914* (London, 1966)

Ayida, A. A. and. Onitiri, H.M.A., eds. *Reconstruction and Development in Nigeria*. Proceedings of a 1969 National Conference. Ibadan: Oxford University Press.

Ayida, A., A., The Nigerian Revolution, 1966-76,' Presidential Address to Nigerian Economic Society, 1971 (Ibadan, 1973).

Ayida, A.A., *Reflections on Nigerian Development* (Malthouse, Lagos, 1987).

Aylmer, G., *The State's Servants: The Civil Service of the English Republic*, 1649-1660 (Oxford, 1973).

Azikiwe, N., My Odyssey: an Autobiography (London, 1971).

Bach, D. and Gazibo, M. (eds), *Neo-patrimonialism in African States* (Cambridge 1982)

Baldwin, K.D.S., The Niger Agricultural Project: an experiment in African development (Oxford, 1957);

Bangura, Yusuf, 'Structural Adjustment and the Political Question,' in *ROAPE* 37.

Baptiste, F. A., 'The Relations between the Western Region and the Federal Government of Nigeria' (M.A. thesis, University of Manchester, 1965).

Barnett, A.S., 'The Gezira Scheme: Production of Cotton and the Reproduction of Underdevelopment,' Taylor & Francis Ltd, 2013

Bauer, P.T., *West African Trade* (Cambridge, 1954).

Bauer, West African Trade; H. C. Kriesel, Marketing of Groundnuts in Nigeria, Cocoa Marketing in Nigeria, Cotton Marketing in Nigeria (East Lansing and Ibadan, 1968-69)

Baumann, H. Connolly, C. and Whitney, J. 'A Situation Report on Agricultural Credit in Nigeria,' *CSNRD* 3 (1966)

Bayart, J. F., *The State in Africa* (London, 1989, 1993, 2009).

Beckman, B. , and J. Lonsdale, 'Moral ethnicity and political tribalism,' *Unhappy Valley* (London 1972).

Beckman, B. and Andrae, G., *The Wheat Trap: Bread and Underdevelopment in Nigeria* (London 1985).

Beckman, B. , 'Bakalori: Peasants versus State and Capital,' *Nigerian Journal of Political Science*, 4, 1-2 (1985).

Beckman, B. , 'Interest Groups and the Construction of Democratic Space, in Ibrahim (ed.) *Expanding Democratic Space*, Dakar, 1997

Beckman, B., Eyoh, D. and Kymlicka, W.(eds.), *Ethnicity and Democracy in Africa* (Oxford 2004).

Beckman, B., Review of Williams (ed.), *Nigeria: Economy and Society*, *Review of African Political Economy* 10 (1978);

Beer and Williams, 'The Politics of the Ibadan Peasantry' in The African Review, 5 (1976)

Beer, C.E.F., 'The Farmers and the State in Western Nigeria,' (Ph.D., University of Ibadan, (1971)

Beer, C.E.F., *The Politics of Peasant Groups in Western Nigeria* (Ibadan University Press, 1976)

Beer, S. S., Cocoa, Custom and Socio-Economic Change 'Christianity and the Rise of Cocoa Growing Ibadan and Ondo,' *JHSN*, 4 (1968),

Bernstein, H. (ed.), *Underdevelopment and Development: the Third World Today* (Harmondsworth, 1973).

Berry, *Cocoa, Custom and Socio-Economic Change, and Fathers Work for their Sons: Accumulation, Mobility, and Class Formation in an Extended Yoruba Community* (Berkeley, 1985)

Berry, S*., Cocoa, Custom and Socio-Economic Change in Rural Western Nigeria* (Oxford, 1975), p. 28.

Biersteker, T., *Multinationals, The State, and Control of the Nigerian Economy* (Princeton University Press, 1987)

Bourdillon, B., 'Address to the British Empire Society,' *West Africa*, 30 Jan. 1937

Bray, J.M. 'The Industrial Structure of a Traditional Yoruba Town' (Ph.D thesis, University of Ibadan, 1966).

Brett, E.A., *Capitalism and Underdevelopment in East Africa: the Politics of Economic Change, 1919-1939* (Heinemann, 1973);

Bukharin and Preobrazhensky, *The ABC of Communism* ({1920} Harmondsworth, 1969)

Buntjer, B. 'Whom to Blame: The Farmer or the Extension Workers,' *SAN*, 14, 1 (1972);

Buntjer, B., 'Aspects of Change in rural Zaria,' *SAN*, vol. 12, 2 (1970).

Buxton, Thomas Fowell, *The African Slave Trade and Its Remedy* (London, 1839).

Byerlee, D., 'Indirect Employment and Income Distribution Effects on Agricultural Development Strategies,' *AREP*, 6 (1973).

Chayanov, A. V., *The Theory of Peasant Economy* ({1923} London, 1991),

Clapham, C., *The Nature of the Third World State* (Madison, 1985).

Clarke, I. and Linden, P., *Islam in Modern Nigeria: A Study of a Moslem Community in a Post-Independent State*, (Mainz, 1984).

Clough, P., *Morality and Economic Growth in Rural West Africa: Indigenous Accumulation in Hausaland* (New York/Oxford, 2114)

Cohen, *Labour and Politics in Nigeria* (London, 1975).

Coleman, J.S. *Nigeria: Background to Nationalism* (Berkeley, 1958).

Collins, P., 'Public Policy and the Development of Indigenous Capitalism,' *Journal of Comparative and Commonwealth Studies*, 15, 2 (1977)

Collins, P., 'Public Policy and the Development of Indigenous Capitalism,' *Journal of Comparative and Commonwealth Political Studies* 19, 1997

Collins, P., 'The Political Economy of Indigenization,' *The African Review*, 4 (1975)

Cooke, W. (ed.), *Power and Development* (London, 1995)

Corrigan, P.R.D., 'State Formation and Moral Regulation in 19th Century Britain' (PhD thesis, University of Durham, 1977)

Corrigan, P.R.D., Ramsay, H. and Sayer, D., *Socialist Construction and Marxist Theory* (London, 1978).

Cowen and Shenton, 'The Origins and Course of Fabian Colonialism in Africa,' *Journal of Historical Sociology* 4, 2 (1991), pp. 143-74.

Cowen, M. P. and Shenton, R.W., *Doctrines of Development* (London, 1975).

Crowder, M. and Ikime, O.,(eds.) *West African Chiefs*, University of Ife, Institute of African Studies, Africana Pub. Corp. New York, 1970

Daily Times of Nigeria, *The First Ten Years, Independent Nigeria* (Lagos, 1970)

de Kadt, E. and Williams, G. (eds) *Sociology and Development* (London, 1974, 2001).

Dent, M. 'A Minority Party: The United Middle Belt Congress,' in Mackintosh, Nigerian Government and Politics, Allen & Unwin (Jun. 1966)

Deutsch, J.G. 'Educating the Middleman: Political and Economic History of Statutory Colonial Marketing in Nigeria,' Ph. D. thesis, 1990 , Part VI.

Diamond, L., Kirk-Greene, A.H.M., Oyediran, O. (eds), *Transition without End: Nigerian Politics and Civil Society under Babangida* (Boulder, CO 1997)

Dike, K. O., *Trade and Politics in the Niger Delta, 1830-85* (Oxford, 1956).

Dudley, B.J., 'Federalism and the Balance of Political Power in Nigeria,' *Journal of Commonwealth Political Studies*, 4 (1966);

Dudley, B.J., *An Introduction to Nigerian Government and Politics* (Macmillan, London, 1982)

Dudley, B.J., *Instability and Political Order- Politics and Crisis in Nigeria* (Ibadan, 1973);

Dudley, B.J., *Parties and Politics in Northern Nigeria* (London, 1968)

Duffield, Ian, 'The Business Activities of Duse Mohammed Ali,' *JHSN*, 4 (1969).

Dunn, John ed., *West African States: Failure and Promise* (Cambridge University Press, 1978)

Durkheim, E., *Rules of Sociological Method* {1895} (New York, 1982), p. 35.

Durkheim, E., *The Division of Labour in Society*, (New York, 1964).

Ebong, I. J., 'Nigerian Social Objectives and the Rural Sector,' Rural Development in Nigeria (Proceedings of the 1972 Annual Conference of the Nigerian Economic Society (NES), Ibadan, 1973.

Eicher, C.K. and Liedholm, C. (eds) *Growth and Development of the Nigerian Economy*, East Lansing, 1970,

Ekeh, P., 'Colonialism and the Two Publics in Africa,' *Comparative Studies in Society and History*, 17 (1975).

Engels, F., 'The Peasant Question in France and Germany,' ({Neue Zeit, 1894-1895} 1894), *Selected Works*, vol. 3, and in (CW 28);

Engels, F., Feuerbach, Opposition of the Materialistic and Idealistic Ideology, *German Ideology* I, ch. 1, (illusorischen gemeinschaftlichen Interessen, translated as 'general interest).

Essang and A. F. Mawabonku, 'Determinants and Implications of Rural-Urban Migration: A Case Study of Selected Communities in Western Nigeria,' *NRDS*, 10 and *AREP* 10 (1974).

Essang and Ogunfowora, 'Plantation Agriculture and Labour Use in Southern Nigeria,' *NRDS*, 15 (1975);

Essang, S.M. and Olayide, S.O., 'Economic Development or Income Distribution?' A False Dilemma,' *NJSA*, 1 (1974).

Essang, S.M. 'Agricultural Development and Employment Generation in Nigeria,' *NRDS*, 2 (1972), p. 2.

Essang, S.M. 'Institutional Arrangements and Income Distribution in a Primary Export Economy,' *BRES* 6, 2 (1971) pp. 210-211.

Essang, S.M. 'The Land Surplus Notion and Nigerian Agricultural Development Policy,' *WAJAE*, 2, 1 (1973).

Eyoh, D. and Kymlicka, W. (eds.), *Ethnicity and Democracy in Africa* (Oxford 2004).

Fadipe, N. A., *The Sociology of the Yoruba*, ed. F. O. and Okediji, O.O., (Ibadan, 1970) p. 150.

Falusi, B., 'Multivariate Probit Analysis of Selected Factors Influencing Fertilizer Adoption among Farmers in Western Nigeria,' *NJESS*, 16, 1, (1974).

Famoriyo, O., 'An appraisal of Farm Tenancy Problems in Ife Division,' M. A. Thesis University of Ibadan, 1969).

Fanon, F., *The Wretched of the Earth* [(1961) London, 1966]

Fayemi, A. 'Problems of Agricultural Production in Nigeria and How to Solve them,' Inaugural Lecture, (University of Ibadan, 1972–73)

Federal Government of Nigeria, *Guidelines to the Third National Development Plan, 1975-80* (Lagos, 1973), pp. 68-73.

Federal Government of Nigeria, National Accelerated Food Production Programme, *Third Plan*, pp. 69-73.

Federal Government of Nigeria, *The National Development Plan*, Lagos, 1973.

Federal Government of Nigeria, *The Second National Development Plan*. Lagos, 1970. The plan was critically reviewed in QJA 5, 3 (1971).

Federal Government, Statement of (sic!) Angola, 6 January, 1976, *Nigerian Bulletin on Foreign Affairs*, 6, 1 (1976), p. 2.

Federation of Nigeria, Report of the Commission of Enquiry into the Affairs of Certain Statutory Corporations in Western Nigeria (Chairman: Mr Justice Coker) (Lagos, 1962).

Feldman, D. 'The Economics of Ideology,' in Leys, C. (ed.), *Politics and Change in Developing Countries* (Cambridge, 1969).

Fine, J. C., 'A Re-appraisal of Some Common Assumptions about Agricultural Development in Nigeria,' *Samaru Agricultural Newsletter (SAN)*, 10, 5 (1968).

First, R., *Libya* (Harmondsworth, 1974).

First, R., *The Barrel of a Gun: Power in Africa* (London, 1972)

Forrest, T., The Advance of African Capital: the Growth of Nigerian Private Enterprise (Edinburgh 1986).

Frank, A. G., *Capitalism and Underdevelopment in Latin America* (Harmondsworth, 1967).

Frantz Fanon, *The Wretched of the Earth* ({1963} London, 1966).

Freund, W., *Capital and Labour in the Nigerian Tin Mines* (London 1981),

Freund, W., South Africa as a Developmental State? Changes in the social structure since the end of apartheid and the emergence of the BEE elite,' *Review of African Political Economy* 114 (2012);

Freund, W., *The African Worker* (Cambridge 1988)

Freund, W., *The Making of Contemporary Africa: The Development of African Society since 1800* (Cambridge, 2nd. ed. 1998) add 3rd ed.

Freund, W., *Twentieth-Century South Africa – A Development History* (Cambridge University Press, 2019).

Galetti, R., Baldwin, K.D.S. and Dina, I.O., *Nigerian Cocoa Farmers* (London, 1956);

Garba, Col J. N., Commissioner for External Affairs, to the General Assembly of the United Nations, 7 October, 1975, *Nigerian Bulletin on Foreign Affairs*, 5, 3 and 4 (1975), p. 2.

Gerry, C. and Lebrun, O., 'Petty Producers and Capitalism,' *ROAPE*, 3 (1975);

Gerschenkron, A., *Economic Backwardness in Historical Perspective* (Cambridge MA, 1962)

Gerth, H.H. and C. Wright Mills (eds) *From Max Weber: Essays in Sociology* (New York, 1946, London, 2008),

Girvan, N., 'The Development of Dependency Economics in the Caribbean and Latin America: Review and comparison,' *Social and Economic Studies*, 22, 1973.

Goddard, A.D. 'Changing Family Structures Among the Rural Hausa,' *Africa*, 73, 3, (1973), SRB, 196

Gowon, General, 1974 Budget Speech, *Daily Times*, 2 April, 1974.

Gramsci, A., *Selections from the Prison Notebooks* (London, 1971).

Gutkind, P., Cohen, R. and Copans, J, (eds) *African Labour History* (Beverly Hills and London, 1979)

Gutkind, P.C.W. and Wallerstein, I. (eds), *The Political Economy of Contemporary Africa* (Los Angeles, 1976/1985).

Gutkind, P.C.W. and Waterman, P. (eds), *African Social Studies- A Radical Reader*, Monthly Review Press, 1977

Guyer, J., 'An African Niche Economy: An Essay on Democracy in Rural Nigeria, 1952-1990,' *African Studies Review*, 36 (1997); and

Guyer, J., 'Representation Without Taxation: An Essay on Democracy in Rural Nigeria,' *African Studies Review* 36 (1992).

Guyer, J., Farming to Feed Ibadan (Oxford 1997)

Guyer, J., Representation without Taxation: An Essay on Democracy in Rural Nigeria, 1952-1990, *African Studies Review*, 35, 1(1992).

Hailey, Lord, *Africa Survey* (Oxford, 1940).

Hancock, W.K., *A Survey of British Commonwealth Affairs*, vol. 2, part 2 (Oxford, 1942)

Hargreaves, J., 'The Loaded Pause,' *JHSN*, 7 (1974)

Hargreaves, J., *Prelude to the Partition of West Africa* (London, 1963),

Harriss, B., Cereal Surpluses in the Sudan-Sahelian States (*ICRISAT*, Hyderabad and School of Development Studies, Norwich, 1978).

Hayter, T., *Aid as Imperialism* (Harmondsworth, 1971);

Helleiner, G.K., Peasant Agriculture, Government and Economic Growth in Nigeria (Homewood, Ill, 1966)

Helleiner, G.K., The Fiscal Role of the Marketing Boards in Nigerian Economic Development 1947-1961, Economic Journal, 74, 295 (1964)

Heyer, J., Roberts, P. and Williams, G. (eds), *Rural Development in Tropical Africa* (Basingstoke, 1982).

Higazi, A., 'The Jos Crisis: a Current Nigerian Tragedy,' (Friedrich Ebert-Stiftung, Abuja, 2/2011), p. 3.

Hill, P., *Rural Hausa- a village and setting* (Cambridge, 1972)

Hill, P., *Studies in Rural Capitalism* (Cambridge, 1970)

Hinchcliffe, K. 'Labour Aristocracy – A Northern Nigerian Case Study,' *JMAS*, 12 (1974).

Hodgkin, T., *Nationalism in Colonial Africa* (London, 1956)

Hodgkin, T.L., 'The African Middle Class,' Corona 8 (1956)

Huffner, H., Quranic Schools in Northern Nigeria: everyday experiences of youth, faith, and poverty (Cambridge, 2018)

Hogendorn, J., "The Origin of the Groundnut trade in Northern Nigeria," Ph. D. Thesis University of London, (1966)

Hoogvelt, A. 'Indigenization in Kano,' *ROAPE*, 14 (1980).

Hopkins, A. G. *An Economic History of West Africa* (London, 1973).

Hopkins, A. G., 'Economic Aspects of Political Movements in Nigeria and the Gold Coast, 1918-39,' *Journal of African History*, 7 (1966)

Hopkins, A. G.,' The Lagos Strike of 1897,' *Past and Present*, 35 (1966);

Horowitz, D.I., *A Democratic South Africa: constitutional engineering in a divided society*. Berkeley, 1971

Hughes, A. and Cohen, R. 'An Emerging Nigerian Working Class: The Lagos Experience, 1897-1939,' in Gutkind, P., Cohen, R. and Copans, J, (eds) *African Labour History* (Beverly Hills and London, 1979);

Hutton, C. and Cohen, R., 'African Peasants and the Resistance to Change' in Oxaal, *et al.*, *Beyond the Sociology of Development* (London 1975)

Hyslop, Jonathan (ed.), African Democratisation in an Era of Globalisation (Johannesburg, 1999).

I.L.O. Mission, 'Draft of a Preliminary Request'; Essang, 'Agricultural Development and Employment Generation in Nigeria,' *NRDS*, 2.

Ibrahim, J. (ed.) *Expanding Democratic Space in Nigeria* (Dakar, 1997).

Ibrahim, J.I., 'Ethno-religious mobilisation and the sapping of democracy' in Hyslop (ed.) African Democratisation in an Era of Globalisation (Johannesburg, 1999).

Ibrahim, Jibrin, 'The Politics of Religion in Nigeria: the Parameters of the 1987 Crisis in Kaduna State,' *ROAPE*, 45, 46 (1989), p. 65, and pp. 65-82.

Idachaba, F. S., 'The "Demonstration Effect" of Farm Institutes and Settlements: Theory and Evidence,' *BRES*, 8, 2;

Idusogie, E. O., Olayide and Olatunbosun, 'Implications of Agricultural Wastes on Nigerian Nutrition and Economy,' *BRES* 8, 2 (1973) pp. 258-259

Ijose, A. and Abaelu, J. N., 'Institutional Credit for Small Holder Farmers: A Case Study of the Western Nigerian Agricultural Credit Corporations'

Ikime, O. and Osoba, S.O., 'Indirect Rule in British Africa,' *Tarikh*, 3, 3 (New York, 1970)

Ikime, O., 'Reconsidering Indirect Rule,' *JHSN*, 4 (1968)

Ikime, O., *Merchant Prince of the Niger Delta* (London, 1968)

International Bank for Reconstruction and Development (IBRD), *The Economic Development of Nigeria* (Baltimore 1955)

International Monetary Fund, *Survey of African Economics*, vol. 6 (Washington D.C., 1975).

J. de St Jorre, *The Nigerian Civil War* (Hodder and Stoughton, London, 1972)

Jackson, C., 'Hausa Women on Strike,' *ROAPE* 13, 1978

Jeffries, R., 'Labour Aristocracy? A Ghana Case Study,' *ROAPE*, 3 (1975)

Jeffries, R., *Class, Power and Ideology in Ghana: The Railwaymen of Sekondi* (Cambridge, 1978).

Jega, Attahiru, *Democracy, Good Governance and Democracy In Nigeria* (Ibadan, 2007)

Jinadu, A., Olagunju, T. and Oyovbaire, S. (eds), *Transition to Democracy in Nigeria* (Ibadan, 1997).

Johnson, C., MITI and the Japanese Miracle, 1925-1975 (Palo Alto, CA, 1982), p. 19;

Johnson, C., *Who Governs? The Rise of the Developmental State* (London, 1996).

Johnson, G.L. *et al.*, Strategies and Recommendations for Nigerian Rural Development, 1969-1986, *CSNRD* (Lagos and East Lansing, 1969) http://pdf.usaid.gov/pdf_docs/PNAAE469.pdf

Johnson, M.. 'Cotton Imperialism in West Africa,' *African Affairs*, 291 (1974).

Johnson, Samuel (Rev) *History of the Yoruba: from the Earliest Times to the Beginning of the British Protectorate* ({ed. O. Johnson, 1921}, London 2010).

Jolly, R. *et al. Third World Employment* (Harmondsworth, 1973).

Jolly, R. *et al.*, *Third World Employment* (Harmondsworth, 1973).

Jones, T. L. *et al.*, 'A Proposed Agricultural Credit Programme for Nigeria,' *CSNRD*, 4 (1966)

Jones, G.I., The Trading States of the Oil Rivers (Oxford, 1963)

Jones, W. O., 'Measuring the Effectiveness of Agricultural Marketing in Contributing to African Development,' *Food Research Institute Studies* (*FRIS*) 9, 3 (1970)

Joseph, R., 'Class, State, and Prebendal Politics in Nigeria,' *Journal of Comparative and Commonwealth Politics*, 21 (1983);

Joseph, R., 'Political Parties and Ideology in Nigeria,' *ROAPE*, 13 (1979).

Joseph, R., *Democracy and Prebendal Politics in Nigeria: the Rise and Fall of the Second Republic* (Cambridge, 1987)

Kane, O., *Muslim Modernity Postcolonial Nigeria: A Study of the Society for the Removal of Innovation and Reinstatement of Tradition* (Leiden, 2003).

Kautsky, K., *The Agrarian Question* (1894)

Kay, G., 'Introduction' to *The Political Economy of Colonialism in Ghana* (Cambridge, 1972).

Kayode, M.O. and Otobo, D. (eds), *Allison Akene Ayida: the Quintessential Public Servant* (Malthouse, Lagos, 1984)

Kilby, P., *Industrialisation in an Open Economy: Nigeria 1945-66* (Cambridge, 1969).

King, R., Co-operative Policy and Village Development in Northern Nigeria,' in Heyer, J., Roberts, P. and Williams, G. (eds), *Rural Development in Tropical Africa* (Basingstoke, 1982)

King, R., *Farmers Co-operatives in Northern Nigeria*, Institute for Agricultural Research, Zaria, 1976)

Kirk-Greene, A.M.H. (ed.), *Crisis and Conflict in Nigeria: a Documentary Sourcebook, 1966-70* (2 vols.) (London, 1971)

Kolawole, M., 'Mechanization of the Small Farm: Possibilities and Problem,' *WAJAE* 1, 1 (1972);

Koll, M., *Crafts and Co-operation in Western Nigeria* (Freiburg, 1969)

Kriesel, *Cocoa Marketing in Nigeria*, *Consortium for the Study of Nigerian Rural Development*, East Lancing and Ibadan, 1969.

Laurent, C. K. et. al. 'Agricultural Investment Strategy in Nigeria,' *CSNRD*, 26 (1969), p. 23.

Law, R. (ed.), *From Slave Trade to 'Legitimate' Commerce: The commercial transition in nineteenth-century West Africa* (Cambridge, 1995).

Lenin, "On Cooperation", in Lenin, *Collected Works*, vol. 33 ({1923} Moscow, 1960).

Lenin, *Imperialism, The Highest Stage of Capitalism* (1916) in *Selected Works* (in one vol.) (Moscow, 1968) p. 215.

Lenin, V.I., 'Preface' (1907) to Development of Capitalism, and The Agrarian Programme of Social Democracy in the First Russian Evolution vol. 14 (1907)

Lenin, V.I., The Development of Capitalism in Russia {1899} (*Collected Works*, vol. 3, p. 177).

Lenin, What is to be Done? ({1902}, Oxford 1962, and in *Collected Works*, vol. 5. (Moscow, 1970).

Lewis, W.A., *Reflections on Nigeria's Economic Growth* (Paris, 1967)

Leys, C. (ed.), *Politics and Change in Developing Countries* (Cambridge, 1969).

Leys, C., 'Capital Accumulation, Class Formation and Dependency. The Significance of the Kenyan Case,' *Socialist Register* (1978)

Leys, C., *Underdevelopment in Kenya* (London 1975)

Lloyd, P.C., 'Craft Organization in Yoruba Towns,' *Africa*, 23 (1953)

Lloyd, P.C., 'Integration,' 'Local Government in Yoruba Towns' (D.Phil, University of Oxford, 1958); Post and Jenkins, Price of Liberty. Part III.

Lloyd, P.C., 'The Integration of New Economic Classes into Local Government in Western Nigeria,' *African Affairs*, 53 (1953).

Lloyd, P.C., *Power and Independence: Urban Africans' Perceptions of Social Inequality* (London, 1974).

Loimeier, R., *Islamic Reform and Political change in Northern Nigeria* (Evanston, IL, 1997)

Lubeck, P. 'Protests under Semi-industrial Capitalism,' The Maitatsine Riots in Kano: An Assessment,' in Peel, J.D.Y. and C. Stewart (eds), *Popular Islam South of the Sahara* (Manchester, 1985), pp. 76-77.

Lubeck, P., 'Labour in Kano since the Petroleum Boom,' *ROAPE*, 13 (1979).

Lubeck, P., 'Unions, Workers and Consciousness in Kano,' and 'Economic Security' in Sandbrook, R. and Cohen, R. (eds). *The Development of an African Working Class* (London, 1976).

Lubeck, P., *Islam and Urban Labour in Northern Nigeria: the Making of an Islamic Working Class* (Cambridge, 1986).

Luckham, R., *The Nigerian Military* (Cambridge, 1971)

Lugard, F., 'The Extension of British Influence (and Trade) in Africa,'
    Proceedings, Royal Colonial Institute, 27 (1896), p. 7.
Lugard, *The Dual Mandate in British Tropical Africa* (London, 1922)
Lukpata, V.I., 'Revenue Allocation Formulae in Nigeria: a Continuous
    Search,' International Journal of Public Administration and
    Management Research, 2, 2 (2013), p. 35.
M. Watts, *Silent Violence: Food, Family and Peasantry in Northern
    Nigeria* (Berkeley 1983);
M. Woo-Cummings, *The Developmental State* (Ithaca NY, 1999);
Mackintosh, J.P. *Nigerian Government and Politics* (London, 1966)
Mackintosh, John, *Nigerian Government and Politics*, Allen & Unwin
    (Jun. 1966)
Madunagu, E., Forces in the current power struggle in Nigeria,
    Pambazuka News, 29 June 2018
Mannheim, K., *Ideology and Utopia* (London, 1940).
Mao Zedong (Tse-tung), 'Analysis of Classes in Chinese Society,' *Selected
    Works*, vol. 1 (Peking, 1965).
Mars, J., 'Extra-territorial Enterprises' in M. Perham (ed.), *Mining,
    Commerce and Finance in Nigeria* (London, 1948);
Marshall, R., *Political Spiritualities: the Pentecostal Revolution in Nigeria*
    (Chicago, 2009)
Marx and Engels, *The German Ideology* ({1846})
Marx and Engels, *The Manifesto of the Communist Party*, and the
    Prefaces.
Marx, K., 'Preface' to A Contribution to the Critique of Political
    Economy ({1859} CW, 29) pp. 263-4),
Marx, K., 'Preface' to the Russian Edition of the Manifesto of the
    Communist Party ({1882} (CW 29), (MW 45)
Marx, K., *Capital*, 1976, vols. 1
Marx, K., The Future Results of British Rule in India' {22 July 1853})
    'Preface' to the first German edition of Capital, vol. 1 ({1867}
    Harmondsworth, 1976) p. 91, in Marx, K. and Engels, F., *Collected
    Writings*, (CW, vols. 12, 32a)
Marx, The Eighteenth Brumaire of Louis Bonaparte (1852).
Mason, E.S. and Asher, R.E., *The World Bank Since Bretton Woods*
    (Washington, 1973);

McFadzean, Sir Frank, Chairman of Shell, Preface to their 1976 Annual Report, *Financial Times*, 14 May 1976.

McLellan, D., *Karl Marx: Selected Writing*, 2nd ed. (Oxford, 2000)

McPhee, A., *The Economic Revolution in British West Africa* (London, 1926).

Meillasoux, C., 'Introduction' to *The Development of Indigenous Trade and Markets in West Africa* (Oxford, 1971).

Melson and Wolpe (eds), Nigeria, Panter-Brick (ed.), *Nigerian Politics and Military Rule: Prelude to Civil War* (London, 1970)

Melson, R. and H. Wolpe (eds) *Nigeria: Modernization and the Politics of Communalism* (East Lansing 1972)

Mkandawire, T*., Thinking About Development States in Africa*, United Nations University (1996).

Moore, B., *The Social Origins of Dictatorship and Democracy* (New York, 1966)

Mosley, P., J. Harragin, and J. Toye, *The Politics of Aid: the World Bank and Policy-based Lending*, vol. 1. (Oxford 2009).

Muhammed, Gen. Murtala, Address to the Extraordinary Summit Conference of the Organization of African Unity, 11 January, 1976, in *Nigerian Bulletin on Foreign Affairs*, 6, 1 (1976), p. 10.

Mustapha, A. R. 'Ethnicity and the Politics of Democratization in Nigeria,' in B. Berman, D. Eyoh, and W. Kymlicka, (eds.), *Ethnicity and Democracy in Africa* (Oxford 2004).

Mustapha, A. R., and M.U. Bunza, 'Contemporary Islamic Sects & Groups in Northern Nigeria,' in Mustapha A.R.,(ed.), *Sects and Social Disorder: Muslim Identities and Conflicts in Northern Nigeria* (Woodbridge, 2014).

Mustapha, A.R. and Ehrhardt, D. eds, *Creed and Grievance Muslim-Christian Relations & Conflict Resolution in Nigeria*. 2018.

Mustapha, A.R. and Gamawa, A.R., Challenges of Legal Pluralism: Sharia law and its aftermath, in Mustapha, A.R. and Ehrhardt, D., *Creed and Grievance Muslim-Christian Relations & Conflict Resolution in Nigeria*. 2018,

Mustapha, A.R., 'Ethnicity and Democratization in Nigeria; Case Study of Zangon Kataf," in J. Ibrahim (ed.), *Expanding Democratic Space in Nigeria* (Dakar, 1994).

Nadel, S. F., 'The Concept of Social Elites,' *International Social Science Bulletin*, 8 (1956).

Nduka, O., 'The Anatomy of Rationalization,' *Nigerian Opinion*, 7, 1 (1971)

Nduka, O., Western Education and the Nigerian Cultural Background (Ibadan, 1964)

Newlyn, W. T., 'A Study of Costs of Mechanized Agriculture in Nigeria,' West African Institute of Social and Economic Development (WAISER), (n.d., c. 1954);

Nigeria, Public Service Review Commission: Main Report and Government Views on the Report of the Public Service Commission (Chairman: J. Udoji)) (Lagos, 1974),

Nigeria, Report of the Advisory Committee on Aids to African Businessmen (Lagos, 1959).

Nigeria, Second and Final Report of the Wages and Salaries Review Commission 1970-1971 (Chairman: S.O. Adebo), (Lagos, 1971)

Nolutshungu, S.C., Fragments of a Democracy: Reflections on Class and Politics in Nigeria," *Third World Quarterly*, 30 (1) (1992), p. 101.

Norman and E. B. Simmonds, 'Determination of Relevant Research Priorities for Farm Development in West Africa,' SRB 204 (1973),

Norman, 'Interdisciplinary Research,' *ACE*, 6 (1971), pp. 34–8;

Norman, D. W., 'Initiating Change in Traditional Agriculture,' *Samaru Research Bulletin*, 7 (1970).

Norman, D.W., 'Interdisciplinary Research on Rural Development. The Experience of the Rural Economy Research Unit in Northern Nigeria,' Overseas Liaison Committee, *American Council on Education, ACE*, 6 (1974).

Norman, D.W., 'Economic Analysis of Agricultural Production and Labour Utilization among the Hausa in the North of Nigeria,' African Rural Employment Papers, Michigan State University, (AREP), 5 (1973).

Norman, D.W., 'Economic Analysis,' *AREP*, 4, pp. 5, 16;

Norman, Land and Labour Relationships,' *SMP*, 19, (1967)

Nove, Alec, *An Economic History of the USSR* ({1969} Harmondsworth, 1993).

Nwajiaku, K., Heroes and Villains: Ijaw Narratives of the Nigerian Civil War,' *African Development*, XXXIV, 1, (1) 2009.

Nwajiaku-Dahou, K., 'The Political Economy of Oil and "Rebellion", in Nigeria's Niger Delta,' *ROAPE* 132, pp. 299-300.

O'Connell, J., 'The Political Class and Nigeria's Economic Growth,' *Nigerian Journal of Economic and Social Studies* 8 (1966)

Obi, C., The Impact of Oil and Nigeria's Revenue Allocation System: Problems and Prospects for National Reconstruction, in Amuwo, K. *et al.,* (eds) *Federalism and Political Restructuring in Nigeria* (Ibadan, 1998).

Ogunfowora, O. and Norman, 'Farm firm Normative Fertiliser Demand Response in the North-Central State of Nigeria,' *Journal of Agricultural Economics*, 24, 2 (1973

Ogunfowora, O., 'Farm Survey as a Data Base for Analysis and Planning,' Nigerian Rural Development Study, Rural Development Papers, Department of Agricultural Economics, University of Ibadan (*NRDS*) 14 (1974), pp. 1-2.

Ogunfowora, O., 'Income and Employment Potential of Credit and Technology in Peasant Farming,' *NRDS*, 9 (1973).

Ogunfowora, O., Essang and Olayide, 'Capital and Credit in Nigerian Agricultural Development,' *NRDS*, 6 (1972).

Okediji, O.O., 'Motivating Youths to Settle in Rural Area' (NISER, mimeo).

Okigbo, P., `Economic Implications of the 1979 Constitution of the Federal Republic of Nigeria' in Nigerian Economic Society, *The Nigerian Economy: A Political Economy Approach* (Longman, London, 1986).

Okigbo, P., *Presidential Commission on Revenue Allocation*, 1980.

Okri, B., *Infinite Riches* (Orion, 1999).

Okugu, 'The outlook for Nigerian oil: 1985-2000: Four scenarios,' *ROAPE*, 17 (1986)

Okurume, 'The Food Crop Economy in Nigerian Agricultural Policy,' *CSNRD*, 31 (1969) pp. 91-92;

Okurume, G. E., *The Food Crop Economy in Nigerian Agricultural Policy* (East Lansing and Ibadan, 1969)

Olakanpo, O., 'A Preliminary Report on Indigenous Enterprise in Distributive Trades in Nigeria,' NISER, mimeo, (Ibadan, c. 1967).

Olatunbosun, D. 'Western Nigerian Farm Settlement: an Appraisal,' Journal of Development Administration, JDA, 5, 3, (1971) NISER, 75

Olatunbosun, D. 'Western Nigerian Farm Settlements,' *JDA*, 5, 3, pp. 427-428;

Olatunbosun, D. and Olayide, S.O., 'Effects of the Marketing Boards on the Output and Income of Primary Producers' in Onitiri, H.M.A. and Olatunbosun, D. (eds) *The Marketing Board System.*

Olatunbosun, D., 'The Farm Settlement: A Case Study of an Agricultural Project in Nigeria,' *BRES*, 6, 1, (1971)

Olatunbosun, D., 'Trends and Prospects of Nigeria's Agricultural Exports,' in Onitiri and Olatunbosun, ed. NISER (1972).

Olatunbosun, D., *Nigeria's Neglected Rural Majority* (Ibadan, 1975)

Olayemi and Oni, 'Costs and Returns in Peasant Cocoa Production: A Case Study of Western Nigeria,' *BRES*, 6, 2 (1971) p. 147.

Olayemi, 'Some Economic Characteristics,' *BRES*, 7, 2

Olayemi, J. K., 'Some Economic Characteristics of Peasant Agriculture in the Cocoa Belt of Western Nigeria,' Bulletin of Rural Economics and Sociology, (*BRES*), 7, 2 (1972).

Olayemi, J.K. and Oni, S. 'Asymmetry in Price Response: A Case Study of Western Nigerian Cocoa Farmers,' *NJESS*, 14, 3 (1972).

Olayide and Olatunbosun, 'New Dimensions in the Administration of Agriculture in Nigeria,' *QJA* 6, 1 (1971).

Olayide *et al.*, A Quantitative Analysis of Food Requirements, Supplies and Demands in Nigeria, 1968-1985, (Federal Department of Agriculture, Lagos 1972), pp. 68-69.

Olayide, 'Research on Rural Integrated Development, Employment and Food Production in the Guinea Savannah Zone of Nigeria,' *NRDS*, 1 (1971)

Olayide, 'Stimulating Integrated Rural Development through Research,' *NRDS*, 18 (1975).

Olukoshi, A., 'Economic Crisis, Structural Adjustment and the Coping Strategies of Manufacturers in Kano, Nigeria,' United Nations Institute for Social Development, DP 77, 1996.

Oni, Comrade O. and Onimade, B., *Economic Development of Nigeria: The Socialist Alternative* (Ibadan. 1975), pp. 187-188.

Oni, S. A., 'Increased Food production through Agricultural Innovations in Nigeria,' West African Journal of Agricultural Economics, *WAJAE* 1, 1 (1972).

Onitiri, H.M.A. and D. Olatunbosun (eds), *The Marketing Board System* (Ibadan, 1972)

Opeke, L. K., 'Rapporteur,' *WAJAE*, 1, 1, (1972);

Osaghae, E., Onwudiwu, E. and Suberu, R. (eds), *The Nigerian Civil War and its Aftermath* (Ibadan, 2002).

Osifo, D. E. and Anthonio, Q.B.O., 'Costs and Returns: A Study of Upland Paddy Production under Traditional Farming Conditions of the Wasimi and Ilaro Areas of the Western State of Nigeria,' *NJESS*, 12, 3 (1970)

Osoba, 'Ideological Trends in the Nigerian National Liberation Movement and the Problems of National Identity, Solidarity, Motivation, 1934-1965' Ibadan, 27 (1969)

Osoba, 'Ideological Trends,' and 'The Deepening Crisis of the Nigerian Bourgeoisie,' *ROAPE*, 13 (1979).

Osoba, 'Ideology and Planning for National Economic Development 1946-72' in M. Tukur and T. Olagunju (eds), *Nigeria in Search of a Viable Polity* (Zaria, 1975).

Osoba, 'The Colonial Antecedents and Contemporary Development of Nigerian Foreign Policy,' (PhD thesis, Moscow State University, 1967).

Osoba, S, 'Corruption in Nigeria: historical perspectives,' *ROAPE*, 69 (1996).

Osoba, *The Nigerian power elite* ({1970} New York), p. 377.

Osuntokun, A., 'Agricultural Credit Strategies,' *AID,* 6, 3.

Osuntokun, A., 'Agricultural Credit Strategies for Nigerian Farmers,' Spring Review of Small Farmer Credit, *AID*, 6, (1973)

Othman, S. and Williams, G., 'Politics, Power and Democracy in Nigeria' in J. Hyslop (ed.) *African Democracy in an Era of Globalization* (Johannesburg, 1999).

Othman, Shehu, 'Classes, Crises and Coup': the Demise of Shagari's Regime,' *African Affairs*, 83 (1984);

Othman, Shehu, 'Nigeria: "Power for Profit": Class, Corporatism and Nationalism in the Military' in D.C. O'Brien, J. Dunn, and R.

Rathbone (eds), *Contemporary West African States* (Cambridge, 1989).

Othman, Shehu, 'Nigeria': Power for Profit: Class, corporatism and factionalism in the military,' in O'Brien, D.C., Dunn, J. and Rathbone, R. (eds) *Contemporary West African States*. (Cambridge, 1989).

Otite, O. and Albert, I. (eds) *Community Conflict in Nigeria: Management, Resolution, and Transformation* (Ibadan, 1999)

Otobo, D., 'The Nigerian General Strike of 1981,' *Review of African Political Economy*, 1981, Vol. 22, pp.65-81

Otobo, D., 'The Political Clash in the Aftermath of the Nigerian General Strike of 1981,' *Review of African Political Economy*, 1982, Vol.25, pp. 104-112

Oxaal., I. Barnett, T. and Booth, D. (eds), *Beyond the Sociology of Development* (London 1975)

Oyediran, O. and Agbaje, A. (eds), *Nigeria: Politics of Transition and Governance* (Dakar, 1999).

Oyovbaire, S., `The Politics of Revenue Allocation' in Panter-Brick, (ed.) *Soldiers and Oil; and Federalism in Nigeria: A Study in the Development of the Nigerian State* (London, 1985), pp. 162-200.

Oyovbaire, S., *West Africa*, 4 November, 1974.

Panter-Brick (ed.), *Nigerian Politics and Military Rule: Prelude to the Civil War* (London, 1969).

Panter-Brick, (ed.) *Soldiers and Oil; and Federalism in Nigeria: A Study in the Development of the Nigerian State* (London, 1985)

Patel and 'Strategy for Revolutionizing Maize Production,' *BRES*, 8, 2

Patel and Agboola, 'Strategy,' *BRES*, 8, 2 (1973).

Patel, A. U. and Agboola, A. A. 'Strategy for Revolutionizing Maize Production in a Nigerian Village,' *BRES*, 8, 2 (1973).

Patel, A. U. and Antonio, 'An Analysis of Selected Factors that Influence the Adoption of Improved Practices among Tobacco Farmers in the Western State,' *NAJ*, 8, 2 (1971).

Peace, A. 'Industrial Conflict in Nigeria,' in E. de Kadt and Williams (eds) *Sociology and Development* (London, 1974, 2001).

Peace, A. *Choice, Class, and Conflict: A Study of Southern Nigerian Factory Workers* (Hassocks, 1979), pp. 49-79.

Peace, A., 'The politics of transporting,' *Africa* 58, 1 (1988)

Peel, J.D.Y. '*Olaju*: a Yoruba conception of development,' *Journal of Development Studies*, 14 (1978). Parts IV and V.

Peel, J.D.Y. and Stewart, C. (eds), *Popular Islam South of the Sahara* (Manchester, 1985).

Peel, J.D.Y., *Aladura: a Religious Movement among the Yoruba* (London, 1968).

Peel, J.D.Y., *Christianity, Islam, and Orisha Religion: Three Traditions in Comparison and Interaction*, University Press, 2016.

Perham, M. (ed.), *Mining, Commerce and Finance in Nigeria* (London, 1948);

Petras, J. and Morley, M. 'The Venezuelan Development 'Model' and U.S. Policy, *Development and Change*, 7 (1976).

Philip Corrigan, 'Appeals to Society': An Examination of how the Ideology of the State was Materialized in Britain before 1850' (BA dissertation, Department of Sociology, University of Durham, unpublished, 1973).

Philips, A. O. 'The Concept of Development,' *Review of African Political Economy* (*ROAPE*) 8 (1977) M.P. Cowen and R.W. Shenton, 'The Invention of Development' in Doctrines, pp. 3-59, and in W. Cooke (ed.), *Power and Development* (London, 1995), pp. 27-63

Pitcher, A., Moran, M.H. and Johnston, M., 'Rethinking patrimonialism and neo-patrimonialism in Africa,' *African Studies Review* 52 (2009)

Post, K. and G. Jenkins, *The Price of Liberty: Personality and Politics in Colonial Nigeria* (Cambridge, 1973).

Post, K. and Vickers, M., *Structure and Conflict in Nigeria* (London, 1973).

Post, K., Adegoke Adelabu, Africa in Ebullition: Being a handbook of freedom for Nigerian nationalists (Lagos, 1952).

Post, K., *The New States of West Africa* (London, 1964)

Post, K., *The Nigerian Federal Elections of 1959: Politics and administration in a developing political system* (Oxford, 1963)

Post, K.W.J., ' "Peasantisation" and Rural Political Movements in Western Africa,' Archives Europeиnnes de Sociologie, 13 (1972),

Post, K.W.J., *Arise Ye Starvelings: the Jamaican Labour Rebellion of 1938 and its aftermath* (The Hague, 1978).

Poulantzas, 'The Capitalist State, *NLR*, 95 (1976)

Poulantzas, N., *Political Power and Social Classes* (London, 1973)

Purvis, M. J., 'A Study of the Economics of Tractor Use in Oyo Division of the Western State,' *Consortium for the Study of Nigerian Rural Development (CSNRD)*, Michigan State University and NISER, 17 (1968).

Purvis, M. J., 'Report on a Survey of Oil Palm Rehabilitation Scheme in Eastern Nigeria,' *CSNRD*, 10 (1967)

R. Galletti, K.D.S. Baldwin and I. Dina, *Nigerian Cocoa Farmers* (Oxford, 1956).

R.L. Sklar, *Nigerian Political Parties* (Princeton, 1963),

Raphael, D. D., *Adam Smith* (Oxford, 1985).

Redfield, R., *Peasant Society and Culture* (Chicago, 1956), pp. 18-19.

Remy, D., 'Underdevelopment and the Experience of Women,' in R. Reiter (ed.) *Towards an Anthropology of Women* (New York, 1975)

Report of the (Adebiyi) Tribunal of Inquiry into the Activities of Trade Unions (Lagos 1977).

Report of the Commission Appointed to Enquire into the Fears of Minorities and the Means of Allaying Them (Chairman: Henry Willink). Cmd, 505, 1958.

Report of the Commission of Enquiry into the Affairs of Certain Statutory Corporations in Western Nigeria (Chairman, Justice Coker) (Lagos, 1962).

Report of the Commission of Enquiry into the Civil Disturbances which occurred in certain parts of the Western State of Nigeria in the month of December, 1968 (Chairman: Justice Ayoola) (Ibadan, 1969).

Report of the Commission of Enquiry into the Disorders in the Eastern Provinces of Nigeria, Col. 256 (London, 1950) (The Fitzgerald Report).

Report of the Commission of Enquiry into the Marketing of West African Cocoa (Chairman, W. Nowell) Cmnd. 5485 (London, 1938);

Report of the Constitution Drafting Committee (Lagos 1976), vol. 1, p. v.

Report of the Tribunal appointed to enquire into allegations on the Official Conduct of the Premier of, and certain persons holding Ministerial and other Public Offices in the Eastern Region of Nigeria, Cmd. 51 (London 1957) (The Foster Sutton Report).

Rhodes, R. (ed.) *Imperialism and Underdevelopment* (New York, 1970)

Ricardo de Oliveira, *Oil and Politics in the Gulf of Guinea* (London, 2007)

Ricardo, D., *On the Principles of Political Economy and Taxation* (Harmondsworth, 1971)

Roberts, P., 'The Sexual Politics of Labour: Rural Women in Western Nigeria and Hausa Niger,' in K. Young, et al., *Serving Two Masters,* (New Delhi, 1988)

Rodgers, E. M. Ashcroft, J. R. and Roling, N., *Diffusion of Innovation in Brazil, India and Nigeria,* (1970).

Roider, W., *Farm Settlements for Socio-economic Development: The Western Nigerian Case* (Munich, 1971).

Rupley, L. 'Revenue Allocation Once Again' and 'The Next Revenue Allocation,' *West Africa,* 1, 8 July 1974 and 6 January 1975.

Russell, B. and Russell, A., *German Social Democracy* (London, 1896)

Sandbrook, R. and Cohen, R. (eds), *The Development of an African Working Class* (London, 1976).

Sayer, D., *Marx's Method: Ideology, Science and Critique in Capital* (Hassocks, 1979)

Shenton, R. and L. Lennihan, 'Capital and Class: Peasant Differentiation in Northern Nigeria,' *Journal of Peasant Studies,* 9, 1 (1981)

Shenton, R.W. and Watts, M., 'Capitalism and Hunger in Northern Nigeria,' *ROAPE,* 15 (1980).

Shenton, R.W. and Freund, W., 'The Incorporation of Northern Nigeria into the World Capitalist Economy,' *ROAPE,* 13 (1979).

Shenton, R.W., *The Development of an African Capitalism* (Oxford, 1986)

Sklar, 'Contradictions in the Nigerian Political System,' *JMAS,* 3 (1965)

Sklar, 'Political Science and National Integration,' *Journal of Modern African Studies,* 5 (1967).

Sklar, R. and C.S. Whitaker, 'Nigeria,' in J. Coleman and C.G. Rosberg, eds. *Political Parties and National Integration in Tropical Africa* (Berkeley, 1964);

Sklar, R., 'Political Science and National Integration – A Radical Approach,' *Journal of Modern African Studies* 5, 1 (1967)

Smith, Adam, *An Inquiry into the Nature and Causes of the Wealth of Nations* (1759) (Chicago, 1982)

Smith, Adam, *The Theory of Moral Sentiments* {1759} A.L. Macfie and
    D.D. Raphael (eds), (Indianapolis, 1984)
Stolper, W.F., *Planning without Facts: Lessons in Resource Allocation
    from Nigeria's Development* (Cambridge, Mass., 1966).
Stremlau, J.J., The International Politics of the Nigerian Civil War, 1967-
    1970 (Princeton, 1977)
Stremlau, J.J., *The International Politics of the Nigerian Civil War, 1967-
    1970* (Princeton University Press, 1977).
Teriba, O., 'Rural Credit and Rural Development in Nigeria,' *NES.* p.
    173.
Thandika Mkandawire, 'Thinking about Developmental States in Africa,'
    Cambridge Journal of Economics (2012)
Thomas, W. I. and Thomas, Dorothy Swaine, *The Child in America:
    Behavior Problems and Programs* (New York, 1928), pp. 571-2.
Tiffen, M., *The Enterprising Peasant, Economic Development in Gombe
    Emirate North Eastern State, Nigeria 1900–1968* (London, 1976).
Toyo, E., 'An Open Letter to the Nigerian Left,' *ROAPE*, 32 (1985)
Trotsky, L., *History of the Russian Revolution* ({1930} London, 1934)
Tseayo, J. 'The Emirate System and Tiv Reaction to Pagan Status in
    Northern Nigeria' in Williams (ed.), *Nigeria: Economy and Society*
    (London, 1976).
Tukur, M. and Olagunju, T. (eds), *Nigeria in Search of a Viable Polity*
    (Zaria, 1975).
Turi Muhammadu, 'Private Sector versus Public Sector,' New Nigerian
    (Kaduna) 1 May, 1973.
Udo, R. K. 'Sixty Years of Plantation Agriculture in Southern Nigeria,
    1902-62,' *Economic Geography*, 41, 4 (1965)
Upton, M., 'Socio-economic Survey of Some Farm Families in Nigeria,
    Social and Psychological Factors,' *BRES*, 3, 2 (1968);
Upton, M., *Agriculture in South-Western Nigeria* (University of Reading,
    1967)
Usoro, E. J., 'Observed Disparity in Nigerian Rural Poverty,' Poverty in
    Nigeria, *Proceedings of the 1975 Annual Conference*, Bagauda Lake,
    Kano, Nigerian Economic Society (NES)
Usoro, E., *The Nigerian Oil Palm Industry* (Ibadan, 1974)

van Allen, J. ' "Sitting on a Man": Colonialism and the Lost Political
    Institutions of Igbo Women,' *Canadian Journal of African Studies* 6,
    2 (1972).
van den Borne, B. and Roling, N., 'Extension Workers and Farmer
    Characteristics,' *BRES*, 8, 1 (1973)
Wade, R., *Governing the Market: Economic theory and the role of
    government in East Asian industrialization* (Princeton NJ, 1990);
Walicki, A., *The Controversy over Capitalism* (Oxford, 1969).
Wallace, T., *Rural Development through Irrigation* (Zaria, 1979)
Wallerstein, I., (ed.) *Social Change* (New York, 1966).
Ward-Price, H., *Land Tenure among the Yoruba* (Lagos, 1933);
Warren, Bill, 'Imperialism and Capitalist Industrialisation,' *New Left
    Review*, 81 (1973)
Waterman, P. 'Conservatism amongst Nigerian workers' in Williams, G.
    (ed.) *Nigeria: Economy and Society* (London, 1975).
Waterman, P., 'Communist Theory in the Nigerian Trade Union
    Movement,' *Politics and Society* (1973).
Waterman, P., 'The 'Labour Aristocracy' in Africa,' *Development and
    Change*, 7 (1975).
Waterman, P., *Industrial Relations and the Control of Labour Protest in
    Nigeria* (The Hague, 1977).
Weber, 'Politics as a Vocation,' {1918, published 1999, London, 1948), p.
    128.
Weber, M., *Economy and Society* vol. 1 ({1921} (New York, 1968), pp.
    265-8.
Weber, M., *The Religion of China: Confucianism and Taoism* ({1915}
    Glencoe, 1951)
Weeks, 'Employment: Does it Matter?' in R. Jolly *et al. Third World
    Employment* (Harmondsworth, 1973).
Weeks, J. 'Employment, Growth and Foreign Domination in
    Underdeveloped Countries,' *Review of Radical Political Economics*,
    4 (1972).
Weeks, J. 'Wage Policy and the Colonial Legacy,' *JMAS*, 9 (1971).
Weeks, J., 'Imbalance between the Centre and Periphery and the
    "Employment' Crisis" in Kenya,' in Oxaal., I. Barnett, T. and Booth,
    D. (eds), *Beyond the Sociology of Development* (London 1975)

Wells, J.C., Agricultural Policy and Economic Growth in Nigeria, 1962-1968 (Ibadan, 1974).

White Paper on the Second and Final Report of the Wages and Salaries Commission 1970-1971 (Lagos, 1971), esp. pp. 8-10.

Whitehead, C.E., The Political Implications of Social Change in Ghana, 1947-1957,' (B.A. dissertation, Department of Social Theory and Institutions, University of Durham, unpublished, 1968), p. 42-4,

Whitfield, L., The Politics of Aid: African Strategies for Dealing with Donors (Oxford, 2009).

Williams, S. K. T. *et al.*, Second Annual Report. Isoya Rural Development Project, (University of Ife, 1974).

Williams, 'Why is there no agrarian capitalism in Nigeria?' *Journal of Historical Sociology*,1, 4 (1988).

Williams, G. (ed), Special Issue on Nigeria, *ROAPE* 13 (1978)

Williams, G. (ed.), *Nigeria: Economy and Society* (London, 1975).

Williams, G. 'Class Relations in a Neo-colony Political Economy: the case of Nigeria' in Gutkind, P. and P. Waterman (eds), *African Social Studies; a radical reader*, New York 1977.

Williams, G., 'Agriculture in Nigeria,' and J. Derrick, 'Farming in Nigeria,' *West Africa*, 16 and 23 July, 1979.

Williams, G., 'In Defence of History,' *History Workshop Journal*, 7 (1979).

Williams, G., 'Les contradictions de la Banque Mondiale et le crise l'Ÿtat en Afrique' en L'Ÿtat contemporaine en Afrique, sous la direction de Emmanuel Terry' (Paris, 1987), p. 363.

Williams, G., 'Marketing without and with Marketing Boards in Nigeria,' *ROAPE* 34 (1985)

Williams, G., 'Studying Development and Explaining Policy,' *Oxford Development Studies*, 31 (1) 2003.

Williams, G., 'Taking the Part of Peasants: rural development in Nigeria and Tanzania,' in P.C.W. Gutkind and Wallerstein, I. (eds), *The Political Economy of Contemporary Africa* (Los Angeles, 1976/1985).

Williams, G., 'The Political Sociology of Western Nigeria,' B. Phil. thesis (University of Oxford 1967),

Williams, G., 'The Social Stratification of a Neo-colonial Political Economy: Western Nigeria,' in C.H. Allen and R.W. Johnson (eds),

African Perspectives: Papers in the History, Politics and Economics of Africa: Presented to Thomas Hodgkin (Cambridge 1970).

Williams, G., 'The World Bank and the Peasant Problem,' in J. Heyer, P. Roberts and Williams, G. (eds), *Rural Development in Tropical Africa* (Basingstoke, 1982).

Williams, G., 'Why Structural Adjustment is Necessary and Why it Doesn't Work,' Debates, *ROAPE* 60, 1994.

Williams, G., Democracy as idea and Democracy as Process in Africa, *Journal of African-American History*, 86, 4, 2003.

Williams, G., *Review of Post and Jenkins, The Price of Liberty*, in *African Affairs*, 73, 265 (1974).

Williams, G., The Nigerian Civil War at www.gavinwilliams.org (website in progress), and The Origins of the Nigerian Civil War (Milton Keynes, 1982).

Williams, G., The Political Sociology of Western Nigeria, B. Phil. thesis, University of Oxford, 1967. Revised January 1980

Williams, Gavin, ed. *Nigeria: Economy and Society*, Rex Collings, London, 1976.

Williams, S. K. T., 'Rural Poverty to Rural Prosperity: a Strategy for Development in Nigeria,' Inaugural Lecture, (University of Ife, 1973.

Wolf, E., 'On Peasant Rebellions,' *International Social Science Journal*, 21 (1969).

Wood, A., *The Groundnut Affair*, (London, 1950).

Wright Mills, C., *The Power Elite* (Oxford, 1956).

Yahaya, A. D. &. Goddard, 'A Socio-economic Study of Three Villages in the Sokoto Close-settled Zone,' *SMP*, 33 (1970);

Yahaya, A. D. `Nigerian Public Administration under Military Rule: The Experience of the Northern States' in O. O. Adamolekun (ed.), *Nigerian Public Administration, 1960-1980* (Heinemann, Ibadan, 1985)

Ye. Preobrazhensky. *The New Economics* ({1924, 1926} Oxford, 1965).

Index

www.ingramcontent.com/pod-product-compliance
Lightning Source LLC
Chambersburg PA
CBHW022303280326
41932CB00010B/964